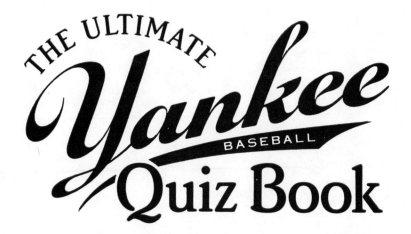

THE ULTIMATE

Yankee

BASEBALL

Quiz Book

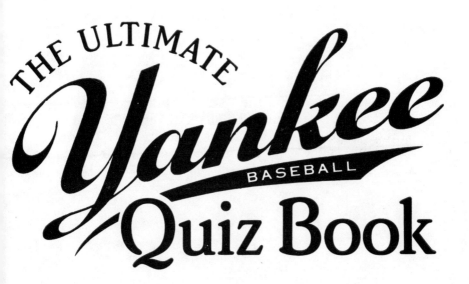

THE ULTIMATE Yankee BASEBALL Quiz Book

UPDATED EDITION
DOM FORKER

BELL PUBLISHING COMPANY
NEW YORK

To Babe, Lou, and Earle . . . Joe, Bill, and Red . . .
Tommy, Phil, and Charlie . . . Allie, Vic, and
Eddie . . . Mickey, Whitey, and Roger . . . Thurm,
Graig, and Cat . . . Ron, Dave, and Willie . . .
thanks for the memories

A Lou Reda book.

Copyright © 1989, 1982 by Dom Forker
All rights reserved.

This 1989 edition is published by Bell Publishing Company,
distributed by Crown Publishers, Inc., 225 Park Avenue South,
New York, New York 10003, by arrangement
with Lou Reda Productions.

Printed and Bound in the United States of America

ISBN 0-517-68015-7
h g f e d c b a

Contents

Introduction

I've been to a lot of World Series games that involved New York Yankee baseball, but I've never seen a Yankee contest that for drama and suspense and history could match the playoff final between the Yankees and the Royals on October 14, 1976.

Luck played a great role in my being a witness to history that night. On the day before the game, a teaching friend and colleague, Vince Fitz, asked me if I wanted to accompany him to the playoff finale. He and his wife, Elaine, had bought a pair of box seats to the three Yankee home games. To them it was a dream come true. But unfortunately the dream had some nightmarish elements. The seats, it turned out, were right smack behind the right-field foul pole. After two nights of peering around the round yellow pole—it's wider than you'd think—Elaine had had it. She decided to watch Game Five on television, in the comfort of her living room.

Vince, knowing of my love affair with the Yankees, asked me if I would like to accompany him. I did not hesitate. Twice in my life I failed to go to a Yankee World Series game that I had fully planned to attend. On both occasions it was because other friends of mine had backed out at the last moment. The first time Don Larsen pitched his no-hitter; the second time Reggie Jackson hit three home runs. I said, "Yes."

We got to Yankee Stadium early that evening, thinking that maybe we could make some type of a swap that would improve our viewing vantage point. After circumambulating Yankee Stadium a couple of times, without success, we decided it was time for a beer. We stopped in a bar, under the El tracks, in a spot where Ruth's and Mantle's best shots never reached. But their pictures, along with those of other Yankee greats of the past, adorned the walls. We got into a conversation about Yankee history with a wiry, low-keyed fellow who was seated next to us. His name was Bob. Soon our conversation switched to our present predicament.

Bob, who was placid but streetwise, told us, "Don't worry. I don't even have a ticket. But it's still early. Pretty soon things will start to happen."

Well, it was six o'clock and things weren't happening fast enough for Vince and me, so we strolled around Yankee Stadium a few more times. But the only action that we ran across was a few arrests of scalpers by undercover men. (The following morning's newspapers recounted that there were 78 such arrests.) We returned somewhat glumly to our right-field watering hole. It was seven o'clock. Game time was only one hour away.

"Don't worry," our friend Bob repeated. "Pretty soon now things are going to start happening." We didn't know whether he was a Pollyanna or a prophet. He turned out to be both.

Within a few minutes of our return, a portly, bald, middle-aged gentleman announced that he had box seats for sale. A bus from Perth Amboy, he said, with 50 people on it had broken down on the New Jersey Turnpike. He had to get rid of the tickets. For cost!

We bought two tickets and sold the originals, for cost, to two college students who didn't seem to mind that they were behind an obstruction. As we took our seats—behind the Royals' third-base dugout—we had the feeling that we were in for a most enjoyable evening. When we looked behind us and saw the smiling I-told-you-so face of Bob, we *knew* that the evening's script was going to have a happy ending.

But shortly after we had settled into our seats, we became temporarily unsettled. John Mayberry reached the right-field seats with a two-run homer off Ed Figueroa in the top of the first. But the Yankees, who would be paced by Mickey Rivers, Chris Chambliss, and Thurman Munson that night, bounced back with two runs to tie in their half of the first.

The game seesawed back and forth the rest of the night. Kansas City took a 3–2 lead in the second on a run-scoring single by Buck Martinez. But the Yankees scored a pair of runs in both the third and the sixth to lead 6–3 going to the eighth.

At that time there was a feeling of euphoria in New Yankee Stadium. The Yankees, of course, had a great tradition. Up until that moment the Bronx Bombers had won 29 pennants and 20 world championships. But they had not won a pennant in 12 years nor a world title in 14 years. Yankee fans were not used to such dry periods of time. They needed a thirst-quencher.

But with one swing of the bat George Brett removed that sense of euphoria and replaced it with an ominous pall of gloom. He hit a three-run homer in the top of the eighth, off reliever Grant Jackson, to knot the score at 6–6. The big stadium was silenced.

Much has been written about the "animals" who inhabit Yankee Stadium. The Dodgers of 1977–78 characterized it as a zoo. They couldn't wait to depart from New York. And they did so, two years in a row, without the world title. Sparky Lyle, who was an integral part of that setting for many years, called it the Bronx Zoo. But it was certainly not a jungle on that particular night. The crowd was very partisan. Almost completely partisan. Pro-Yankees and anti-Royals. But not hostilely anti-Royals. The spectators had come to see the Yankees win. The fact that they were playing Kansas City was incidental. And when Brett's home run changed the picture of the game, the crowd was destroyed. The mood had suddenly changed from "There's no way that we're going to lose this game" to "Maybe, somehow, we're destined to lose this game." Twelve years of famine had created a lot of Doubting Thomases among the Yankees' legions of followers.

Forlornly, we sat back in our seats, sensing impending defeat. But we felt a tap on our shoulders and turned around to see the still-smiling face of Bob, a throwback to the Yankee fan's omniscient confidence of the past, assuring us, "Don't worry, pretty soon things are going to start happening."

3

It didn't happen immediately. The Yankees failed to score in the bottom of the eighth. Everyone was sure the game would end in the ninth. It was sudden death. The entire season had come down to one inning. Jackson's replacement survived a tense top of the inning. There were two hairline plays at second. On both of them shortstop Fred Stanley ranged far to his right on infield grounders and threw to second, to Willie Randolph, just in time to get the force on the sliding Royals. Either play could have gone either way.

In the bottom of the ninth, there was the feeling among the crowd that one of the Yankees was going to hit one out. Chambliss led off. Munson was on deck. We sat back in our seats, this time relaxed, waiting for "something to happen." We didn't have to wait too long. Relief pitcher Mark Littell's first pitch to Chambliss soared into the night. It was one of the most beautiful sights I have ever seen. From our third-base vantage spot we could see the ball disappear into the night, just above the fence and just beneath the lights which illuminated the scene. It was truly a scene to behold.

As Chambliss circled the bases—with some difficulty, I might add, because of some overexuberant fans who tried to abscond with him as a souvenir—a sense of oneness developed in the partisan crowd. Here and there grown men ecstatically embraced each other. Vince and I, in fact, shared that expression of joy with our newfound friend Bob.

I hope that you can share that joy, too, as you peruse these pages. Turn each page with the feeling that "something is going to happen, soon" and you will not be disappointed. For with the Yankees it always does.

The events of that evening are, I am sure, indelibly impressed upon the minds of every fan who saw that game. But there's one important fact about that game that might not so readily come to mind. Who was the Yankee relief pitcher who took Jackson's place on the mound in the ninth inning and ultimately got credit for the win?

Answer: Dick Tidrow

4

The Ground Rules

The ground rules of this game are simple. There are 2,900 questions in this book. The answers are given at the end of each chapter. Check your answers, and give yourself one point for each correct answer. Then, using the Scorebook page at the back of the book, divide your total correct answers by 2,900 to find your winning percentage. Use the Yankee Winning Percentages chart to compare your results with the Yankees' best and worst winning percentages from 1903–1988, and find out where you fit in with Yankee success or failure!

Some of the questions are repeated with a different wrinkle. That's only natural—pitchers set up hitters the same way.

What kind of winning percentage can *you* score? If you score above .714, you're in a class by yourself. On the other hand, if you score between .714 and .329, you're like all the other Yankee teams between 1903 and 1988.

But it's not going to be easy—and that's the way it should be. Over the years, great Yankee teams have repeatedly risen to the occasion. And they've been swinging against pitchers like Cy Young, Walter Johnson, Eddie Plank, Lefty Grove, Bob Feller, Hal Newhouser, Early Wynn, and Nolan Ryan.

You will be, too. Good luck.

CHAPTER ONE

Billy's Boys

---

1. WHO'S WHO

You can use the following list as a guide to the answers* in this quiz:

Chris Chambliss	Catfish Hunter
Ron Davis	Reggie Jackson
Bucky Dent	Sparky Lyle
Brian Doyle	Thurman Munson
Ed Figueroa	Graig Nettles
Goose Gossage	Lou Piniella
Ron Guidry	Mike Torrez
Don Gullett	Bill White

1) _____ Who was the first pitcher born in Puerto Rico to win 20 games in the major leagues?

2) _____ Who won the Rookie of the Year Award with Kansas City in 1969?

3) _____ Who hit the home run, off Mark Littell of the Royals, to clinch the 1976 pennant?

4) _____ Who pitched in 420 games for the Yankees without starting even *one* time?

5) _____ Who was the last Yankee to win an MVP Award?

6) _____ Who has hit more home runs at his position than any other player in the history of the American League?

7) _____ Who was the winning pitcher in the Yankees' only division playoff game in history?

8) _____ Who was the former Yankee who lost that game?

*Answers to quizzes will be found at the end of each chapter.

9) _____ Who was the Yankee (late 1970s to early 1980s) who twice hit more than 40 home runs?

10) _____ Who was the last major leaguer to hit .300 and drive home 100 runs for three straight years?

11) _____ Who was the last major leaguer to perform the feat before the preceding player? (He has something to say about every present-day Yankee game.)

12) _____ Who was the only American League relief pitcher to win the Cy Young Award before Rollie Fingers of the 1981 Brewers copped the honor?

13) _____ Who was the last Yankee to win the home-run title outright?

14) _____ Who has the highest winning percentage for one season of any pitcher who has ever won 20 games?

15) _____ Who hit the key three-run homer in the 1978 playoff game against the Red Sox?

16) _____ Who, in the eighth inning of that historic game, hit the home run that proved to be the decisive run?

17) _____ Who was the leading hitter for the Yankees in the 1978 World Series?

18) _____ Who was the former Yankee who pitched the last perfect game in the majors before the Indians' Len Barker performed the feat in 1981?

19) _____ Who won the Rookie of the Year Award with Cleveland in 1971?

20) _____ Who was the Yankee opening-game pitcher in the 1977 World Series who started the World Series opener *against* the Pinstripers the preceding season?

21) _____ Who has struck out more batters in one season than any other Yankee pitcher in history?

22) _____ Who was the Yankee on the 1981 roster (he later became a Pinstripe pilot) who hit .300 seven times?

23) _____ Who was the relief pitcher from this era who, four times, has posted an ERA of less than 2.00?

24) _____ Who posted a then-club-record 35 saves in one season? (He pitched in two World Series for the Yankees.)

25) _____ Who was the 1979 relief pitcher who won 14 out of 16 decisions?

2. TRUE OR FALSE

Mark *T* or *F* for "true" or "false" before each statement.

1) ___ Tommy John has three times won 20 or more games in a season.

2) ___ He has had more 20-game seasons in his years with the Yankees than he had in his other 20 major league seasons.

3) ___ Thurman Munson collected more hits in one season than any other catcher in Yankee history.

4) ___ Thurman Munson had a .300 lifetime average.

5) ___ Graig Nettles began his major-league career with the Indians.

6) ___ Reggie Jackson has never hit .300.

7) ___ Roy White managed to hit .300 in at least one major-league season.

8) ___ Don Gullett never won 20 games in a season.

9) ___ Mike Torrez has never won 20 games in a season.

10) ___ Reggie Jackson has won an MVP Award during his career.

11) ___ Willie Randolph won the Rookie of the Year Award.

12) ___ Bobby Murcer hit more than 30 home runs in a season.

13) ___ He also hit better than .325 in a season.

14) ___ Chris Chambliss has hit .300 in a season.

15) ___ He has also driven home 100 runs in a season.

16) ___ Mickey Rivers won a stolen-base crown.

17) ___ Jim Mason was the only player to homer in his only official World Series at bat.

18) ___ Chris Chambliss has hit 20 home runs in a season.

19) ___ Graig Nettles has not hit a home run in four World Series.

20) ___ Billy Martin led one of his teams to a pennant before he came to the Yankees.

21) ___ Fran Healy never hit a home run with the Yankees.

22) ___ Thurman Munson never hit 20 home runs in a season.

23) ___ Catfish Hunter won 20 games in a season five years in a row.

24) ___ Mickey Rivers hit well over .300 in each of the three playoff series in which he appeared.

25) ___ Bobby Bonds, in his one year in New York, hit 30 or more home runs and stole 30 or more bases.

3. MATCH ONE

Match the players in the left-hand column with the cities in the right-hand column where they were born.

1) ___ Reggie Jackson   a) Colorado Springs, Colo.
2) ___ Ron Guidry   b) Newark, N.J.   ,
3) ___ Goose Gossage   c) Tampa, Fla.
4) ___ Graig Nettles   d) Holly Hill, S.C.
5) ___ Bucky Dent   e) St. Paul, Minn.
6) ___ Rick Cerone   f) Wyncote, Pa.
7) ___ Dave Winfield   g) Savannah, Ga.
8) ___ Lou Piniella   h) Oklahoma City, Ok.
9) ___ Bobby Murcer   i) San Diego, Cal.
10) ___ Willie Randolph   j) Lafayette, La.

4. MATCH TWO

Match the players in the left-hand column with the minor-league cities in the right-hand column where they first springboarded to the majors.

1) __ Tommy John   a) Appleton
2) __ Bob Watson   b) Rocky Mount
3) __ Jerry Mumphrey   c) None; he played his first professional baseball in the majors.

4) __ Goose Gossage   d) San Antonio
5) __ Dennis Werth   e) Portland
6) __ Elliott Maddox   f) Indianapolis
7) __ Oscar Gamble   g) Arkansas, Tex.
8) __ Dave Revering   h) El Paso
9) __ Dave Winfield   i) Columbus
10) __ Rudy May   j) Oklahoma City

5. MATCH THREE

Match the players in the left-hand column with the teams in the right-hand column with which they first played in the majors.

1) __ Larry Milbourne   a) Pirates
2) __ Sparky Lyle   b) Angels
3) __ Tommy John   c) Phillies
4) __ Jim Spencer   d) Indians
5) __ Fred Stanley   e) White Sox
6) __ Willie Randolph   f) Red Sox
7) __ Bucky Dent   g) Twins
8) __ Eric Soderholm   h) Senators
9) __ Grant Jackson   i) Pilots
10) __ Jim Kaat   j) Astros

Answers

1. Who's Who

1) Ed Figueroa (20–9 in 1978)
2) Lou Piniella
3) Chris Chambliss
4) Sparky Lyle
5) Don Mattingly (1985)
6) Graig Nettles (319)
7) Ron Guidry (1978)
8) Mike Torrez
9) Reggie Jackson (47 for 1969 A's and 41 for 1980 Yankees)
10) Thurman Munson (1975–77)
11) Broadcaster Bill White (1962–64)
12) Sparky Lyle (1977)
13) Graig Nettles (1976)
14) Ron Guidry (.893 in 1978)
15) Bucky Dent
16) Reggie Jackson
17) Brian Doyle (.438)
18) Catfish Hunter (1968 A's)
19) Chris Chambliss
20) Don Gullett
21) Ron Guidry (248 in 1978)
22) Lou Piniella
23) Goose Gossage (1.84 with 1975 White Sox, 1.66 with 1977 Pirates, 0.77 with 1981 Yankees, and 1.82 with 1985 Padres)
24) Sparky Lyle (1972)
25) Ron Davis (14–2 in 1979)

2. True or False

1) True (1977, 1979, and 1980)
2) True
3) True (193 in 1977)
4) False (.292)
5) False (1967 Twins)
6) False (.300 in 1980)
7) False
8) True
9) False (20–9 with 1975 Orioles)
10) True (1973)
11) False
12) True (33 in 1972)
13) True (.331 in 1971)
14) True (.304 in 1975)
15) False
16) True (1975 Angels)
17) True (1976)
18) False
19) True
20) False
21) True
22) False (20 in 1973)
23) True (1971–75)
24) True (.348, .391, and .455)
25) True (32 and 30)

3. Match One

1) f
2) j
3) a
4) i
5) g

6) b
7) e
8) c
9) h
10) d

4. Match Two

1) e
2) j
3) a
4) g
5) i

6) b
7) d
8) f
9) c
10) h

5. Match Three

1) j
2) f
3) d
4) b
5) i

6) a
7) e
8) g
9) c
10) h

Historical Interlude
Number One

The 1978 playoffs between the Yankees and the Royals did not go to a fifth game, but the action in Games Three and Four was just as tense as the fifth-game dramatics of the previous two years.

After two lopsided games—the Yankees won Game One 7–1 and the Royals copped Game Two 10–4—New York and Kansas City played each other the way American League fans had come to expect.

In both games, as usual, the Yankees had to battle from behind. George Brett was the Royal batting star of Game Three. He hit three home runs and just missed a fourth. In each case the pitching victim was Catfish Hunter, who was no stranger to throwing gopher balls.

The Royals took a 5–4 lead in the top of the eighth on two runs that were not the result of a Brett four-base blast. But in the bottom of the same inning, Roy White singled and scored in front of a Yankee clutch hitter who clubbed one of relief pitcher Doug Bird's fast balls 430 feet into the visitors' bullpen for the game-winning homer. Winner Goose Gossage shut Kansas City off in the ninth inning.

In Game Four, Dennis Leonard and Ron Guidry hooked up in a pitchers' duel. Leonard allowed only four hits. Guidry granted seven. But two of the hits off Leonard were home runs.

The Royals jumped out on top (again!) in the visitors' half of the first. Brett (that name again!) hit a lead-off triple and scored on Hal McRae's single. The Yankees knotted the score in the bottom of the second on Graig Nettles' solo shot. White hit the game-winner in the sixth.

After Amos Otis led off the Royals' ninth with a double, Gossage replaced Guidry and shut the door in Kansas

City's face with a strikeout of Clint Hurdle and outfield flies by Darrell Porter and Pete LaCock.

The Yankees won the game, 2–1, and the series, 3–1.

Looking back to that series, I'm inclined to believe that the turning point of the four-game set was the game-winning home run in Game Three. (It was only the second time that a player had hit a ball in that spot.) Doug DeCinces had hit the first ball to reach that area.

Who hit the second?

Answer: Thurman Munson

CHAPTER TWO

The Highlanders

6. WHO'S WHO

You can use the following list as a guide to the answers in this quiz:

Frank Baker	Bill Hogg
Ray Caldwell	Harry Howell
Hal Chase	Tom Hughes
Jack Chesbro	Long Tom Hughes
Ty Cobb	Ray Keating
Wid Conroy	Willie Keeler
Birdie Cree	Fritz Maisel
Bert Daniels	George Mogridge
Lefty Davis	Les Nunamaker
Patsy Dougherty	Wally Pipp
Kid Elberfeld	Bob Shawkey
Russ Ford	Ed Sweeney
George "Rube" Foster	Jack Warhop
John Ganzel	Jimmy Williams
Joe Gordon	Cy Young
Clark Griffith	Guy Zinn
Bruno Haas	

1) _____ Who was the only Highlander to win at least one home-run title?

2) _____ Who was the only other Highlander to hit as many as ten home runs in a season? (Previously, he had won four consecutive home-run titles with another American League team.)

3) _____ Who was the first Highlander pitcher to win a game in a New York uniform? (On the same day, he became the first Highlander to hit a triple.)

16

4) _____ Who, in 1917, became the first left-handed pitcher to hurl a no-hitter at Fenway Park? (He is still the only lefty to throw a no-hitter at Fenway.)

5) _____ Who was the Highlander pitcher who, in 1915, yielded Babe Ruth's first major-league home run? (It was at the Polo Grounds. Remember, now, Ruth was playing with the Red Sox at the time.)

6) _____ Who set a record by getting hit with pitches three times in one *day*?

7) _____ Who tied a major-league record for first basemen by making 22 putouts in a nine-inning game?

8) _____ Who was the Athletic pitcher—throwing his first game in the majors—who walked a record 16 Highlanders in one game? (He also added three wild pitches in New York's 15–0 rout.)

9) _____ Who was the Red Sox pitcher who no-hit the Yankees in 1908? (Earlier, he had pitched a no-hitter in the National League and a perfect game in the American League.)

10) _____ Who was the pitcher who hurled nine and two-thirds innings of no-hit ball in relief as the Highlanders downed the Browns in 17 innings, 7–5?

11) _____ Who was the shortstop who tied a major league record by getting all four of his team's hits in a 3–2 win over Philadelphia?

12) _____ Who was the catcher who threw out three consecutive Tiger baserunners trying to steal second base in the first inning?

13) _____ Who was the first player to decide an extra-inning 1–0 game with a home run? (He did it for Washington in 1906, but he played for New York in 1904. He was a pitcher, by the way.)

14) _____ Who was the outfielder who set a major league record by stealing home twice in the same game?

15) _____ Who was the first of three Yankees (Highlanders) to hit three triples in one game?

16) _____ Who was the Yankee right-hander who hurled a no-hitter for nine innings, but lost the game, 5–0, in 11 innings?

17) _____ Who was the pitcher who had 16–, 18–, and 19–win seasons for New York, but didn't pitch a no-

hitter until the season after the Yankees traded him to the Red Sox, who quickly traded him to the Indians? (He pitched it against the Yankees, of course.)

18) _____ Who was the Highlanders' first starting—and losing—pitcher in a major-league game? ("Happy Jack" had the last laugh, though—he won 21 games that season.)

19) _____ Who was the first official at batsman in a Highlander uniform?

20) _____ Who was the pitcher who, in 1913, yielded a second-inning single to Charlie Deal, then pitched no-hit ball the rest of the way, en route to a 6–0 shutout? (He struck Ty Cobb out the only two times the "Georgia Peach" would face him that day.)

21) _____ Who hit the first home run in the franchise's history? (Wid Conroy later homered in the same game.)

22) _____ Who was the competitive opponent who got fined $100 and suspended for ten days because he climbed into the stands at the Polo Grounds and punished a verbal assailant?

23) _____ Who pitched the first shutout for the Highlanders? (He also happened to be their manager.)

24) _____ Who was the slugger whom the Yankees acquired in 1904 in a trade for Bob Unglaub? (The year before, he became the first player to hit two home runs in a World Series game.)

25) _____ Who was the Red Sox righty—he won two games in the World Series the year before—who no-hit New York in 1916?

26) _____ Who was the 23-game winner (1916) who later became a Yankee manager?

27) _____ Who, in one season, started a record 51 games and completed a record 48 contests? (He also pitched 454 and two-thirds innings. But that was not a record!)

28) _____ Who batted .300 or better a record four times with the Highlanders?

29) _____ Who was the Highlander outfielder who hit .300 three times?

30) _____ Who was the Highlander infielder who

batted .300 twice? (In 1916 he won the batting title with the Reds. Lifetime, he hit .291.)

31) _____ Who, from the 1908 staff, turned in the poorest winning percentage by a Highlander pitcher who had 20 or more decisions in one year? (He faded from the major-league scene the following year.)

32) _____ Who, in 1906, set the club record for singles (166) in a single season? (Earle Combs tied the mark in 1927.)

33) _____ Who set the club record for stolen bases (74) in a single season?

34) _____ Who had the longest hitting streak of the era (27 games) with the Highlanders?

35) _____ Who hit 22 triples in 1911, the club's second all-time high? (Earle Combs holds the club record with 23.)

36) _____ Who drove home 99 runs in 1916, the high in this department for that era?

37) _____ Who holds the club's all-time record for stolen bases—248?*

38) _____ Who was the catcher from this era who led the league in fielding percentage one season?

39) _____ Who was the pitcher who turned in the highest fielding percentage (1.000) at his position for one season in the history of the franchise?

40) _____ Who threw the most shutouts by a righty in one season in the history of the club?

41) _____ Who, in addition to Jack Chesbro, appeared in more than 50 games in a season?

42) _____ Who was the only club rookie to strike out more than 200 batters in a season?

43) _____ Who, in addition to Hal Chase, was the only player in the Highlander era to steal 30 or more bases four times?

44) _____ Who amassed the highest single-season batting average of this era?

45) _____ Who was the pitcher whom the Highlanders paid the Athletics $85,000 for in 1915? (He won 168 games in New York and four times won 20 or more games in a season.)

*Set in 1913, it has since been beaten.

46) _____ Who was the manager who piloted the club to 419 wins in almost six seasons?

47) _____ Who was the Highlanders' first team president?

48) _____ Who was the second baseman who led the Highlanders in doubles a club-high three times?

49) _____ Who compiled the highest single-season slugging percentage (.513) of this era?

50) _____ Who got an era-high 193 hits in one season?

7. THE ORIGINALS

Select the original Highlanders—those who played in the new franchise's very first major-league game—from the following multiple-choice groups:

1) __ 1B: a. John Ganzel b. Hal Chase c. Charlie Mullen d. Wally Pipp

2) __ 2B: a. Frank LaPorte b. Jimmy Williams c. Roger Peckinpaugh d. Hack Simmons

3) __ SS: a. Jack Martin b. Jack Knight c. Neal Ball d. Herman Long

4) __ 3B: a. Roy Hartzell b. Frank Baker c. Fritz Maisel d. Wid Conroy

5) __ OF: a. Danny Hoffman b. Willie Keeler c. Elmer Miller d. Harry Wolter

6) __ OF: a. Dave Fultz b. Tim Hendryx c. Birdie Cree d. Bert Daniels

7) __ OF: a. Hugh High b. Guy Zinn c. Clyde Engle d. Lefty Davis

8) __ C: a. Monte Beville b. Red Kleinow c. Jack O'Connor d. Les Nunamaker

9) __ P: a. Jesse Tannehill b. Clark Griffith c. Jack Chesbro d. Harry Howell

8. WHERE'D THEY PLAY: PRE-HIGHLANDERS

Match the original Highlanders in the left-hand column with the major-league team in the right-hand column with which they last played before New York.

1) __ Merle Adkins   a) Orioles
2) __ Jack Chesbro   b) Tigers
3) __ Tim Jordan   c) White Sox
4) __ Kid Elberfeld   d) Senators
5) __ Dave Fultz   e) Pirates
6) __ John Ganzel   f) Phillies
7) __ Pat Greene   g) Dodgers
8) __ Clark Griffith   h) Red Sox
9) __ Willie Keeler   i) Giants
10) __ Herman Long   j) Athletics
11) __ Pat McCauley   k) Braves

9. WHERE'D THEY PLAY: WITH THE HIGHLANDERS

In this quiz all you have to do is to identify where the players listed below played: pitcher, catcher, infield, or outfield. There are seven catchers, six at the other positions. Mark *P, C, I,* or *O* before each name.

1) __ Walt Alexander   6) __ Joe Lake
2) __ Jimmy Austin   7) __ Monty Beville
3) __ Charlie Baumann   8) __ Bill Donovan
4) __ Edgar Hahn   9) __ Clarence Vance
5) __ Charlie Hemphill   10) __ Ed Sweeney

11) __ Irish McIlveen	19) __ Slow Joe Doyle
12) __ Earl Gardner	20) __ John Gossett
13) __ Patsy Dougherty	21) __ Bill Reynolds
14) __ Urban Shocker	22) __ Jesse Tannehill
15) __ Walter Clarkson	23) __ John Priest
16) __ Frank Delahanty	24) __ Bill McKechnie
17) __ Clyde Engle	25) __ Cozy Dolan
18) __ Lou Criger	

10. 20-GAME WINNERS

Five pitchers in the history of the Highlanders won 20 or more games in at least one season. How many of them can you name?

1) _____ (1)	4) _____ (2)
2) _____ (1)	5) _____ (3)
3) _____ (1)	

Answers

6. Who's Who

1) Wally Pipp (1916–17)
2) Frank Baker (10 in 1916)
3) Harry Howell (1903)
4) George Mogridge
5) Jack Warhop
6) Bert Daniels (1913)
7) Hal Chase (1906)
8) Bruno Haas (1915)
9) Cy Young
10) Ray Caldwell (1917)
11) Kid Elberfeld (1903)
12) Les Nunamaker (1903)
13) Long Tom Hughes
14) Guy Zinn (1912)
15) Hal Chase (1906)
16) Tom Hughes (1910)
17) Ray Caldwell (1919)
18) Jack Chesbro (1903)
19) Lefty Davis (1903)
20) Ray Keating
21) John Ganzel
22) Ty Cobb (1912)
23) Clark Griffith (1903)
24) Patsy Dougherty
25) George "Rube" Foster
26) Bob Shawkey (1930)
27) Jack Chesbro (1904)
28) Willie Keeler
29) Birdie Cree
30) Hal Chase (.323 in 1906 and .315 in 1911)
31) Bill Hogg (4–16)
32) Willie Keeler
33) Fritz Maisel (74 in 1914)
34) Hal Chase (1907)
35) Birdie Cree
36) Wally Pipp
37) Hal Chase
38) Ed Sweeney (1912)
39) Harry Howell (1903)
40) Russ Ford (8 in 1910)
41) Bob Shawkey (53 in 1916)
42) Russ Ford (209 in 1910)
43) Wid Conroy
44) Birdie Cree (.348)
45) Bob Shawkey
46) Clark Griffith
47) Joe Gordon (1903–06)
48) Jimmy Williams
49) Birdie Cree (1911)
50) Hal Chase

7. The Originals

1) a
2) b
3) d
4) d
5) b

6) a
7) d
8) c
9) c

8. Where'd They Play: Pre-Highlanders

1) h
2) e
3) a
4) b
5) j
6) i

7) f
8) c
9) g
10) k
11) d

9. Where'd They Play: With the Highlanders

1) C
2) I
3) I
4) O
5) O
6) P
7) C
8) P
9) P
10) C
11) O
12) I
13) O

14) P
15) P
16) O
17) O
18) C
19) P
20) C
21) C
22) P
23) I
24) I
25) I

10. 20-Game Winners

1) Jack Powell
2) Al Orth
3) Bob Shawkey

4) Russ Ford
5) Jack Chesbro

Historical Interlude Number Two

Waite Hoyt weaved an enviable World Series record: six wins and four losses, three of which were of the one-run variety.

But the toughest game that he lost—with the most bizarre World Series ending—took place on October 5, 1921, in the eighth and final game between the two New York teams.

Hoyt, in the Yankees' first World Series, did not allow an earned run in 27 innings of pitching. But he did give up two unearned runs, one of which came in the first inning of this fateful game. Shortstop Roger Peckinpaugh made an error that allowed the Giants' only run—and the game's only run—to cross the plate.

In the home half of the ninth inning, it appeared that the Yankees might get even or better. Babe Ruth, who had been sidelined by an infected arm and a wrenched knee, grounded out in a pinch-hitting appearance. But Aaron Ward drew a free pass before the unbelievable play that closed the curtain on the 1921 World Series. Frank Baker, of home-run fame in World Series play, drilled a sharp shot to the left of the Giant second sacker. It appeared destined for right field. But John McGraw's feisty second baseman had other ideas. He dove to his left, gloved the ball, and threw to first baseman George Kelly to nail Baker.

Ward, who was running with the crack of the bat, thought that the ball was a sure hit, so he never hesitated when he reached second. He kept right on running to third. Kelly, the surprised but opportunistic first baseman, pegged a strike to third basemen Frankie Frisch, who applied the tag to the startled Ward. It was the first—and remains the only—time that the World Series ended in that fashion.

Who was the Giant second baseman who put the machinery of that play into motion?

25

CHAPTER THREE

Murderers' Row

11. WHO'S WHO

You can use the following list as a guide to the answers in this quiz:

Joe Dugan	Bill Piercy
Everett Scott	Ken Williams
Carl Mays	Lefty O'Doul
Jack Quinn	Joe Wood
Bobby Veach	Herb Pennock
Ben Paschal	Wilcy Moore
Tom Zachary	Earle Combs
Ed Barrow	Bob Meusel
Sam Jones	Howard Ehmke
Waite Hoyt	Pee Wee Wanninger
Mark Koenig	Babe Ruth
Wally Pipp	George Halas
Bob Shawkey	Hal Chase
Willis Hudlin	Harry Harper
Urban Shocker	

1) _____ Who was the only 20-game winner on the famed 1927 club?

2) _____ Who has the most wins and saves in World Series play without a reversal?

3) _____ Who was the relief ace who posted a 19–7 record with 13 saves in 1927? (He pitched a 4–3 complete-game win in the windup of the 1927 World Series sweep.)

4) _____ Who was the .280 lifetime hitter whom the Yankees acquired from the Red Sox in 1923? (A steady performer, he played in five World Series for the Pinstripers, batting .333 in 1926.)

5) _____ Who was the dependable infielder from the 1927 team who later played in World Series with two different teams *against* the Yankees?

6) _____ Who was the first baseman whom Lou Gehrig replaced in the lineup? (Many people know him because of the "headache" he experienced in 1925, but few people realize that he twice won home-run crowns.)

7) _____ Who was the Yankee lead-off batter who hit .325 over a 12-year career? (Three times he delivered more than 200 hits.)

8) _____ Who was the shortstop whose record 1,307 consecutive-games-played-in streak came to an end in 1925? (It was later broken, of course, by teammate Lou Gehrig's 2,130-game mark.)

9) _____ Who pitched a 12-inning 0–0 tie against the immortal Walter Johnson in 1919? (He was also the oldest pitcher in history—47—to pitch in the World Series.)

10) _____ Who got suspended for ten days in 1924 for charging Tiger pitcher Bert Cole and taking a wild swing at the beleaguered Bengal? (The altercation precipitated a riot by the Tiger fans which resulted in a forfeiture to the Yankees. In that melee, by the way, Babe Ruth and Ty Cobb exchanged swings and vile epithets.)

11) _____ Who was the future Yankee pitching ace who hurled both ends of a doubleheader against the Pinstripers in 1919, tossed complete games, and came away with a split after 18 innings of toil?

12) _____ Who was the pitcher who tripled and doubled to set the major-league mark for most extra bases by a pitcher in the same inning?

13) _____ Who was the pitcher who defeated the Athletics 23 consecutive times?

14) _____ Who was the Tiger pitcher who, in 1920, defeated the Yankees 1–0 in the American League's shortest game? (He later set a World Series record by striking out 13 batters in one game.)

15) _____ Who was the only player ever to pinch-hit for Babe Ruth?

16) _____ Who was the Cleveland pitcher who served up Babe Ruth's 500th home run?

17) _____ Who was the Yankee pitcher—he was a 26-game winner that season—whose fastball resulted in the death of Indian shortstop Ray Chapman, baseball's only on-the-field fatality?

18) _____ Who was the Yankee pitcher who was suspended for ten days for attacking home-plate umpire Brick Owens?

19) _____ Who was the pitcher who, after a year-long battle, was awarded to the Yankees? (He had jumped to the Federal League when he was the property of the Yankees, but he wished to return to the majors as the property of the White Sox. He was worth fighting over: he won well over 200 career games.)

20) _____ Who became the second Yankee to collect three triples in one game?

21) _____ Who was the future Yankee pitcher—he won 240 major-league games—who yielded Babe Ruth's last home run as a tenant of the Polo Grounds? (The same Red Sox pitcher also surrendered Ruth's first home run as a tenant of Yankee Stadium.)

22) _____ Who was the veteran Yankee pitcher—he won 188 career games—who died of heart failure at the age of 38? (A four-time 20-game winner, he posted an 18–6 mark in the year before his death.)

23) _____ Who was the infielder whom Lou Gehrig pinch-hit for to begin his streak of playing in 2,130 consecutive games?

24) _____ Who hit a record-tying three sacrifice flies in one game?

25) _____ Who was the Red Sox pitcher who gave up a controversial lead-off single to Whitey Witt, then retired 27 consecutive batters?

26) _____ Who set a major-league mark by hitting two inside-the-park home runs in one game?

27) _____ Who was the Red Sox pitcher who granted Lou Gehrig's first major-league home run?

28) _____ Who hit grand slams in consecutive games twice in the same year? (Two years before, he also hit grand slams in consecutive games.)

29) _____ Who was the pitcher whom Babe Ruth roughed up for his 60th home run of the 1927 season?

30) _____ Who was the Yankee pitcher who hurled the only Sunday game of his career en route to a 3–0 World Series win?

31) _____ Who was the first relief pitcher to win an ERA title?

32) _____ Who was the first Yankee pitcher to win a game in the "House That Ruth Built?" (He was also the first pitcher—in the same game—to hit a home run in Old Yankee Stadium.)

33) _____ Who was the Red Sox manager—he was later general manager of the Yankees—who converted Babe Ruth from the mound to the outfield?

34) _____ Who was the outfielder—he later gained fame as a coach in another sport—whom Babe Ruth replaced in right field with the Yankees?

35) _____ Who was the Yankee pitcher who holds the record of most games won without a defeat in the same season?

36) _____ Who three times hit more than 20 triples in a season?

37) _____ Who was the only non-Yankee to win a home-run title in the 1920s?

38) _____ Who was the Yankee pitcher of the 1920s who switched to the outfield and compiled a .349 lifetime average?

39) _____ Who was the deft-fielding first baseman—he has been called the greatest fielding first sacker in the history of the game—who was "chased" from baseball after the 1919 season for alleged gambling irregularities?

40) _____ Who was the outfielder who set an American League mark by hitting for the cycle three times in his career? (Babe Herman did it in the National League.)

41) _____ Who was the pitcher, a 200-plus-game winner, who did not throw a keep-the-runner-close toss to first base in five years?

42) _____ Who was the onetime Yankee pitcher who hurled a league record 22 consecutive years in the big leagues?

43) _____ Who set a club record for right-handed pitchers when he struck out 15 batters in one game?

44) _____ Who hit a club-record 17 home runs in one month?

45) _____ Who was the onetime three-game winner in the World Series who hit two home runs in a 19-inning 3–2 win over the Yankees in 1919? (The second home run won the game.)

46) _____ Who was the pitcher whom some club owners tried to bar from their parks because they objected to his trade to the Yankees by the Red Sox?

47) _____ Who was the 1921 pitcher who tied a major-league mark by hitting three opposing batters in one inning?

48) _____ Who was suspended indefinitely and fined $5,000 for insubordination and other infractions?

49) _____ Who was the only pitcher from this era to pitch a no-hitter?

50) _____ Who was the Yankee pitcher from this era who threw two one-hitters?

12. THE YANKEES' FARM TEAM

The Yankees became the greatest team of the 1920s—and perhaps any other decade—because they traded for, bought, and stole from the Red Sox some of the greatest talent ever developed in baseball. The Red Sox were the greatest team of the 1910s—four pennants and four world titles—and undoubtedly would have been the greatest team of the 1920s, and perhaps of all time, had they not committed extraordinarily bad front-office mistakes. Below you will find 50 Yankees of that era. Twenty of them were acquired from the Red Sox. How many of them can you pick out? Check the correct names.

Ernie Shore
Del Pratt
Roger Peckinpaugh
Duffy Lewis

Frank Baker
Muddy Ruel
Carl Mays
Babe Ruth

Jack Quinn
Ping Bodie
George Mogridge
Waite Hoyt
Harry Harper
Bob Meusel
Whitey Witt
Mike McNally
Wally Schang
Aaron Ward
Everett Scott
Lou Gehrig
Pee Wee Wanninger
Benny Bengough
Sam Jones
Ben Paschal
Urban Shocker
Joe Bush
Joe Dugan
Tony Lazzeri
Mark Koenig

Earle Combs
Pat Collins
Elmer Smith
Mike Gazella
George Pipgras
Harvey Hendrick
Ray Morehart
Johnny Grabowski
Cedric Durst
Herb Pennock
Howard Shanks
Leo Durocher
Gene Robertson
Steve O'Neill
Wilcy Moore
Bobby Veach
Bill Dickey
Lyn Lary
Sammy Byrd
Red Ruffing
Ben Chapman

13. PITCHING GEMS

See if you can match the following pitchers with their lifetime records (it's no wonder that the Yankees won so many pennants and world titles): Bob Shawkey, George Mogridge, Jack Quinn, Carl Mays, Waite Hoyt, Sam Jones, Joe Bush, Herb Pennock, Urban Shocker, Wilcy Moore, George Pipgras, Tom Zachary, and Red Ruffing. (It adds up to a record of 2,448–1,881.)

1) _____ (273–225)   8) _____ (196–181)
2) _____ (242–217)   9) _____ (188–117)
3) _____ (240–162)   10) _____ (185–191)
4) _____ (237–182)   11) _____ (134–129)
5) _____ (229–217)   12) _____ (102–73)
6) _____ (207–126)   13) _____ (51–44)
7) _____ (196–152)

14. MATCHING AVERAGES

Match the 1927 every-day players—reputed to be the greatest lineup in history—in the left-hand column with their batting averages of that year in the right-hand column. An *r* after the name indicates reserve. (One letter in the right-hand column may be used twice.)

1) __ Lou Gehrig   a) .317
2) __ Tony Lazzeri   b) .356
3) __ Ray Morehart (r)   c) .373
4) __ Mark Koenig   d) .337
5) __ Joe Dugan   e) .309
6) __ Bob Meusel   f) .275
7) __ Earle Combs   g) .269
8) __ Babe Ruth   h) .285
9) __ Ben Paschal (r)   i) .256
10) __ Pat Collins

15. DOUBLE-DIGIT FOUR-BASE BLOWS

Seven Yankees, in addition to Babe Ruth, Lou Gehrig, and Tony Lazzeri, hit ten or more home runs in a season during this era. How many of them can you name?

1) _____   5) _____
2) _____   6) _____
3) _____   7) _____
4) _____

Answers

11. Who's Who

1) Waite Hoyt (22–7)
2) Herb Pennock (5 wins, 3 saves)
3) Wilcy Moore
4) Joe Dugan
5) Mark Koenig (Cubs, 1932; Giants, 1936)
6) Wally Pipp
7) Earle Combs
8) Everett Scott
9) Jack Quinn
10) Bob Meusel
11) Carl Mays
12) Bob Shawkey (1923)
13) Carl Mays
14) Howard Ehmke
15) Bobby Veach (1925)
16) Willis Hudlin (1929)
17) Carl Mays (1920)
18) Waite Hoyt (1923)
19) Jack Quinn
20) Earle Combs (1927)
21) Herb Pennock
22) Urban Shocker
23) Pee Wee Wanninger
24) Bob Meusel
25) Howard Ehmke
26) Ben Paschal (1925)
27) Bill Piercy
28) Babe Ruth
29) Tom Zachary
30) Carl Mays
31) Wilcy Moore (1927)
32) Bob Shawkey (1923)
33) Ed Barrow
34) George Halas
35) Tom Zachary (12–0 in 1929)
36) Earle Combs (23 in 1927, 21 in 1928, and 22 in 1930)
37) Ken Williams (1922)
38) Lefty O'Doul
39) Hal Chase
40) Bob Meusel
41) Sam Jones
42) Sam Jones (1914–35)
43) Bob Shawkey (1919)
44) Babe Ruth (1927)
45) Joe Wood
46) Carl Mays
47) Harry Harper
48) Babe Ruth (1922)
49) Sam Jones (1923)
50) Bob Shawkey

12. The Yankees' Farm Team

1) Ernie Shore
2) Duffy Lewis
3) Carl Mays
4) Babe Ruth
5) Waite Hoyt
6) Harry Harper
7) Mike McNally
8) Wally Schang

9) Everett Scott
10) Sam Jones
11) Joe Bush
12) Joe Dugan
13) Elmer Smith
14) George Pipgras
15) Harvey Hendrick
16) Herb Pennock
17) Howard Shanks
18) Steve O'Neill
19) Bobby Veach
20) Red Ruffing

13. Pitching Gems

1) Red Ruffing
2) Jack Quinn
3) Herb Pennock
4) Waite Hoyt
5) Sam Jones
6) Carl Mays
7) Bob Shawkey
8) Joe Bush
9) Urban Shocker
10) Tom Zachary
11) George Mogridge
12) George Pipgras
13) Wilcy Moore

14. Matching Averages

1) c
2) e
3) i
4) h
5) g
6) d
7) b
8) b
9) a
10) f

15. Double-Digit Four-Base Blows

1) Frank Baker
2) Wally Pipp
3) Aaron Ward (twice)
4) Bob Meusel (six times)
5) Ben Paschal
6) Bill Dickey
7) Ben Chapman

Historical Interlude
Number Three

The final game of the 1926 World Series has gone down in baseball history as one of the most exciting finishes in the annals of the Fall Classic.

With the visiting Cardinals leading the Yankees 3–2 in the bottom of the sixth, Jesse Haines developed a finger blister while the Yankees loaded the bases with two outs. Rogers Hornsby, the manager of St. Louis, decided to replace Haines with Grover Alexander, who had already won two games in the Series. Alexander, one of the all-time greats of the hill, had to face Tony Lazzeri, a long-ball-hitting rookie. On the second pitch of the confrontation, Lazzeri almost decisively won the duel: he hit a long line drive to left that tailed a few feet left of the foul pole. Three pitches later, Alexander struck Lazzeri out on a sweeping curve ball.

Settling down into a groove, Alexander mowed the Yankees down in order in both the seventh and eighth innings. Before he faced Babe Ruth, with two outs, in the ninth, he had retired nine consecutive batters. Suddenly, working overcautiously, he walked the Babe. But he was still not out of danger, for he had to face Bob Meusel, who had won the home-run crown the year before.

On the first pitch to Meusel, however, Ruth pulled the unexpected: he tried to steal second base. But the Redbird catcher threw a strike to Rogers Hornsby to nail Ruth, who had become the first and only base runner to make the last out of a World Series on an attempted steal.

After the Series ended, Cardinal owner Sam Breadon traded manager Hornsby to the Giants and named his catcher the team's manager. Maybe the backstop's final throw of the 1926 World Series had something to do with Breadon's decision.

Who was that veteran of 21 seasons who stopped the Yankees in 1926 and led the Cardinals in 1927?

Answer: Bob O'Farrell

35

CHAPTER FOUR

McCarthy's Men

16. WHO'S WHO

You can use the following list as a guide to the answers in this quiz:

Babe Dahlgren	Tony Lazzeri
Ben Chapman	Wilcy Moore
Red Ruffing	Bill Dickey
Sammy Byrd	Monte Pearson
Joe Beggs	Frankie Crosetti
Lefty Grove	Charlie Root
Lyn Lary	Spud Chandler
Red Rolfe	Bump Hadley
Lefty Gomez	Russ Van Atta
Lou Gehrig	Jake Powell
Joe DiMaggio	Myril Hoag
Joe Sewell	Johnny Broaca
George Selkirk	Earle Combs

1) _____ Who was the first modern-day player to hit four home runs in a game?

2) _____ Who hit a club-record 15 home runs by a right-handed batter in one month?

3) _____ Who was the Yankee pitcher who ended Mickey Cochrane's career when he hit the Tiger manager in the head with a high hard one in 1937?

4) _____ Who was the Cub pitcher against whom Babe Ruth "called his shot" in the 1932 World Series?

5) _____ Who was the first baseman who replaced Lou Gehrig the day the "Iron Horse's" consecutive-game streak came to an end?

6) _____ Who was the outfielder who set a record for rookies when he scored 132 runs?

7) _____ Who was called "Babe Ruth's Legs"?

8) _____ Who was the outfielder who got a club-rookie-record 206 hits in 1936?

9) _____ Who struck out a club-record-low three times in one season?

10) _____ Who was the two-time 20-game winner, ERA titlist, and MVP selectee who was 30 when he came to the Yankees as a rookie?

11) _____ Who was the Yankee outfielder who led the league in stolen bases three years in a row?

12) _____ Who, in addition to Lou Gehrig (152), Joe DiMaggio (125), Tony Lazzeri (109), and Bill Dickey (107), drove in over 100 runs in 1936?

13) _____ Who holds the club record of most home runs by a rookie?

14) _____ Who was the only Yankee pitcher to win 20 games in four consecutive seasons?

15) _____ Who was the infielder who drove home a league-record 11 runs in one game?

16) _____ Who was the third baseman who averaged only eight strikeouts per year for 14 seasons?

17) _____ Who was the first Yankee to win the Triple Crown?

18) _____ Who was the pitching star who batted .300 eight times?

19) _____ Who was the last Yankee to total more than 400 bases in a season?

20) _____ Who hit two grand slams in the same game?

21) _____ Who was the rookie who got a record-tying four singles in his first major-league game? (He tied the record set by Casey Stengel in 1912.)

22) _____ Who set the modern-day record of reaching base safely seven times in a nine-inning game?

23) _____ Who was the outfielder who got suspended for ten days for getting in a slugfest with the Red Sox' Joe Cronin?

24) _____ Who got touched for three grand slams by Jimmie Foxx in 1938?

25) _____ Who got a record six hits in six at bats in a nine-inning game?

26) _____ Who, in addition to pitching a complete-

game 15–4 win, hit two home runs and two singles in a 1936 game?

27) _____ Who was the 1934 pitcher who tied a major-league record by striking out five times in one game?

28) _____ Who, in addition to Earle Combs, got two doubles in the same inning to help set the mark of most players getting two two-base hits in the same inning?

29) _____ Who was fined $1,000 and suspended 30 days for breaking Senator outfielder Carl Reynolds' jaw in 1932?

30) _____ Who was the Yankee outfielder who was suspended for ten days for voicing threatening comments toward black people over a Chicago radio station?

31) _____ Who hit a record-tying two inside-the-park home runs in the same game? (He added a third home run in that contest.)

32) _____ Who was the former Yankee relief ace who shut out the Yankees 1–0 in 1931? (The next day the Yankees began their 308-game scoring streak that lasted until 1933.)

33) _____ Who was the Athletic pitcher who snapped that streak with a 7–0 shutout?

34) _____ Who was the Yankee pitcher who tied a record by hitting a home run to decide a 1–0 ten-inning game?

35) _____ Who was the Yankee pitcher from this era who threw a 13–0 no-hitter against the Indians?

36) _____ Who was the outfielder who, in the same game, became the third of three Yankees to triple three times in the same game?

37) _____ Who equaled a major-league record in 1932 by striking out two times in the same inning? (He whiffed four of the first five times he batted that day.)

38) _____ Who was the Hall-of-Famer who yielded Hall-of-Famer Ted Williams' first major-league hit—a double—in 1939? (The pitcher whiffed Williams his first two times at bat.)

39) _____ Who was the trailblazer of a rare triple steal in 1932?

40) _____ Who came down with amyotrophic lateral sclerosis in 1939?

41) _____ Who was the outfielder whose great career came to a crashing end when he ran into the outfield wall in St. Louis and fractured his skull?

42) _____ Who made a base-running error—he left the base paths thinking that Lou Gehrig's home run had been caught—that cost the "Iron Horse" the 1931 home-run title? (Babe Ruth and Gehrig tied for the league lead with 41 home runs each.)

43) _____ Who was the infielder who led the league in hits with 213 in 1939?

44) _____ Who hit 46 home runs in his second year in the majors?

45) _____ Who was the four-time 20-game winner from this era who led the league in winning percentage— he was 26–5—with an .839 mark in 1934?

46) _____ Who, from this era, pitched more complete games (261) than any other Yankee pitcher in the Pin-stripers' history?

47) _____ Who, from this era, threw two one-hitters?

48) _____ Who, in addition to Earle Combs, pinch-hit for Lou Gehrig in the 1930s?

49) _____ Who got caught attempting to steal a club-record 23 times in 1931?

50) _____ Who got hit by pitches a club-record 15 times in 1938?

17. FOUR-TIME WORLD CHAMPS

Which 12 of the following 28 players suited up for *all four* of the four consecutive world title teams of 1936–39? Check the correct names.

Lou Gehrig   George Selkirk
Tony Lazzeri   Jake Powell
Frankie Crosetti   Joe DiMaggio
Red Rolfe   Bill Dickey

Roy Johnson	Monte Pearson
Myril Hoag	Bump Hadley
Joe Glenn	Lefty Gomez
Ben Chapman	Johnny Broaca
Jack Saltzgaver	Pat Malone
Art Jorgens	Johnny Murphy
Don Heffner	Jumbo Brown
Bob Seeds	Ted Kleinhans
Dixie Walker	Kemp Wicker
Red Ruffing	Steve Sundra

18. THE 1932 WORLD CHAMPS

Which 13 players from the preceding list (Quiz 17) played on the other Yankee championship team (1932) of the 1930s? Put an X beside the correct names.

19. McCARTHY'S MEN'S MATCHUPS

The group of players referred to in these quizzes was the most remarkable collection of baseball players ever assembled on one team up until that time. No previous team had ever won world titles in four straight years. No team, in fact, had ever dominated for three straight years. Their record would stand until 1953, when another select group of Yankees finally eclipsed it. Let's zero in on those 1936–39 Yankees now and see if we can match 25 of the names in Quiz 17, "Four-Time World Champs," to the statements below.

1) _____ He batted .306 over an 18-year career and won a batting title in the National League with a mark of .357 in 1944.

2) _____ He hit safely in 61 consecutive games in the Pacific Coast League.

3) _____ A .302 lifetime hitter, he was traded by the Yankees to make way for Joe DiMaggio and by the Red Sox to make way for Ted Williams.

4) _____ He most probably would have won 300 games had not World War II interrupted his career.

5) _____ He lost two games for the Cubs in the 1929 World Series, but he twice won 20 games for the Bruins.

6) _____ He had 0.00 ERA marks in four of the six World Series in which he pitched. (Overall, he had a 1.10 ERA in post-season play.)

7) _____ He was called "Lou Gehrig's Caddy."

8) _____ He scored more than 100 runs in each of 13 consecutive seasons.

9) _____ He hit two home runs, a triple, and a double in one game.

10) _____ He was only a substitute outfielder, but he batted .300 in the 1937 World Series—with a home run in the final game—and .400 in the 1938 World Series.

11) _____ As one of two backups to Bill Dickey, he hit one home run in six years. (Traded to the Browns in 1939, he hit four round-trippers.)

12) _____ He batted over .300 for four consecutive years after replacing Babe Ruth in right field.

13) _____ He led the league in strikeouts (99) and stolen bases (27) in 1938. (He struck out a league-leading 105 times in 1937.)

14) _____ He and Red Ruffing (22) were pitchers who drove in 20 or more runs in 1936. (In 1939 he batted .321.)

15) _____ In 1934 he led the league in wins (26), winning percentage (.839), ERA (2.33), complete games (25), innings pitched (281.2), strikeouts (158), and shutouts (6).

16) _____ This glue-man of the infield averaged .309 with the bat from 1936 to 1939.

17) _____ He averaged 26 home runs, 115 RBI, and .327 at the bat during this four-year period.

18) _____ Obtained from Washington during the 1936 season, he batted .306 during the regular year for the

Yankees. (In the World Series he made a valuable contribution, chipping in with ten hits. He never batted higher than .265 in the last seven years of his career, though.)

19) _____ He was born in Norway.

20) _____ He had a losing career record (161–165) with six major-league clubs, but with the Yankees during that four-year span, he weaved a 46–26 mark.

21) _____ He turned in an 11–1 mark for the Yankees in 1939. (Lifetime he was 56–41 for three American League teams. In 1943, his last full season in the majors, he turned in a 15–11 record.)

22) _____ In four seasons this relief pitcher saved only two games with the Yankees; in four seasons with the Giants (1938–41) he saved 27 games. (In his last two seasons in the majors—1940–41—he led the National League with seven and eight saves, respectively.)

23) _____ He was a utility infielder for the 1934–37 Yankees. (He played most of his 11-year career in St. Louis.)

24) _____ This 10–7 lifetime pitcher was 7–3 as a spot starter for the 1937 Yankees.

25) _____ He averaged 13 wins per season in his first three years (1934–36) in the big leagues; then he jumped the team for two years. (In 1939 he returned to the majors to wrap up his career, 4–2, with the Indians.)

Answers

16. Who's Who

1) Lou Gehrig (1932)
2) Joe DiMaggio (15 in July 1937)
3) Bump Hadley
4) Charlie Root
5) Babe Dahlgren (1939)
6) Joe DiMaggio (1936)
7) Sammy Byrd
8) Joe DiMaggio
9) Joe Sewell (1932)
10) Spud Chandler (1937)
11) Ben Chapman (1931–33)
12) George Selkirk (107)
13) Joe DiMaggio (29 in 1936)
14) Red Ruffing (1936–39)
15) Tony Lazzeri (1936)
16) Joe Sewell
17) Lou Gehrig (1934)
18) Red Ruffing
19 Joe DiMaggio (418 in 1937)
20) Tony Lazzeri (1936)
21) Russ Van Atta (1933)
22) Ben Chapman (two doubles and five walks in 1936)
23) Jake Powell (1938)
24) Joe Beggs
25) Myril Hoag (1934)
26) Red Ruffing
27) Johnny Broaca
28) Lyn Lary (1932)
29) Bill Dickey
30) Jake Powell (1938)
31) Ben Chapman (1932)
32) Wilcy Moore
33) Lefty Grove (1933)
34) Red Ruffing (1932)
35) Monte Pearson (1938)
36) Joe DiMaggio
37) Frankie Crosetti
38) Red Ruffing
39) Ben Chapman
40) Lou Gehrig
41) Earle Combs (1934)
42) Lyn Lary (1931)
43) Red Rolfe
44) Joe DiMaggio (1937)
45) Lefty Gomez
46) Red Ruffing
47) Lefty Gomez
48) Myril Hoag (1935)
49) Ben Chapman
50) Frankie Crosetti

17. Four-Time World Champs

1) Lou Gehrig
2) Frankie Crosetti
3) Red Rolfe
4) George Selkirk
5) Joe DiMaggio
6) Bill Dickey

7) Art Jorgens
8) Red Ruffing
9) Monte Pearson

10) Bump Hadley
11) Lefty Gomez
12) Johnny Murphy

18. The 1932 World Champs

1) Lou Gehrig
2) Tony Lazzeri
3) Frankie Crosetti
4) Bill Dickey
5) Myril Hoag
6) Joe Glenn
7) Ben Chapman

8) Jack Saltzgaver
9) Art Jorgens
10) Red Ruffing
11) Lefty Gomez
12) Johnny Murphy
13) Jumbo Brown

19. McCarthy's Men's Matchups

1) Dixie Walker
2) Joe DiMaggio
3) Ben Chapman
4) Red Ruffing
5) Pat Malone
6) Johnny Murphy
7) Jack Saltzgaver
8) Lou Gehrig
9) Tony Lazzeri
10) Myril Hoag
11) Joe Glenn
12) George Selkirk
13) Frankie Crosetti

14) Monte Pearson (20)
15) Lefty Gomez
16) Red Rolfe
17) Bill Dickey
18) Jake Powell
19) Art Jorgens
20) Bump Hadley
21) Steve Sundra
22) Jumbo Brown
23) Don Heffner
24) Kemp Wicker
25) Johnny Broaca

Historical Interlude
Number Four

Babe Ruth captured the attention of the nation on October 2, 1932, for on that historic day he allegedly "called his shot."

The Yankees had won the first two games of the World Series before traveling to Chicago's Wrigley Field. The Cub fans and players were riding Ruth unmercifully for criticizing the Bruin players for failing to award former Yankee infielder Mark Koenig a full share of their Series cut.

But Ruth relished the attention.

In the first inning Earle Combs reached second on a two-base throwing error by shortstop Billy Jurges. Bruin pitcher Charlie Root, obviously upset, proceeded to walk Joe Sewell, something he did not want to do with Ruth coming to the plate. On a 2–0 count, Ruth cracked a three-run homer.

The third time that Ruth came to the plate, in the fifth inning, the Yankees were leading, 4–3. In the interim, he had misplayed a ball in right field, much to the delight of the Cub supporters. Before Root got a chance to pitch to the Babe in the fifth, Ruth allegedly pointed his bat toward the center-field bleachers, saying, in effect, "This is where the ball is going to land." The stage had been set for one of the most dramatic moments in baseball history.

Ruth deliberately took two strikes, which he dutifully noted by raising first one finger and then two after the calls. Then he proceeded to deposit the ball in the exact spot to which he had pointed his bat. Coincidentally, that was the 15th and last home run that Ruth hit in Series play.

Lost in the fanfare of that day were the exploits of another Yankee, who hit two home runs, including the game-winner.

Who was this Yankee great who played in the shadow of Ruth?

Answer: Lou Gehrig

45

CHAPTER FIVE

The War Years

20. WHO'S WHO

You can use the following list as a guide to the answers in this quiz:

Oscar Grimes	Johnny Lindell
Paul Schreiber	Tuck Stainback
Ernie Bonham	Joe Page
Hank Borowy	Jim Turner
Buddy Hassett	Mike Milosevich
Bud Metheny	Joe DiMaggio
Russ Derry	Chet Laabs
Paul Waner	George Stirnweiss
Red Ruffing	Nick Etten
Spud Chandler	Hersh Martin
Johnny Sturm	Frankie Crosetti

1) _____ Who was the player with 3,152 hits who wound up his career with the 1945 Yankees?

2) _____ Who, despite the fact that he batted .357 and hit 30 home runs in 1941, was offered a $2,500 cut for 1942 because "there's a war on"? (He ultimately signed for a $6,250 raise.)

3) _____ Who was the batting-practice pitcher—he hadn't played in the major leagues for 20 years—who made two relief appearances for the 1945 Yankees?

4) _____ Who, after nine years in the minor leagues, got the call to spring training in 1944—Phil Rizzuto was in the Navy—and played 124 games for the Yankees in 1944–45? (When Rizzuto returned from the Navy in 1946, his replacement returned to Kansas City.)

5) _____ Who hit two home runs against the Yankees

on the last day of the 1944 season to help gain the Browns their first and only pennant?

6) _____ Who was the Yankee infielder who committed three errors in one inning in 1944?

7) _____ Who was the Yankee pitching great who returned from the service midway through the 1945 season—30 pounds overweight—and finished the season 7–3?

8) _____ Who became one of only three pitchers to win 20 games while splitting the season between teams in opposite leagues?

9) _____ Who, in 1943, led the league in wins (20), winning percentage (.833), ERA (1.64), and complete games (20)?

10) _____ Who was the last Yankee (pre-Rickey Henderson) to win the stolen-base crown?

11) _____ Who, in addition to Spud Chandler, was the only Yankee pitcher to win 20 games during the war years?

12) _____ Who was the lefty-hitting first baseman in 1942 who batted .284 during the regular season and .333 in the World Series?

13) _____ Who was the Yankees' regular first baseman in 1941—his only major-league season—who went into the service and never returned to the big-league scene?

14) _____ Who was the only player in history to win a slugging crown with a sub-.500 percentage?

15) _____ Who won the home-run title in 1944?

16) _____ Who was the Yankee who won a batting crown with a mark below .310?

17) _____ Who was the outfielder who hit four doubles in one game to tie a major-league record?

18) _____ Who was the Yankee outfielder who batted .302 in 1944? (He had played four years with the Phillies before the war.)

19) _____ Who was the 1944 outfielder who batted .300, hammered 18 home runs, and drove home 103 runs?

20) _____ Who was the pitcher who posted a 17–12 record with a 2.64 ERA in 1944?

21) _____ Who was the infielder who drove home a league-high 111 runs in 1945?

22) _____ Who, in 1944, led the league at his position in putouts (433), assists (481), and fielding percentage (.982)?

23) _____ Who led all centerfielders in putouts (468) in 1944?

24) _____ Who was the right fielder who averaged ten home runs per season from 1943 to 1945 with a high of 14 in 1944? (He lasted to get three at bats in the postwar era.)

25) _____ Who was the 1945 center fielder who led the league by participating in six double plays?

26) _____ Who was the .225-hitting part-time out-fielder of 1945—he had 253 at bats—who hit 13 home runs? (He played for the Phillies in 1946 and the Cardinals, briefly, in 1947.)

27) _____ Who was the 1945 infielder who led the league in errors (31) at his position?

28) _____ Who committed 37 errors at his position but finished only third highest in the league? (Cass Michaels of the White Sox committed 47, and Eddie Lake of the Red Sox committed 40.)

29) _____ Who was the relief pitcher who led the American League with ten saves in 1945?

30) _____ Who was the 1944–45 pitcher—he failed to pick up a save in either year—who twice in the late 1940s led the league in saves?

21. WORLD WAR II LINEUP

In 1944 the Yankees tried to defend the title they had won the previous three years. They failed, however. With a lineup of players that was generally foreign to Yankee followers of 1941–43, they finished in third place, six games behind the pace-setting Browns. Do you remember the starters on that wartime team? Select them from the following multiple-choice groups:

1) __ 1B: a. Johnny Sturm b. Buddy Hassett **c.** George McQuinn d. Nick Etten

2) __ 2B: a. Gerry Priddy b. George Stirnweiss **c.** Don Savage d. Joe Buzas

3) __ SS: a. Mike Milosevich b. Frankie Crosetti **c.** Don Savage d. Hank Majeski

4) __ 3B: a. Red Rolfe b. Joe Buzas c. Oscar Grimes d. Billy Johnson

5) __ OF: a. Paul Waner b. Johnny Lindell c. Johnny Cooney d. Tuck Stainback

6) __ OF: a. Ed Levy b. But Metheny c. Russ Derry d. Larry Rosenthal

7) __ OF: a. Roy Weatherly b. George Selkirk **c.** Frenchy Bordagaray d. Hersh Martin

8) __ C: a. Rollie Hemsley b. Buddy Rosar c. Mike Garbark d. Ken Silvestri

9) __ SP: a. Hank Borowy b. Atley Donald c. Monk Dubiel d. Ernie Bonham*

10) __ RP: a. Jim Turner b. Joe Page c. Bill Zuber d. Mel Queen**

22. WORLD WAR II VETS

Which ten of the following 20 players served in the armed forces during World War II? Check the correct names.

Nick Etten	Roy Weatherly
Buddy Hassett	Mel Queen
George Stirnweiss	Hank Borowy
Rollie Hemsley	Atley Donald
Billy Johnson	Marius Russo
Frankie Crosetti	Russ Derry
Hank Borowy	Aaron Robinson
Ernie Bonham	Charles Wensloff
Johnny Lindell	Johnny Murphy
Joe Page	Bill Bevens

* The starting pitcher with the most wins.
** The relief pitcher with the best overall record.

Answers

20. Who's Who

1) Paul Waner
2) Joe DiMaggio
3) Paul Schreiber
4) Mike Milosevich
5) Chet Laabs
6) Oscar Grimes
7) Red Ruffing
8) Hank Borowy (1945)
9) Spud Chandler (1943)
10) George Stirnweiss (1944–45)
11) Ernie Bonham (21–5 in 1942)
12) Buddy Hassett
13) Johnny Sturm
14) George Stirnweiss (.476 in 1945)
15) Nick Etten (22)
16) George Stirnweiss (.309 in 1945)
17) Johnny Lindell (1944)
18) Hersh Martin
19) Johnny Lindell
20) Hank Borowy
21) Nick Etten
22) George Stirnweiss (second base)
23) Johnny Lindell
24) Bud Metheny
25) Tuck Stainback
26) Russ Derry
27) Oscar Grimes
28) Frankie Crosetti
29) Jim Turner
30) Joe Page (1947 and 1949)

21. World War II Lineup

1) d
2) b
3) a
4) c
5) b
6) b
7) d
8) c
9) a (17–12)
10) a (4–4, 35 appearances, and 7 saves)

22. World War II Vets

Buddy Hassett
Rollie Hemsley
Billy Johnson
Johnny Lindell
Roy Weatherly

Mel Queen
Marius Russo
Aaron Robinson
Charles Wensloff
Johnny Murphy

Historical Interlude Number Five

Necessity is the mother of invention, they say.

Baseball players can well relate to that truism. For example, there have been many players who came up to the majors as pitchers who ended up everyday players. Joe Wood, Babe Ruth, and Lefty O'Doul are three good examples. On the other hand, there have been many players who came up to the big leagues as everyday players who became pitchers. Bucky Walters, Jimmie Foxx, and Bob Lemon are three who come to mind.

But there haven't been too many players who came up to the majors one way, switched the other way, and returned to the former way before their big-league careers were over.

The player in question happened to be one of these rare cases. In 1942, as a rookie, he won two games, both of them in relief, for the Yankees. For the following eight years he played the outfield for the Yankees and the Cardinals (mostly the Yankees). Careerwise, he was a .273 hitter. Three times during his 12-year career, he batted .300.

Released at the end of the 1950 season, he returned to the minors, where he developed a new pitch—a knuckle ball. In 1953 he returned to the majors as a pitcher, first for the Pirates and then for the Phillies.

In his final season in the majors, he proved conclusively that he was a better hitter than he was a pitcher. At the plate he batted .303, hit four home runs, and drove home 17 runs. On the mound he logged a 6–17 record. That was his final year in the majors.

Who was that former Yankee with the checkered career?

Answer: Johnny Lindell

51

CHAPTER SIX

Stengel's Story

23. WHO'S WHO

You can use the following list as a guide to the answers in this quiz:

Tom Morgan	Don Larsen
Fred Hutchinson	Phil Rizzuto
Bobby Shantz	Johnny Lindell
Bob Cerv	Joe Page
Gene Woodling	Enos Slaughter
Ernie Bonham	Johnny Mize
Cliff Mapes	Bobo Newsom
Frank Hayes	Joe DiMaggio
Johnny Sain	Bob Grim
Charlie Keller	Ted Williams
Ryne Duren	Harry Simpson
Vic Raschi	Jerry Coleman
Gil McDougald	Bob Turley
Allie Reynolds	Mel Allen
Mickey Mantle	Eddie Lopat
Whitey Ford	Jim Konstanty

1) _____ Who, in 1950, tied a record for balks in one game (4) and balks in a season (6)?

2) _____ Who led the American League in pinch hits from 1951 to 1953?

3) _____ Who hit the line drive that struck Herb Score in the face and prematurely ended the premier pitcher's career?

4) _____ Who slugged the ball for 14 total bases en route to hitting for the cycle in a 1948 game? (He homered twice, tripled, doubled, and singled.)

5) _____ Who hit one of Pedro Ramos' change-up pitches off the upper facade in right field in 1956? (It failed to clear the roof by only 18 inches.)

6) _____ Who was the "plowboy" who tied a major-league record by hitting three batters in the same inning of a 1954 game?

7) _____ Who no-hit Cleveland 1–0 in 1951? (He was a former Indian.)

8) _____ Who was the one-time Indian whose homer proved to be the difference in that no-hit game?

9) _____ Who was the winning pitcher in the game in which the Yankees tied the record of copping 19 consecutive games?

10) _____ Who was the much-traveled pitcher who won his first game as a Yankee and his 200th game as a major leaguer in the Yankees' 18th consecutive win of that streak?

11) _____ Who was the Tiger righty who shut the Yankees out 2–0 to bring that record-tying streak to a screeching halt?

12) _____ Who tied the American League record for consecutive strikeouts by fanning six straight Athletics in 1956?

13) _____ Who was the 1953 pitcher who set an American League record by driving home seven runs in one game?

14) _____ Who was the 1952 part-time player who gained the distinction of having homered in all 16 major-league parks?

15) _____ Who became the first pitcher in American League history to throw two no-hitters in the same year?

16) _____ Who was the feared hitter whom he had to "retire" twice to nail down the final out of a no-hitter? (Yogi Berra dropped a foul pop just before he caught a foul pop.)

17) _____ Who was the former Yankee—he played for other teams, too—who holds the mark for the most three-home-run games?

18) _____ Who was the most recent Yankee rookie pitcher to win 20 games?

19) _____ Who was the MVP winner with another

American League team who pitched in the World Series with the Yankees in the late 1950s?

20) _____ Who was the first switch hitter to win a batting crown?

21) _____ Who was the Yankee strongman from this era who hit 12 career pinch-hit homers?

22) _____ Who was the only Yankee pitcher to throw a perfect game?

23) _____ Who was the only Yankee pitcher to throw two no-hitters in one season?

24) _____ Who was the Yankee outfielder who tied for the league lead in triples in both 1956 and 1957?

25) _____ Who was the only Yankee to hit 40 home runs but fail to drive home 100 runs in that season?

26) _____ Who was the onetime Yankee 20-game winner who died in 1949 after an emergency appendectomy operation while he was on the staff of the Pirates?

27) _____ Who was the old-timer who was given his release on "Old-Timers" Day?

28) _____ Who was the Indian catcher who hit a home run to decide Bob Feller's 1–0 no-hitter against the Yankees in 1946?

29) _____ Who copped the Triple Crown during this era?

30) _____ Who was the Yankee outfielder who wore two numbers (3 and 7) that were eventually retired by the Yankees?

31) _____ Who was the only Yankee right-hander to win the Cy Young Award?

32) _____ Who was the Yankee who outdueled Mel Parnell of the Red Sox on the final day of the 1949 season to clinch the pennant for the Yankees?

33) _____ Who got a three-run bases-loaded hit in that dramatic 5–3 victory?

34) _____ Who, on the preceding day, hit an eighth-inning homer to give the Yankees a 5–4 win that pushed them into a first-place tie with the fading Red Sox?

35) _____ Who, in the same game, held the Red Sox scoreless over the last six and one-third innings of the contest to allow the Yankees to come back from a 4–0

deficit and win one of the most emotionally charged games in their history?

36) _____ Who, in the 1940s, played against the Yankees in two World Series and, in the 1950s, played with them in three World Series?

37) _____ Who was the player in 1949 who missed the first half of the season because of a heel injury and then returned to hit .346 down the stretch?

38) _____ Who led the league in home runs (39) and RBI (155) in 1948?

39) _____ Who was the former Yankee pitching great who yielded the first major-league home run that was hit by Hank Aaron?

40) _____ Who was the Yankee outfielder who made only one error, for a fielding percentage of .997, in 1947?

41) _____ Who was the Yankee outfielder who made only one error, for a .996 mark, in 1953?

42) _____ Who was the steady left-hander who compiled an .800 winning percentage (16–4) in 1953? (He also led the league with a 2.42 ERA.)

43) _____ Who was the former National League great who picked up a league-leading 22 saves in 1954?

44) _____ Who was the only Yankee outfielder during this era to lead the league in assists?

45) _____ Who, in his first seven years in the majors, did not have an ERA above 3.00? (He won ERA titles in 1956 and 1958.)

46) _____ Who was tne 1957 acquisition who led the league in ERA (2.45) that year?

47) _____ Who was the Yankee outfielder of 11 years who had a career slugging average of .518? (In his first eight years—when he was healthy—his average was .536.)

48) _____ Who was the Yankee pitcher (20–6) who was 8–0 in relief without *one* save?

49) _____ Who was a World Series opening-game starter *against* the Yankees who later during this era posted a 7–2 record with 11 saves *for* the Yankees?

50) _____ Who was the relief pitcher from the late 1950s who led the league in saves (20) in 1958 and ERA (1.88) in 1960?

24. THE KANSAS CITY EXPRESS, PART I

Kansas City used to be one of the Yankees' top farm teams in the American Association. In the late 1950s many followers of American League action felt that Kansas City still was a Yankee farm team. The Yankees sent to the Athletics many well-known—but timeworn—names. Occasionally they traded for or bought back some of these veterans in the field. Back in those late 1950s, you truly needed a scorecard to tell a Yankee from an Athletic. In this first quiz you're going to be asked to pick from the lists below the 25 players that New York dealt to Kansas City during this era. Check the correct names.

Ewell Blackwell	Don Bollweg
Joe Collins	Vic Raschi
Gene Woodling	Allie Reynolds
Jerry Coleman	Jim McDonald
Bill Skowron	Bob Kuzava
Tom Gorman	Mickey McDermott
Dick Kryhoski	Billy Hunter
Eddie Lopat	Johnny Mize
Harry Byrd	Bill Miller
Enos Slaughter	Ray Scarborough
Gil McDougald	Irv Noren
Ellie Howard	Bob Hogue
Bob Turley	Joe Ostrowski
Johnny Sain	Johnny Schmitz
Eddie Robinson	Ralph Terry
Tommy Byrne	Ralph Branca
Jim Konstanty	Billy Martin
Tom Sturdivant	Charlie Silvera
Bob Cerv	Ted Gray
Bobby Richardson	Woodie Held
Tony Kubek	Bob Grim
Bobby Shantz	Jim Coates
Tom Morgan	Sal Maglie

Harry Simpson	Hank Bauer
Al Cicotte	Norm Siebern
Murry Dickson	Kent Hadley
Bobby Del Greco	Dale Long
Johnny James	Elmer Valo
Johnny Kucks	Jesse Gonder
Clete Boyer	Don Larsen
Fritzie Brickell	Luis Arroyo
Ralph Houk	Bill Stafford
Eli Grba	Marv Throneberry
Jerry Lumpe	Ken Hunt
Gary Blaylock	George Wilson
Jim Bronstad	Andy Carey

25. THE KANSAS CITY EXPRESS, PART II

In this quiz you're going to be asked to pick out the 15 players from the 40 listed below whom the Yankees acquired from Kansas City during this period. Check the correct names.

Bill Renna	Al Cicotte
Harry Byrd	Eli Grba
Enos Slaughter	Harry Simpson
Jim Konstanty	Dale Long
Bobby Shantz	Elmer Valo
Art Ditmar	Virgil Trucks
Jim McDonald	Luis Arroyo
Ray Scarborough	Bill Stafford
Ralph Branca	Eddie Robinson
Clete Boyer	Billy Hunter
Ted Gray	Duke Maas
Tommy Byrne	Murry Dickson
Tony Kubek	Irv Noren
Jim Coates	Woodie Held
Ryne Duren	Ralph Terry

Johnny Kucks   Bob Turley
Tom Sturdivant   Roger Maris
Hector Lopez   Joe DeMaestri
Norm Siebern   Tom Morgan
Don Larsen   Bob Cerv

26. YANKEE NATIONAL LEAGUE FARM TEAMS

During the 1950s the Yankees sought down-the-stretch insurance from National League teams. Below you will find the names of National League players who were basically acquired for September pennant runs. All you have to do is to match the player in the left-hand column with the team in the right-hand column from which he was acquired. (Teams can be used more than once.)

1) ___ Johnny Mize   a) Giants
2) ___ Johnny Hopp   b) Reds
3) ___ Johnny Sain   c) Pirates
4) ___ Johnny Schmitz   d) Cardinals
5) ___ Ewell Blackwell   e) Phillies
6) ___ Enos Slaughter   f) Braves
7) ___ Jim Konstanty   g) Dodgers
8) ___ Sal Maglie
9) ___ Gerry Staley
10) ___ Dale Long

Answers

23. Who's Who

1) Vic Raschi
2) Johnny Mize
3) Gil McDougald (1957)
4) Joe DiMaggio
5) Mickey Mantle
6) Tom Morgan
7) Allie Reynolds
8) Gene Woodling
9) Vic Raschi (1947)
10) Bobo Newsom
11) Fred Hutchinson
12) Whitey Ford
13) Vic Raschi
14) Johnny Mize
15) Allie Reynolds (1951)
16) Ted Williams
17) Johnny Mize (6)
18) Bob Grim (1954)
19) Bobby Shantz (1957, 1960)
20) Mickey Mantle (1956)
21) Bob Cerv
22) Don Larsen (1956)
23) Allie Reynolds (1951)
24) Harry Simpson
25) Mickey Mantle (1958 and 1960)
26) Ernie Bonham
27) Phil Rizzuto (1956)
28) Frank Hayes
29) Mickey Mantle (1956)
30) Cliff Mapes
31) Bob Turley (1958)
32) Vic Raschi
33) Jerry Coleman
34) Johnny Lindell
35) Joe Page
36) Enos Slaughter
37) Joe DiMaggio
38) Joe DiMaggio
39) Vic Raschi (1954)
40) Joe DiMaggio
41) Gene Woodling
42) Eddie Lopat
43) Johnny Sain
44) Mickey Mantle (20 in 1954)
45) Whitey Ford
46) Bobby Shantz
47) Charlie Keller
48) Bob Grim (1954)
49) Jim Konstanty (1955)
50) Ryne Duren

24. The Kansas City Express, Part I

Ewell Blackwell
Tom Gorman
Dick Kryhoski

Enos Slaughter
Johnny Sain
Eddie Robinson

Tom Sturdivant
Bob Cerv
Tom Morgan
Mickey McDermott
Billy Hunter
Irv Noren
Ralph Terry
Billy Martin
Woodie Held
Bob Grim

Harry Simpson
Murry Dickson
Johnny Kucks
Jerry Lumpe
Hank Bauer
Norm Siebern
Don Larsen
Marv Throneberry
Andy Carey

25. The Kansas City Express, Part II

Bill Renna
Enos Slaughter
Bobby Shantz
Art Ditmar
Clete Boyer
Ryne Duren
Harry Simpson
Virgil Trucks

Duke Maas
Murry Dickson
Ralph Terry
Hector Lopez
Roger Maris
Joe DeMaestri
Bob Cerv

26. Yankee National League Farm Teams

1) a
2) c
3) f
4) g
5) b

6) d
7) e
8) g
9) b
10) a

Historical Interlude
Number Six

The curtain closer of the 1949 season included a lot of drama. It also contained a Yankee first.

Both the Red Sox and the host Yankees were tied for first with one game left to play. So, in effect, the game was sudden death for the pennant. Mel Parnell and Vic Raschi, two of the best pitchers of that era, took the mound. It turned out to be a classic confrontation.

Phil Rizzuto tripled to lead off the bottom of the first and scored on Tommy Henrich's ground out. That's the way it stood until the bottom of the eighth.

One of the key decisions of the game was made in the top of the eighth. Red Sox manager Joe McCarthy was faced with the dilemma of letting Parnell hit for himself or letting someone else bat for him. Parnell was pitching a masterful game. But the Red Sox needed runs, and they were running out of time. McCarthy decided to pinch-hit. The Red Sox failed to score and were forced to go to Ellis Kinder, another 20-game winner. But Kinder didn't have it. The Yankees scored four runs—three of them on a bases-loaded hit by rookie Jerry Coleman—and the Red Sox' three counters in the ninth fell two runs short.

It's the Red Sox' ninth that interests me, though. After Bobby Doerr's extra-base hit scored runs two and three, Joe DiMaggio voluntarily took himself out of the game for a defensive replacement.

Just over viral pneumonia, which had kept him in bed and out of the lineup for two weeks, DiMaggio faulted himself for failing to catch Doerr's drive. He felt that two steady legs would have made the difference. So he told manager Casey Stengel to put someone with solid underpinning in his place.

DiMaggio's replacement proceeded to catch a fly ball en route to the 5–3 finish. The game actually ended when Birdie Tebbetts, with runners on base, lifted a pop foul by the first-base boxes. First baseman Tommy Henrich leaned into the stands to make the final putout.

Who was that substitute outfielder, with the nickname "Tiger," who became the first player ever to replace Di-Maggio for defensive purposes?

Answer: Cliff Mapes

CHAPTER SEVEN

The Major's Men

27. WHO'S WHO

You can use the following list as a guide to the answers in this quiz:

Bill Fischer

Jack Reed

Al Downing

Duke Sims

Jake Gibbs

Luis Arroyo

Tom Tresh

Hoyt Wilhelm

Earl Wilson

Fred Talbot

Roger Maris

Lindy McDaniel

Mel Stottlemyre

Tracy Stallard

Roy White

Stu Miller

Thurman Munson

Dooley Womack

Stan Bahnsen

Ellie Howard

Joe Pepitone

Horace Clarke

Mickey Mantle

Johnny Miller

Fred Stanley

Bobby Richardson

Clete Boyer

Whitey Ford

Denny McLain

Bobby Murcer

1) _____ Who set a record by receiving four intentional bases on balls and tied a record by drawing five walks in the same game?

2) _____ Who hit a ball in 1963 that experts agree would have traveled over 600 feet if it had not been stopped by the facade that majestically perches above the third tier of Yankee Stadium?

3) _____ Who was the Kansas City hurler who threw the ball to the preceding hitter?

4) _____ Who pitched eight and one-third innings of

scoreless baseball while establishing a major-league record by passing 11 hitters?

5) _____ Who was the rookie who hit two home runs in one inning in 1962?

6) _____ Who hit his only major-league home run in the 22nd inning to decide the longest game in Yankee history?

7) _____ Who pitched 13 innings of almost perfect relief and became a winner on his team's home run in the 13th inning?

8) _____ Who was the infielder who hit the home run to decide the game referred to in the preceding question?

9) _____ Who struck out the side on nine pitches in 1967?

10) _____ Who was the last Yankee before Don Mattingly to lead the league in RBI?

11) _____ Who became the first and only Yankee to homer in his first official major-league at bat?

12) _____ Who hit the final grand slam home run in Old Yankee Stadium?

13) _____ Who hit the last Yankee home run in Old Yankee Stadium?

14) _____ Who threw the pitch that Roger Maris hit for home run No. 61 in 1961?

15) _____ Who has been the only player in history to fail to win the home-run title with more than 50 home runs?

16) _____ Who led the American League in at bats from 1962 to 1964?

17) _____ Who was the former quarterback for Ole Miss who caught for the Yankees in the 1960s?

18) _____ Who has been the only Yankee outfielder to play a "full" season without committing an error?

19) _____ Who was the last pitcher to no-hit the Yankees?

20) _____ Who was the switch-hitting Yankee infielder who led the American League in at bats in 1969–70?

21) _____ Who was the first of the Yankee lefties to win the Cy Young Award?

22) _____ Who was the pitcher who chalked up a

career winning percentage of .690, the best figure for hurlers with 200 or more victories?

23) _____ Who was the bullpen specialist who was Whitey Ford's "savior" in 1961?

24) _____ Who was one of the two brothers—the Yankee one, of course—who hit a home run in the 1964 Series?

25) _____ Who was the Yankee right fielder who made only one error in 1964? (He fielded .996.)

26) _____ Who was the other Yankee outfielder who made only one error in 1964? (His average was .996, too.)

27) _____ Who, in addition to Mickey Mantle and Roger Maris, was the only Yankee to drive home 100 runs in one season during this period?

28) _____ Who was the Oriole pitcher who served up Mickey Mantle's 500th home run in 1967?

29) _____ Who got involved in a fight with Carlton Fisk at Fenway Park in 1973?

30) _____ Who hit a grand slam home run for the Yankees in Game Six of the 1964 World Series?

31) _____ Who, before Ron Guidry, had the best winning percentage for a Yankee left-hander with 20 or more wins in a season?

32) _____ Who was the season strikeout leader from this era who later won 20 games for the 1971 Dodgers?

33) _____ Who won 20 games in 1965 and lost 20 games the following season?

34) _____ Who was the right-handed pitcher who picked up 29 saves in 1970?

35) _____ Who was the Tiger righty who threw the pitch that Mickey Mantle hit for his 535th home run? (It pushed Mantle past Jimmie Foxx on the all-time home-run list.)

36) _____ Who threw the pitch that Mickey Mantle hit for his 536th and last home run? (This pitcher hit 35 career homers.)

37) _____ Who was the righty relief pitcher who finished a record 48 games in one season with the Yankees?

38) _____ Who had a dismal 1–9 record in 1967?

39) _____ Who was the infielder who played in a club-record 162 games in 1962?

40) _____ Who is the former Yankee pitcher who tied a major-league record by spraying five hits—four singles and a double—in one game?

41) _____ Who hit a club-record 17 sacrifice flies in 1971?

42) _____ Who was the most recent Yankee—he was a 1972 outfielder—to score five runs in one game?

43) _____ Who has recorded more at bats in one season (692) than any other Yankee?

44) _____ Who was the Yankee from this era who led the league in fielding at his position in back-to-back years?

45) _____ Who won the Golden Glove Award at his position from 1961 to 1965?

46) _____ Who won the Rookie of the Year Award in 1968?

47) _____ Who won the Rookie of the Year Award in 1962?

48) _____ Who hit for the highest average in one season during this era?

49) _____ Who was the last Yankee before Don Mattingly to collect 200 or more hits in one season?

50) _____ Who was the only Yankee from this era to steal more than 30 bases in a season?

28. THE MAJOR'S TROOPS

Which ten of the following 25 players first performed for the Yankees during Ralph Houk's tenure as manager (1961–63 or 1966–73)? (The relevant players do not include those who came to New York during the reigns of Casey Stengel, Yogi Berra, or Johnny Keane.) Check the correct names.

Hector Lopez   Jim Coates
Johnny Blanchard   Al Downing

Luis Arroyo
Rollie Sheldon
Clete Boyer
Ralph Terry
Bud Daley
Hal Reniff
Mel Stottlemyre
Pete Mikkelsen
Pedro Ramos
Chris Chambliss
Phil Linz

Marshall Bridges
Jim Bouton
Roy White
Bobby Murcer
Gil Blanco
Roger Repoz
Tommy Tresh
Fritz Peterson
Stan Bahnsen
Joe Pepitone

29. FIVE IN A ROW

The Yankees of 1960–64 equaled the record set by the 1949–53 Pinstripers—they won five pennants in a row. Ten Yankees were in uniform for that unique string. (One of them concluded the string with one year of managing.) How many of them can you name? (Coaches don't count.)

1) _____
2) _____
3) _____
4) _____
5) _____

6) _____
7) _____
8) _____
9) _____
10) _____

30. NO BIG DEAL

The Yankees continued to deal with National League teams during the 1960s and the 1970s, but without the success of the late 1940s and the 1950s. (The only really good interleague swap that the Yankees made during this period was the one that acquired Lindy McDaniel, which later led to the acquisition of Lou Piniella.) Match the acquired players in the left-hand column with teams in the right-hand column from which they were obtained.

1) __ Robin Roberts	a)	Braves
2) __ Marshall Bridges	b)	Cubs
3) __ Stan Williams	c)	Phillies
4) __ Bob Friend	d)	Cardinals
5) __ Bill Robinson	e)	Reds
6) __ Charley Smith	f)	Dodgers
7) __ John Boccabella	g)	Astros
8) __ Dick Simpson	h)	Pirates
9) __ Nate Coleman	i)	Expos
10) __ Gary Waslewski	j)	Giants

31. YOU NEED A SCORECARD

Some of the Yankees who played during this era are as obscure as those who took the places of the Yankee stars of the World War II years. Below you will find 20 players from this era. All you have to do is to identify them by the position which they played: *P* for pitcher, *C* for catcher, *I* for infielder, *O* for outfielder.

1) __ Lu Clinton	11) __ Joe Verbanic
2) __ Ray Barker	12) __ Mike Ferraro
3) __ Jack Cullen	13) __ Thad Tillotson
4) __ Bill Henry	14) __ Tom Shopay
5) __ John Kennedy	15) __ Len Boehmer
6) __ Bill Tillman	16) __ Gerry Moses
7) __ Billy Bryan	17) __ Frank Baker
8) __ Ross Moschitto	18) __ Bobby Mitchell
9) __ Cecil Perkins	19) __ John Cumberland
10) __ Ron Woods	20) __ Bernie Allen

Answers

27. Who's Who

1) Roger Maris (1962)
2) Mickey Mantle
3) Bill Fischer
4) Mel Stottlemyre (1970)
5) Joe Pepitone
6) Jack Reed (1962)
7) Lindy McDaniel (1973)
8) Horace Clarke
9) Al Downing
10) Roger Maris (142 in 1961)
11) Johnny Miller (1966)
12) Fred Stanley (1973)
13) Duke Sims (1973)
14) Tracy Stallard
15) Mickey Mantle (54 in 1961)
16) Bobby Richardson
17) Jake Gibbs
18) Roy White (1971)
19) Hoyt Wilhelm (1958)
20) Horace Clarke
21) Whitey Ford (1961)
22) Whitey Ford
23) Luis Arroyo
24) Clete Boyer
25) Roger Maris
26) Tom Tresh
27) Joe Pepitone (100 in 1964)
28) Stu Miller
29) Thurman Munson
30) Joe Pepitone
31) Whitey Ford (.862 in 1961)
32) Al Downing
33) Mel Stottlemyre
34) Lindy McDaniel
35) Denny McLain (1968)
36) Earl Wilson (1968)
37) Dooley Womack (1967)
38) Fred Talbot
39) Bobby Richardson
40) Mel Stottlemyre (1964)
41) Roy White
42) Bobby Murcer
43) Bobby Richardson (1962)
44) Joe Pepitone (1965–66)
45) Bobby Richardson
46) Stan Bahnsen
47) Tom Tresh
48) Ellie Howard (.348 in 1961)
49) Bobby Richardson (209 in 1962)
50) Horace Clarke (33 in 1969)

28. The Major's Troops

1) Al Downing (1961)
2) Rollie Sheldon (1961)
3) Bud Daley (1961)
4) Hal Reniff (1961)
5) Marshall Bridges (1962)
6) Jim Bouton (1962)
7) Tommy Tresh (1961)
8) Fritz Peterson (1966)
9) Stan Bahnsen (1966)
10) Joe Pepitone (1962)

29. Five in a Row

1) Bobby Richardson
2) Tony Kubek
3) Clete Boyer
4) Roger Maris
5) Mickey Mantle
6) Ellie Howard
7) Hector Lopez
8) Whitey Ford
9) Johnny Blanchard
10) Yogi Berra

30. No Big Deal

1) c
2) e
3) f
4) h
5) a
6) d
7) b
8) g
9) j
10) i

31. You Need a Scorecard

1) O
2) I
3) P
4) P
5) I
6) C
7) C
8) O
9) P
10) O
11) P
12) I
13) P
14) O
15) I
16) C
17) I
18) O
19) P
20) I

Historical Interlude Number Seven

Bobby Richardson had an up-and-down World Series career—ranging from highs of .406, .391, and .367 to lows of .214, .148, and .000—but the 1960 and 1964 Fall Classics brought out the best in the Yankee second baseman.

A light-hitting .266 lifetime batter, he turned slugger in the 1960 get-together with the Pirates. He got 11 hits, including two doubles, two triples, and a grand slam homer, for a batting average of .367. He also drove home a record 12 runs in that Series and slugged for a .667 average.

During the regular season those same numbers were anemic: batting average .252, home runs 1, RBI 26, and slugging percentage .298.

In 1964 Richardson got a record 13 hits that were good for a .406 average. The only other player who got 13 hits in World Series play was Lou Brock, who reached that total in a losing cause for the 1968 Cardinals.

Richardson could relate to Brock. When he set his RBI record in 1960 and his total-hit mark in 1964, the Yankees lost also.

In 1960 another Yankee drove home what would have been—except for Richardson's heroics—a record 11 runs. Do you recall the name of Richardson's teammate?

Answer: Mickey Mantle

CHAPTER EIGHT

Player Positions

32. THE PITCHERS

Place the following pitchers in the order of their mound tenure with the Yankees: Jack Chesbro, Whitey Ford, Mel Stottlemyre, Mike Torrez, Russell Ford, Ron Guidry, Herb Pennock, Red Ruffing, Allie Reynolds, and Spud Chandler.

1) _____ (1903–09)
2) _____ (1909–13)
3) _____ (1923–33)
4) _____ (1930–42, 1945–46)
5) _____ (1937–47)
6) _____ (1947–54)
7) _____ (1950, 1953–67)
8) _____ (1964–74)
9) _____ (1977)
10) _____ (1975–)

33. THE CATCHERS

Place the following catchers in the order that they called the signals for the Pinstripers: Bill Dickey, Thurman Munson, Wally Schang, Yogi Berra, Mike Garbark, Ellie Howard, Aaron Robinson, Jake Gibbs, Deacon McGuire, and Muddy Ruel.

1) _____ (1904–07)
2) _____ (1917–20)
3) _____ (1921–25)
4) _____ (1928–43, 1946)
5) _____ (1944–45)
6) _____ (1943, 1945–47)
7) _____ (1946–63)
8) _____ (1955–67)
9) _____ (1962–71)
10) _____ (1969–79)

34. THE FIRST BASEMEN

Place the following first basemen in the order that they played the initial sack for the Bronx Bombers: Lou Gehrig, Joe Pepitone, Bill Skowron, Wally Pipp, Joe Collins, Chris Chambliss, George McQuinn, Mickey Mantle, Babe Dahlgren, and Buddy Hassett.

1) _____ (1915–25)   6) _____ (1948–57)
2) _____ (1923–39)   7) _____ (1954–62)
3) _____ (1937–40)   8) _____ (1962–69)
4) _____ (1942)   9) _____ (1967–68)
5) _____ (1947–48)   10) _____ (1974–79)

35. THE SECOND BASEMEN

Place the following second basemen in the order that they played the keystone sack for New York: Joe Gordon, Jerry Coleman, Aaron Ward, Billy Martin, Willie Randolph, Tony Lazzeri, Bobby Richardson, George Stirnweiss, Horace Clarke, and Sandy Alomar.

1) _____ (1917–26)   6) _____ (1950–53,
2) _____ (1926–37)   1955–57)
3) _____ (1938–43,   7) _____ (1955–66)
           1946)   8) _____ (1965–74)
4) _____ (1943–50)   9) _____ (1974–76)
5) _____ (1949–57)   10) _____ (1976–)

36. THE THIRD BASEMEN

Place the following third basemen in the order that they manned the hot corner for the Yankees: Graig Nettles, Red Rolfe, Frank Baker, Clete Boyer, Gil McDougald, Joe Dugan, Billy Johnson, Andy Carey, Jerry Kenney, and Bobby Brown.

1) _____ (1916–19, 1921–22)
2) _____ (1922–28)
3) _____ (1931, 1934–1942)
4) _____ (1943, 1946–1951)
5) _____ (1946–54)
6) _____ (1951–57, 1959–60)
7) _____ (1952–60)
8) _____ (1959–66)
9) _____ (1967, 1969–72)
10) _____ (1973–   )

37. THE SHORTSTOPS

Place the following shortstops in the order that they plugged the number-six spot in the Yankee lineup: Phil Rizzuto, Everett Scott, Gil McDougald, Bucky Dent, Tony Kubek, Mark Koenig, Frankie Crosetti, Lyn Lary, Mike Milosevich, and Gene Michael.

1) _____ (1922–25)
2) _____ (1925–30)
3) _____ (1929–34)
4) _____ (1932–48)
5) _____ (1941–42, 1946–56)
6) _____ (1944–45)
7) _____ (1956–59)
8) _____ (1957–65)
9) _____ (1968–73)
10) _____ (1977–   )

38. THE LEFT FIELDERS

Place the following left fielders in the order of their tenure with the Pinstripers: Gene Woodling, Roy White, Bob Meusel, Charlie Keller, Ben Chapman, George Selkirk, Norm Siebern, Ellie Howard, Tommy Tresh, and Yogi Berra.

1) _____ (1920–29)
2) _____ (1930–36)
3) _____ (1934–42)
4) _____ (1939–43, 1945–49, 1952)
5) _____ (1949–54)
6) _____ (1956, 1958–59)
7) _____ (1947-48, 1956–62)
8) _____ (1955–60, 1965)
9) _____ (1962–69)
10) _____ (1965–79)

39. THE CENTER FIELDERS

Place the following center fielders in the order that they played the outfield in New York: Mickey Rivers, Joe Di-Maggio, Earle Combs, Bobby Murcer, Elliott Maddox, Mickey Mantle, Whitey Witt, Johnny Lindell, Ping Bodie, and Jake Powell.

1) _____ (1918–21)
2) _____ (1922–25)
3) _____ (1924–35)
4) _____ (1936–40)
5) _____ (1936–42, 1946–51)
6) _____ (1941–50)
7) _____ (1951–66)
8) _____ (1965–66, 1969–74, 1979–   )
9) _____ (1974–76, 1981)
10) _____ (1976–79)

40. THE RIGHT FIELDERS

Place the following right fielders in the order that they played the outfield for the Bronx Bombers: Roger Maris, Reggie Jackson, Babe Ruth, Hank Bauer. Bobby Bonds, George Selkirk, Tommy Henrich, Bud Metheny, Bobby Murcer, and Willie Keeler.

1) _____ (1903–09)
2) _____ (1920–34)
3) _____ (1934–42)
4) _____ (1937–42, 1946–50)
5) _____ (1943–46)
6) _____ (1948–59)
7) _____ (1960–66)
8) _____ (1965–66, 1969–74, 1979–)
9) _____ (1975)
10) _____ (1977–)

41. THE MANAGERS

Place the following managers in the order that they handled the reins of the Yankees: Bob Shawkey, Casey Stengel, Ralph Houk, Miller Huggins, Yogi Berra, Joe McCarthy, Billy Martin, Frank Chance, Bucky Harris, and Johnny Keane.

1) _____ (1913–14)
2) _____ (1918–29)
3) _____ (1930)
4) _____ (1931–46)
5) _____ (1947–48)
6) _____ (1947–60)
7) _____ (1964)
8) _____ (1965–66)
9) _____ (1961–63, 1966–73)
10) _____ (1975–79)

42. CATCHERS

Match the following catchers with their lifetime averages:
Ellie Howard, Yogi Berra, Thurman Munson, Wally Schang,
and Benny Bengough.

1) _____ (.292)   4) _____ (.274)
2) _____ (.285)   5) _____ (.255)
3) _____ (.284)

43. FIRST BASEMEN

Match the following first basemen with their lifetime
averages: Wally Pipp, Hal Chase, Bill Skowron, Joe Pepitone, and George McQuinn.

1) _____ (.291)   4) _____ (.276)
2) _____ (.282)   5) _____ (.258)
3) _____ (.281)

44. SECOND BASEMEN

Match the following second basemen with their lifetime
averages: Billy Martin, Bobby Richardson, Jerry Coleman, George Stirnweiss, and Del Pratt.

1) _____ (.292)   4) _____ (.263)
2) _____ (.268)   5) _____ (.257)
3) _____ (.266)

45. THIRD BASEMEN

Match the following third basemen with their lifetime averages: Red Rolfe, Clete Boyer, Gil McDougald, Joe Dugan, and Bobby Brown.

1) _____ (.289)   4) _____ (.276)
2) _____ (.280)   5) _____ (.240)
3) _____ (.279)

46. SHORTSTOPS

Match the following shortstops with their lifetime averages: Phil Rizzuto, Frankie Crosetti, Lyn Lary, Tony Kubek, and Everett Scott.

1) _____ (.273)   4) _____ (.249)
2) _____ (.269)   5) _____ (.245)
3) _____ (.266)

47. LEFT FIELDERS

Match the following players with their lifetime averages: Charlie Keller, Gene Woodling, Tommy Tresh, Hector Lopez, and Birdie Cree.

1) _____ (.292)   4) _____ (.269)
2) _____ (.286)   5) _____ (.245)
3) _____ (.284)

48. CENTER FIELDERS

Match the following players with their lifetime averages: Mickey Mantle, Whitey Witt, Ben Chapman, Johnny Lindell, and Irv Noren.

1) _____ (.302)   4) _____ (.275)
2) _____ (.298)   5) _____ (.273)
3) _____ (.287)

49. RIGHT FIELDERS

Match the following players with their lifetime averages: Tommy Henrich, Roger Maris, George Selkirk, Hank Bauer, and Bud Metheny.

1) _____ (.290)   4) _____ (.260)
2) _____ (.282)   5) _____ (.247)
3) _____ (.277)

Answers

32. The Pitchers

1) Jack Chesbro
2) Russell Ford
3) Herb Pennock
4) Red Ruffing
5) Spud Chandler

6) Allie Reynolds
7) Whitey Ford
8) Mel Stottlemyre
9) Mike Torrez
10) Ron Guidry

33. The Catchers

1) Deacon McGuire
2) Muddy Ruel
3) Wally Schang
4) Bill Dickey
5) Mike Garbark

6) Aaron Robinson
7) Yogi Berra
8) Ellie Howard
9) Jake Gibbs
10) Thurman Munson

34. The First Basemen

1) Wally Pipp
2) Lou Gehrig
3) Babe Dahlgren
4) Buddy Hassett
5) George McQuinn

6) Joe Collins
7) Bill Skowron
8) Joe Pepitone
9) Mickey Mantle
10) Chris Chambliss

35. The Second Basemen

1) Aaron Ward
2) Tony Lazzeri
3) Joe Gordon
4) George Stirnweiss
5) Jerry Coleman

6) Billy Martin
7) Bobby Richardson
8) Horace Clarke
9) Sandy Alomar
10) Willie Randolph

36. The Third Basemen

1) Frank Baker
2) Joe Dugan
3) Red Rolfe
4) Billy Johnson
5) Bobby Brown
6) Gil McDougald
7) Andy Carey
8) Clete Boyer
9) Jerry Kenney
10) Graig Nettles

37. The Shortstops

1) Everett Scott
2) Mark Koenig
3) Lyn Lary
4) Frankie Crosetti
5) Phil Rizzuto
6) Mike Milosevich
7) Gil McDougald
8) Tony Kubek
9) Gene Michael
10) Bucky Dent

38. The Left Fielders

1) Bob Meusel
2) Ben Chapman
3) George Selkirk
4) Charlie Keller
5) Gene Woodling
6) Norm Siebern
7) Yogi Berra
8) Ellie Howard
9) Tommy Tresh
10) Roy White

39. The Center Fielders

1) Ping Bodie
2) Whitey Witt
3) Earle Combs
4) Jake Powell
5) Joe DiMaggio
6) Johnny Lindell
7) Mickey Mantle
8) Bobby Murcer
9) Elliott Maddox
10) Mickey Rivers

40. The Right Fielders

1) Willie Keeler
2) Babe Ruth
3) George Selkirk
4) Tommy Henrich

5) Bud Metheny
6) Hank Bauer
7) Roger Maris

8) Bobby Murcer
9) Bobby Bonds
10) Reggie Jackson

41. The Managers

1) Frank Chance
2) Miller Huggins
3) Bob Shawkey
4) Joe McCarthy
5) Bucky Harris

6) Casey Stengel
7) Yogi Berra
8) Johnny Keane
9) Ralph Houk
10) Billy Martin

42. Catchers

1) Thurman Munson
2) Yogi Berra
3) Wally Schang

4) Ellie Howard
5) Benny Bengough

43. First Basemen

1) Hal Chase
2) Bill Skowron
3) Wally Pipp

4) George McQuinn
5) Joe Pepitone

44. Second Basemen

1) Del Pratt
2) George Stirnweiss
3) Bobby Richardson

4) Jerry Coleman
5) Billy Martin

45. Third Basemen

1) Red Rolfe
2) Joe Dugan
3) Bobby Brown

4) Gil McDougald
5) Clete Boyer

46. Shortstops

1) Phil Rizzuto
2) Lyn Lary
3) Tony Kubek

4) Everett Scott
5) Frankie Crosetti

47. Left Fielders

1) Birdie Cree
2) Charlie Keller
3) Gene Woodling

4) Hector Lopez
5) Tommy Tresh

48. Center Fielders

1) Ben Chapman
2) Mickey Mantle
3) Whitey Witt

4) Irv Noren
5) Johnny Lindell

49. Right Fielders

1) George Selkirk
2) Tommy Henrich
3) Hank Bauer

4) Roger Maris
5) Bud Metheny

Historical Interlude
Number Eight

Whitey Ford and World Series records are synonymous.

He set many post-season records, including ones for most wins (10) and most losses (8). But the record that most people relate to is his scoreless string of 33⅔ innings. (That string eclipsed the string of 29⅔ innings which Babe Ruth had weaved for the 1916 and 1918 Red Sox.)

Ford began the string in 1960 when he pitched two shutouts for a total of 18 scoreless innings against the Pirates. In 1961, against the Reds, he hurled 14 innings of shutout ball to break the Babe's record.

The following year, he got by the Giants in the first inning of Game One, but saw his streak get broken in the second inning. The lead-off batter singled. After one was out, Jim Davenport singled him to third. Then Jose Pagan dropped down a bunt for a base hit as the first run in 33⅔ innings against Whitey Ford crossed the plate. Ford then settled down and coasted to a 6–2 win.

In Game Six, Ford lost his first outing since 1958, a 5–2 decision to Billy Pierce. Ford never again won a World Series game. He lost two to the Dodgers in 1963, one in which he yielded only two hits, and one to the Cardinals in 1964.

Flashing back to 1962, I have deliberately withheld the name of the runner who broke Ford's scoreless inning string. He was a longtime Whitey Ford nemesis.

Can you name him?

Answer: Willie Mays

84

CHAPTER NINE

The All-Star Game

50. WHO'S WHO

Identify the following Yankees who have distinguished themselves in All-Star play.

1) _____ Who started the first game for the American League, pitched three scoreless innings, and got the first decision in All-Star competition?

2) _____ Who hit the two-run homer that provided the margin of difference for the American League?

3) _____ Who robbed Chick Hafey of a two-run homer in the eighth to ensure the 4–2 win?

4) _____ Who were the two Yankees, in addition to Jimmie Foxx, Al Simmons, and Joe Cronin, whom Carl Hubbell struck out in succession in 1934?

5) _____ Who was the only pitcher to win three games in All-Star competition?

6) _____ Who was the Yankee skipper who served as a pinch manager for the regular braintrust, who had suffered a nervous breakdown?

7) _____ Who is the Yankee who was the first rookie to start in an All-Star game?

8) _____ Who was the third baseman on the squad that boasted six Yankee starters?

9) _____ Who was an honorary member of the 1939 team?

10) _____ Who was the Yankee manager who was sidelined one year because he was appearing too often?

11) _____ Who was the former Yankee who was one-half of the first fraternal act in an All-Star game?

12) _____ Who was the manager who deliberately held six of his players out of the game?

13) _____ Who managed a record six losers?

14) _____ Who is the former Yankee who was the first rookie pitcher to receive credit for a win?

15) _____ Who is the former Yankee who was selected to the All-Star team in each of his 13 big-league seasons?

16) _____ Who was the manager who dropped his first four decisions?

17) _____ Who is the Hall-of-Famer who lost both of his decisions and posted an 8.25 ERA in six games?

18) _____ Who struck out a record 17 times?

19) _____ Who hit home runs in back-to-back games in the 1930s?

20) _____ Who hit home runs in back-to-back years in the 1950s?

21) _____ Who was the Yankee outfielder who played all three outfield positions during the first four years of the All-Star game?

22) _____ Who made his four hits count for 14 total bases?

23) _____ Who hit a home run when the Yankees hosted their first All-Star game in 1939?

24) _____ Who has been the only Yankee to commit two errors in one game?

25) _____ Who is the former Yankee pitcher who drilled a two-run single en route to a pitching victory?

26) _____ Who has been the last Yankee pitcher (1948) to get credit for a victory?

27) _____ Who is the former Yankee who stroked three doubles?

28) _____ Who drove home a club-high six runs?

29) _____ Who collected a club-high four ribbies in one game?

30) _____ Who struck out a club-high nine batters in five appearances?

51. ANEMIC AVERAGES

The Yankees have an unbelievably low team average, just barely .200, in All-Star play. Can you pick out the 15 Yankees from the following names who have hit even less than .204 in the "Mid-Summer Dream"? Check the correct names.

Ben Chapman
Red Ruffing
Babe Ruth
Jerry Coleman
Joe Gordon
Charlie Keller
Red Rolfe
Johnny Mize
Bobby Bonds
Roy White
Thurman Munson
Gil McDougald
Roger Maris
Bobby Murcer
Bill Dickey

George Stirnweiss
George McQuinn
Phil Rizzuto
Ellie Howard
Hank Bauer
Mickey Mantle
Tommy Henrich
Yogi Berra
Lou Gehrig
Joe DiMaggio
Tony Kubek
Bill Skowron
George Selkirk
Bobby Richardson
Joe Pepitone

52. PITCHING REVERSALS

Yankee pitchers have dropped the last seven decisions in which they have been involved. Whitey Ford has suffered two of the setbacks. How many of the other five moundsmen can you name?

1) _____   4) _____
2) _____   5) _____
3) _____

Answers

50. Who's Who

1) Lefty Gomez (1933)
2) Babe Ruth
3) Babe Ruth
4) Babe Ruth, Lou Gehrig
5) Lefty Gomez
6) Joe McCarthy (1936) for Mickey Cochrane
7) Joe DiMaggio (1936)
8) Red Rolfe (1939)
9) Lou Gehrig
10) Joe McCarthy (1940)
11) Joe DiMaggio (Dom, who played, too, scored Joe with a single in the eighth.)
12) Joe McCarthy (1943) withheld Ernie Bonham, Spud Chandler, Bill Dickey, Joe Gordon, Johnny Lindell, and Charlie Keller because of criticism about the Yankees' dominance of players on the American League team.
13) Casey Stengel
14) Frank Shea (1947)
15) Joe DiMaggio
16) Casey Stengel (1950–53)
17) Whitey Ford
18) Mickey Mantle
19) Lou Gehrig (1936–37)
20) Mickey Mantle (1955–56)
21) Ben Chapman
22) Lou Gehrig
23) Joe DiMaggio
24) Red Rolfe (1937)
25) Vic Raschi (1948)
26) Vic Raschi
27) Joe Gordon
28) Joe DiMaggio
29) Lou Gehrig (1937)
30) Lefty Gomez

51. Anemic Averages

1) Ben Chapman (.143)
2) Jerry Coleman (.000)
3) Joe Gordon (.187)
4) Charlie Keller (.143)
5) Bobby Bonds (.000)
6) Roy White (.000)
7) Thurman Munson (.200)
8) Roger Maris (.117)
9) Bobby Murcer (.091)
10) Ellie Howard (.000)
11) Tommy Henrich (.111)
12) Yogi Berra (.200)
13) Tony Kubek (.000)
14) Bobby Richardson (.091)
15) Joe Pepitone (.000)

52. Pitching Reversals

1) Eddie Lopat
2) Allie Reynolds
3) Mel Stottlemyre
4) Catfish Hunter
5) Goose Gossage

Historical Interlude
Number Nine

Some ordinary players rise to the occasion in a World Series. But when Billy Martin, an average .257 lifetime hitter, gets into a Fall Classic, it seems as though he almost always reaches above himself.

In five World Series as a player, he performed on four world championship teams; in two Fall Classics as a manager, he has directed one title winner.

As a player Martin hit .333 in October action, which was 76 points above his lifetime average. In regular-season play he hit one home run for every 53 times he came to the bat; in post-season play he ripped one homer for every 20 plate appearances.

His last three Series averages were .500, .320, and .296. You can count the number of players who have hit .500 in World Series play on two hands.

In 1953 he hit .500 in six games to tie a record. He also got 12 hits, which set a record.

Some of his key hits in 1952–53 included a three-run game-winning home run, a three-run game-winning triple, and a one-run game-winning (and Series-winning) single.

In 1953, when he hit .500 on 12 hits, he clubbed two home runs, two triples, and two doubles to compile an incredible .938 slugging average. In that same Series he totaled 23 bases, a record at that time.

But Martin stood out in World Series play on defense as well as offense. At one point he did not make an error over 23 consecutive games, a record for second baseman.

Undoubtedly the play for which he is most remembered took place in the seventh inning of the seventh game in 1952. With the bases loaded and two outs, the Dodgers had one of their most feared hitters at the plate. (The score was 4–2 Yankees.) He lifted a towering pop fly just to the left of the pitcher's mound. Relief pitcher Bob

Kuzava froze on the mound. First baseman Joe Collins lost the ball in the high sky. Martin was the Yankees' third and last possibility. He spurted from his position and picked the ball off his shoes as the third Dodger runner got set to cross the plate.

Once again, in the clutch, Martin did not fail the Yankees. If he had not made that breathtaking play, the Yankees would have lost the game, 5–4, and the Series, As it was, they won the game, 4–2, and the Series.

Looking back, you may find it difficult to recall that Dodger clean-up hitter who almost got three RBI—one a game-winner—on a pop fly that traveled no more than 60 feet.

Do you?

Answer: Jackie Robinson

CHAPTER TEN

Rookies and Veterans

53. YANKEE ROOKIES OF THE 1940S

Match the following players with the years in which they officially became major-league rookies: Phil Rizzuto, Yogi Berra, Hank Borowy, Ernie Bonham, Bill Bevens, Tommy Byrne, George Stirnweiss, Jerry Coleman, Eddie Lopat, and Randy Gumpert.

1) _____ (1940)   6) _____ (1945)
2) _____ (1941)   7) _____ (1946)
3) _____ (1942)   8) _____ (1947)
4) _____ (1943)   9) _____ (1948)
5) _____ (1944)   10) _____ (1949)

To be considered a rookie, the player, if a regular, needed 100 official at bats in his first full season and, if a pitcher, either ten decisions or 100 innings of pitching.

54. YANKEE ROOKIES OF THE 1950S

Match the following players with the years in which they officially became major-league rookies: Ellie Howard, Jim Coates, Whitey Ford, Clete Boyer, Marv Throneberry, Mickey Mantle, Billy Martin, Bill Skowron, Tony Kubek, and Bill Renna.

1) _____ (1950)   2) _____ (1951)

3) _____ (1952)	7) _____ (1956)
4) _____ (1953)	8) _____ (1957)
5) _____ (1954)	9) _____ (1958)
6) _____ (1955)	10) _____ (1959)

55. YANKEE ROOKIES OF THE 1960S

Match the following players with the years in which they officially became major-league rookies: Mel Stottlemyre, Stan Bahnsen, Lou Piniella, Bill Stafford, Jim Bouton, Reggie Jackson, Roy White, Horace Clarke, Al Downing, and Eli Grba.

1) _____ (1960)	6) _____ (1965)
2) _____ (1961)	7) _____ (1966)
3) _____ (1962)	8) _____ (1967)
4) _____ (1963)	9) _____ (1968)
5) _____ (1964)	10) _____ (1969)

56. YANKEE ROOKIES OF THE 1970S

Match the following players with the years in which they officially became major-league rookies: Goose Gossage, Barry Foote, Thurman Munson, Ron Guidry, Dave Winfield, Ron Davis, Jim Beattie, Tom Underwood, Chris Chambliss, and Willie Randolph.

1) _____ (1970)	6) _____ (1975)
2) _____ (1971)	7) _____ (1976)
3) _____ (1972)	8) _____ (1977)
4) _____ (1973)	9) _____ (1978)
5) _____ (1974)	10) _____ (1979)

57. CAREER YANKEES

Twenty of the 40 players listed below spent their entire careers with the Yankees. Which ones? Check the correct names.

Phil Ruzzuto
Bob Meusel
Lou Gehrig
Tony Lazzeri
Red Rolfe
Joe Gordon
Jerry Coleman
Yogi Berra
Allie Reynolds
Whitey Ford
Babe Ruth
Tony Kubek
Bill Skowron
Frankie Crosetti
Hank Bauer
Earle Combs
Tommy Henrich
Charlie Keller
Joe Collins
Bobby Brown

Bobby Richardson
Joe Page
Bill Dickey
Lefty Gomez
Spud Chandler
Bill Bevens
Vic Raschi
Gil McDougald
Gene Woodling
Eddie Lopat
Johnny Kucks
Andy Carey
Ellie Howard
Mel Stottlemyre
Herb Pennock
Waite Hoyt
Thurman Munson
Graig Nettles
Roy White
Ralph Houk

58. BREAKING IN

With what teams did these 20 onetime Yankees begin their major-league careers?

1) _____ Babe Ruth   3) _____ Bobby Shantz
2) _____ Johnny Mize   4) _____ Eddie Lopat

5)	_____ Gene Woodling	13)	_____ Allie Reynolds
6)	_____ Roger Maris	14)	_____ Bobo Newsom
7)	_____ Don Larsen	15)	_____ Sal Maglie
8)	_____ Red Ruffing	16)	_____ George McQuinn
9)	_____ Johnny Sain		
10)	_____ Enos Slaughter	17)	_____ Jim Konstanty
		18)	_____ Irv Noren
11)	_____ Wes Ferrell	19)	_____ Virgil Trucks
12)	_____ Jim Turner	20)	_____ Robin Roberts

59. STARTERS AND FINISHERS

The following 20 players either began or concluded their careers with the Yankees. See if you can determine which way it was. Mark *S* for started and *C* for concluded.

1) __ Dixie Walker	11) __ Mark Koenig
2) __ Leo Durocher	12) __ Johnny Murphy
3) __ Paul Waner	13) __ Tony Lazzeri
4) __ Lew Burdette	14) __ Buddy Rosar
5) __ Johnny Allen	15) __ Jim Turner
6) __ Fred Merkle	16) __ Rocky Colavito
7) __ Jackie Jensen	17) __ Cliff Mapes
8) __ Hugh Casey	18) __ Dale Long
9) __ Lefty O'Doul	19) __ Earl Torgeson
10) __ Johnny Mize	20) __ Ron Swoboda

60. BOWING OUT

With what teams did these 20 former Yankees conclude their big-league careers?

1) _____ Roger Maris
2) _____ Babe Ruth
3) _____ Joe Gordon
4) _____ Joe Page
5) _____ Gene Woodling
6) _____ Hank Bauer
7) _____ Billy Johnson
8) _____ Tony Lazzeri
9) _____ Lefty Gomez
10) _____ George Stirnweiss

11) _____ Ernie Bonham
12) _____ Hank Borowy
13) _____ Johnny Lindell
14) _____ Frank Shea
15) _____ Billy Martin
16) _____ Bill Skowron
17) _____ Don Larsen
18) _____ Clete Boyer
19) _____ Johnny Allen
20) _____ Ralph Terry

61. YANKEE FAREWELLS

Below are listed 20 famous Yankee players and the years in which they broke into the major leagues. Can you provide the years in which they bowed out of the "Big Time"?

1) Babe Ruth
   (1914-_____)
2) Red Ruffing
   (1924-_____)
3) Lou Gehrig
   (1923-_____)
4) Joe DiMaggio
   (1936-_____)
5) Tony Lazzeri
   (1926-_____)

6) Phil Rizzuto
   (1941-_____)
7) Red Rolfe
   (1931-_____)
8) Bill Dickey
   (1928-_____)
9) Mickey Mantle
   (1951-_____)
10) Whitey Ford
   (1950-_____)

11) Roger Maris
    (1957–_____)
12) Earle Combs
    (1925–_____)
13) Lefty Gomez
    (1930–_____)
14) Allie Reynolds
    (1942–_____)
15) Vic Raschi
    (1946–_____)
16) Ellie Howard
    (1955–_____)
17) Johnny Mize
    (1936–_____)
18) Catfish Hunter
    (1965–_____)
19) Charlie Keller
    (1939–_____)
20) Tommy Henrich
    (1937–_____)

Answers

53. Yankee Rookies of the 1940s

1) Ernie Bonham (1940)
2) Phil Rizzuto (1941)
3) Hank Borowy (1942)
4) George Stirnweiss (1943)
5) Eddie Lopat (1944)
6) Bill Bevens (1945)
7) Randy Gumpert (1946)
8) Yogi Berra (1947)
9) Tommy Byrne (1948)
10) Jerry Coleman (1949)

54. Yankee Rookies of the 1950s

1) Whitey Ford (1950)
2) Mickey Mantle (1951)
3) Billy Martin (1952)
4) Bill Renna (1953)
5) Bill Skowron (1954)
6) Ellie Howard (1955)
7) Clete Boyer (1956)
8) Tony Kubek (1957)
9) Marv Throneberry (1958)
10) Jim Coates (1959)

55. Yankee Rookies of the 1960s

1) Eli Grba (1960)
2) Bill Stafford (1961)
3) Jim Bouton (1962)
4) Al Downing (1963)
5) Mel Stottlemyre (1964)
6) Horace Clarke (1965)
7) Roy White (1966)
8) Reggie Jackson (1967)
9) Stan Bahnsen (1968)
10) Lou Piniella (1969)

56. Yankee Rookies of the 1970s

1) Thurman Munson (1970)
2) Chris Chambliss (1971)

3) Goose Gossage (1972)
4) Dave Winfield (1973)
5) Barry Foote (1974)
6) Tom Underwood (1975)

7) Willie Randolph (1976)
8) Ron Guidry (1977)
9) Jim Beattie (1978)
10) Ron Davis (1979)

57. Career Yankees

Phil Rizzuto
Lou Gehrig
Red Rolfe
Jerry Coleman
Whitey Ford
Tony Kubek
Frankie Crosetti
Earle Combs
Tommy Henrich
Joe Collins

Bobby Brown
Bobby Richardson
Bill Dickey
Spud Chandler
Bill Bevens
Gil McDougald
Mel Stottlemyre
Thurman Munson
Roy White
Ralph Houk

58. Breaking In

1) Red Sox
2) Cardinals
3) Athletics
4) White Sox
5) Indians
6) Indians
7) Browns
8) Red Sox
9) Braves
10) Cardinals

11) Indians
12) Braves
13) Indians
14) Dodgers
15) Giants
16) Reds
17) Reds
18) Senators
19) Tigers
20) Phillies

59. Starters and Finishers

1) S
2) S

3) C
4) S

5) S	13) S
6) C	14) S
7) S	15) C
8) C	16) C
9) S	17) S
10) C	18) C
11) S	19) C
12) S	20) C

60. Bowing Out

1) Cardinals	11) Pirates
2) Braves	12) Tigers
3) Indians	13) Phillies
4) Pirates	14) Senators
5) Mets	15) Twins
6) Athletics	16) Angels
7) Cardinals	17) Cubs
8) Giants	18) Braves
9) Senators	19) Giants
10) Indians	20) Mets

61. Yankee Farewells

1) 1934	11) 1968
2) 1947	12) 1935
3) 1939	13) 1943
4) 1951	14) 1954
5) 1939	15) 1955
6) 1956	16) 1968
7) 1942	17) 1953
8) 1946	18) 1979
9) 1968	19) 1952
10) 1967	20) 1950

Historical Interlude Number Ten

Pinch-hitters shined in the 1947 World Series.

Cookie Lavagetto, of course, got the most memorable pinch hit of that Fall Classic. His double, with two outs in the ninth inning of Game Four, broke up Bill Bevens' no-hitter and gave the Dodgers a 3–2 victory.

But the Yankees had their pinch-hitting heroes, too. In Game Three, Yogi Berra, a rookie, hit the first pinch-hit home run in World Series history.

The "Golden Boy" tag, however, went to another Yankee rookie, Bobby Brown. He hit safely in his three official pinch-hit appearances to set a major-league record for one Series. In Game Seven he doubled home the tying run for the Yankees and scored what proved to be the winning run of the Series.

In four World Series, Brown batted 1.000, .500, .333, and .357. His lifetime average in World Series play was .439, the all-time high for players who performed in three or more post-season classics.

Looking back upon his career, Brown might concur that he never scored a more important run in his career than the tie-breaking one in Game Seven of 1947. The player who drove him home with a single had three of the Yankees' four game-winning hits in the Series. (Joe Di-Maggio had the other one.) That same player drove home the game-winning run in the first game of the 1949 Series also. So, in effect, in four of the five Yankee wins during that span, he delivered the run that decided the contest.

Who was that reliable player?

Answer: Tommy Henrich

CHAPTER ELEVEN

Nicknames

62. BEFORE OR BETWEEN

Insert the players' nicknames in the appropriate places. In most of the cases, the monikers belong between the players' first and last names. But in other instances they are the player's first names or are part of the first name. In such a situation the player's first name is not given below.

1) _____ Keeler
2) _____ Chesbro
3) Dick _____ Tidrow
4) Jim _____ Hunter
5) Rich _____ Gossage
6) Ron _____ Blomberg
7) George _____ Medich
8) Albert _____ Lyle
9) _____ Piniella
10) _____ Rivers
11) Frank _____ Shea
12) John _____ Mize
13) Billy _____ Martin
14) Ed _____ Ford
15) Tom _____ Morgan
16) Ewell _____ Blackwell
17) Jim _____ McDonald

18) Bob _____ Kuzava
19) Bill _____ Skowron
20) _____ Turley
21) Don _____ Larsen
22) Tom _____ Sturdivant
23) Harry _____ Simpson
24) Sal _____ Maglie
25) _____ Throneberry
26) _____ Bouton
27) Leo _____ Daley
28) Joe _____ Pepitone
29) _____ Linz
30) Marshall _____ Bridges
31) Horace _____ Womack
32) Gene _____ Michael

33) Marius _____ Russo
34) Jim _____ Turner
35) John _____ Hassett
36) George _____ Stainback
37) Billy _____ Johnson
38) George _____ Stirnweiss
39) Bill _____ Zuber
40) Tommy _____ Byrne
41) Paul _____ Waner
42) Joe _____ Page
43) Larry _____ Berra
44) Arthur _____ Metheny
45) Fred _____ Stanley
46) Phil _____ Rizzuto
47) Vic _____ Raschi
48) Steve _____ Souchock
49) Bill _____ White
50) Bobby _____ Brown
51) Ralph _____ Houk
52) _____ Bauer
53) Clarence _____ Marshall
54) Cliff _____ Mapes
55) _____ Lopat
56) Allie _____ Reynolds
57) Waite _____ Hoyt
58) Lou _____ Gehrig
59) Earle _____ Combs

60) Tony _____ Lazzeri
61) Leo _____ Durocher
62) Wilcy _____ Moore
63) Vernon _____ Gomez
64) Charles _____ Ruffing
65) Frankie _____ Crosetti
66) Johnny _____ Murphy
67) Fred _____ Walker
68) Robert _____ Rolfe
69) George _____ Selkirk
70) Joe _____ DiMaggio
71) Irving _____ Hadley
72) Tommy _____ Henrich
73) Ellsworth _____ Dahlgren
74) Spurgeon _____ Chandler
75) Joe _____ Gordon
76) Atley _____ Donald
77) Charlie _____ Keller
78) Warren _____ Rosar
79) Ernie _____ Bonham
80) _____ Jones

103

81) _____ Bush
82) Everett _____ Scott
83) Enos _____ Slaughter
84) Lawton Walter _____ Witt
85) _____ Dugan
86) _____ Meusel
87) George Herman _____ Ruth
88) Carl _____ Mays
89) Frank _____ O'Doul
90) Frank _____ Baker

91) Herb _____ Pennock
92) Ron _____ Guidry
93) Clark _____ Griffith
94) _____ Chase
95) Norman _____ Elberfeld
96) Frank _____ Hahn
97) Jimmy _____ Austin
98) Jim _____ Vaughn
99) Cliff _____ Johnson
100) Graig _____ Nettles

Answers

62. Before or Between

1) "Wee Willie"
2) "Happy Jack"
3) "Dirt"
4) "Catfish"
5) "Goose"
6) "The Boomer"
7) "Doc"
8) "Sparky"
9) "Sweet Lou"
10) "Mick the Quick"
11) "Spec" or "The Naugatuck Nugget"
12) "The Big Cat"
13) "The Kid"
14) "Whitey"
15) "Plowboy"
16) "The Whip"
17) "Hot Rod"
18) "Sarge"
19) "Moose"
20) "Bullet Bob"
21) "Perfect Game"
22) "Snake"
23) "Suitcase"
24) "The Barber"
25) "Marvelous Marv"
26) "Jersey Jim"
27) "Buddy"
28) "Pepi"
29) "Harmonica Phil"
30) "Sheriff"
31) "Dooley"
32) "The Stick"
33) "Lefty"
34) "Milkman"
35) "Buddy"
36) "Tuck"
37) "The Bull"
38) "Snuffy"
39) "Goober"
40) "The Wildman"
41) "Big Poison"
42) "Fireman" or "The Gay Reliever"
43) "Yogi"
44) "Bud"
45) "Chicken"
46) "The Scooter"
47) "The Springfield Rifle"
48) "Bud"
49) "Lefty"
50) "The Golden Boy"
51) "The Major"
52) "Hammering Hank"
53) "Cuddles"
54) "Tiger"
55) "Steadie Eddie"
56) "The Super Chief"
57) "Schoolboy"
58) "The Iron Horse"
59) "The Kentucky Colonel"
60) "Poosh 'em Up"
61) "The Lip"
62) "Cy"

63) "Lefty" or "El Goofy"
64) "Red"
65) "The Crow"
66) "Fireman"
67) "Dixie"
68) "Red"
69) "Twinkletoes"
70) "The Yankee Clipper" or "Jolting Joe"
71) "Bump"
72) "Old Reliable"
73) "Babe"
74) "Spud"
75) "Flash"
76) "Swampy"
77) "King Kong"
78) "Buddy"
79) "Tiny"
80) "Sad Sam"
81) "Bullet Joe"
82) "Deacon"
83) "Country"
84) "Whitey"
85) "Jumping Joe"
86) "Long Bob"
87) "Babe" or "The Bambino" or "The Sultan of Swat"
88) "Sub"
89) "Lefty"
90) "Home Run"
91) "The Knight of Kennett Square"
92) "Louisiana Lightning"
93) "The Old Fox"
94) "Prince Hal"
95) "The Tabasco Kid"
96) "Noodles"
97) "Pepper"
98) "Hippo"
99) "Top Cat"
100) "Puff"

Historical Interlude Number Eleven

They call Reggie Jackson "Mr. October." And with good reason.

In the 1973 World Series, with the A's, Jackson hit .310 and one home run. A year later, he stroked .286 and one four-base blow. In 1977, with the Yankees, he smashed .450 and five home runs. A year later, he cracked .391 and two home runs.

But undoubtedly the 1977 Series was his greatest one.

With his hitting he totaled 25 bases, one better than the former record set by Duke Snider and tied by Lou Brock. Both Snider and Brock needed seven games to amass their totals, though.

Other records that Jackson set were ten runs (one better than Babe Ruth), four consecutive home runs (with one walk in between), four home runs on four consecutive swings, three homers off three different pitchers in one game, three home runs on the first pitch in one game, and three straight homers in one game.

It seems safe to say that many Octobers will pass before any other slugger will have the type of World Series that Jackson had in 1977.

Is it safe to ask who was the former Yankee who held the total base mark for a six-game set before Jackson smashed it? Their paths have a tendency to cross.

Answer: Billy Martin

CHAPTER TWELVE
The Hitters

63. STEPPING INTO THE BOX

Which way did they bat? Mark *L* for left-handed, *R* for right-handed, and *S* for switch-hitter.

1) __ Bob Meusel		16) __ Phil Rizzuto
2) __ Lou Gehrig		17) __ Johnny Lindell
3) __ Wally Pipp		18) __ Tommy Henrich
4) __ Tony Lazzeri		19) __ Billy Johnson
5) __ Bill Dickey		20) __ Joe Pepitone
6) __ Mickey Mantle		21) __ Bill Skowron
7) __ Tom Tresh		22) __ Tony Kubek
8) __ Sandy Alomar		23) __ Joe Collins
9) __ Earle Combs		24) __ George Stirnweiss
10) __ Horace Clarke		25) __ Gene Michael
11) __ Frankie Crosetti		26) __ George McQuinn
12) __ Red Rolfe		27) __ Hank Bauer
13) __ Willie Miranda		28) __ Rusty Torres
14) __ Roy White		29) __ Harry Simpson
15) __ Joe Gordon		30) __ Danny Cater

64. THE YEAR THEY HIT THE HEIGHTS, PART I

Take the following ten pre-1940 hitters and match them up with their best single-season batting averages with the Yankees: Bob Meusel, Wally Pipp, Mark Koenig, Earle Combs, George Selkirk, Charlie Keller, Wally Schang, Ben Chapman, Joe Dugan, and Jake Powell.

1) _____ (.356)   6) _____ (.319)
2) _____ (.337)   7) _____ (.316)
3) _____ (.334)   8) _____ (.312)
4) _____ (.329)   9) _____ (.306)
5) _____ (.319)   10) _____ (.302)

65. THE YEAR THEY HIT THE HEIGHTS, PART II

Take the following post-1940 hitters and match them up with their highest respective season's batting averages with the Yankees: Tommy Henrich, Yogi Berra, Bobby Richardson, Ellie Howard, Mickey Mantle, Thurman Munson, Bobby Murcer, Mickey Rivers, Lou Piniella, and Bill Skowron.

1) _____ (.365)   6) _____ (.319)
2) _____ (.348)   7) _____ (.318)
3) _____ (.331)   8) _____ (.312)
4) _____ (.326)   9) _____ (.308)
5) _____ (.322)   10) _____ (.302)

66. HIGHEST SINGLE-SEASON AVERAGE PER POSITION

Select the player, from the multiple-choice groups for each position, who hit for the highest average in a single season with the Yankees.

1) 1B __ (.379): a. Hal Chase b. Lou Gehrig c. George McQuinn d. Bill Skowron

2) 2B __ (.354): a. Joe Gordon b. George Stirnweiss c. Del Pratt d. Tony Lazzeri
3) SS __ (.324): a. Kid Elberfeld b. Mark Koenig c. Phil Rizzuto d. Gil McDougald
4) 3B __ (.329): a. Red Rolfe b. Frank Baker c. Andy Carey d. Joe Sewell
5) LF __ (.348): a. Bob Meusel b. Birdie Cree c. Gene Woodling d. Lou Piniella
6) CF __ (.381): a. Joe DiMaggio b. Earle Combs c. Mickey Mantle d. Bobby Murcer
7) RF __ (.393): a. Willie Keeler b. Ben Chapman c. Babe Ruth d. Hank Bauer
8) C __ (.362): a. Wally Schang b. Ellie Howard c. Yogi Berra d. Bill Dickey
9) P __ (.374): a. Carl Mays b. Don Larsen c. Red Ruffing d. Tommy Byrne

67. BATTING CHAMPIONS

Only six Yankees have won a batting championship. (One of them did it in consecutive years.) The others won only one title. List the winners from among the following names: Earle Combs, Bob Meusel, Bill Dickey, Babe Ruth, Lou Gehrig, Red Rolfe, Hal Chase, Charlie Keller, Joe DiMaggio, Bobby Murcer, George Stirnweiss, Don Mattingly, and Mickey Mantle.

1) _____   4) _____
2) _____   5) _____
3) _____   6) _____

68. HIGHEST LIFETIME AVERAGE PER POSITION

Select the player, from multiple-choice groups for each position, who hit for the highest lifetime average. Two players are tied for the lead at one position. You need to name both of them to score.

1) 1B __ (.340): a. Wally Pipp b. Hal Chase c. Lou Gehrig d. Bill Skowron

2) 2B __ (.292): a. Joe Gordon b. Bobby Richardson c. Aaron Ward d. Tony Lazzeri

3) SS __ (.279): a. Phil Rizzuto b. Mark Koenig c. Frankie Crosetti d. Kid Elberfeld

4) 3B __ (.312): a. Red Rolfe b. Frank Baker c. Billy Johnson d. Joe Sewell

5) LF __ (.309): a. Bob Meusel b. Charlie Keller c. Gene Woodling d. Birdie Cree

6) CF __ (.325): a. Joe DiMaggio b. Earle Combs c. Mickey Mantle d. Bobby Murcer

7) RF __ (.345): a. Babe Ruth b. George Selkirk c. Willie Keeler d. Tommy Henrich

8) C __ (.313): a. Thurman Munson b. Bill Dickey c. Yogi Berra d. Wally Schang

9) P __ (.273): a. Red Ruffing b. Carl Mays c. Al Orth d. Joe Bush

69. TWO-BASE HITS

Match the following players with their highest single-season double output for the Yankees: Red Rolfe, Joe DiMaggio, Lou Gehrig, Babe Ruth, Bob Meusel, and Don Mattingly.

1) _____ (53)   4) _____ (46)
2) _____ (52)   5) _____ (45)
3) _____ (47)   6) _____ (44)

70. THREE-BASE HITS

Match the following players with their highest single-season triple output with the Yankees: George Stirnweiss, Wally Pipp, Earle Combs, Lou Gehrig, and Birdie Cree.

1) _____ (23)   4) _____ (20)
2) _____ (22)   5) _____ (19)
3) _____ (22)

71. SINGLE-SEASON RBI LEADERS

Select the players from the following multiple choice groups who drove home the most runs in a season at their positions for the Yankees.

1) 1B __ (184): a. Johnny Mize b. Lou Gehrig c. Wally Pipp d. Bill Skowron

2) 2B __ (115): a. Joe Gordon b. Aaron Ward c. Tony Lazzeri d. George Stirnweiss

3) SS __ (107): a. Tom Tresh b. Mark Koenig c. Frankie Crosetti d. Lyn Lary

4) 3B __ (107): a. Clete Boyer b. Red Rolfe c. Billy Johnson d. Graig Nettles

5) LF __ (135): a. Charlie Keller b. Bob Meusel c. Birdie Cree d. Ellie Howard

6) CF __ (167): a. Mickey Mantle b. Bobby Murcer c. Joe DiMaggio d. Earle Combs

7) RF __ (170): a. Babe Ruth b. Roger Maris c. Tommy Henrich d. Reggie Jackson

8) C __ (133): a. Yogi Berra b. Ellie Howard c. Thurman Munson d. Bill Dickey

9) P __ (22): a. Red Ruffing b. Tommy Byrne c. Don Larsen d. Carl Mays

72. JOE DIMAGGIO'S BATTING STREAK

Joe DiMaggio's vital statistics during his 56-game hitting streak are very impressive. How many of the following can you pick out of the multiple-choice groups?

1) __ (Hits) a. 100 b. 112 c. 85 d. 91
2) __ (Avg.) a. .350 b. .408 c. .381 d. .455
3) __ (Runs) a. 37 b. 44 c. 56 d. 75
4) __ (RBI) a. 55 b. 41 c. 70 d. 61
5) __ (HR's) a. 15 b. 10 c. 12 d. 20
6) __ (Tr's) a. 10 b. 0 c. 8 d. 4
7) __ (Db's) a. 26 b. 20 c. 12 d. 16
8) __ (Sg's) a. 46 b. 56 c. 63 d. 40
9) __ (SO's) a. 3 b. 0 c. 7 d. 11
10) __ (BB's) a. 56 b. 35 c. 21 d. 14

73. BATTING STREAKS

Joe DiMaggio, of course, holds the major-league record of hitting safely in 56 consecutive games. At other times during his major-league career, the "Yankee Clipper" compiled hitting streaks of 23, 22, and 20 games, respectively. Seven other Yankees have run up hitting streaks of 20 or more games. How many of them can you name?

1) _____ (29 in 1919)   5) _____ (26 in 1921)
2) _____ (29 in 1931)   6) _____ (20 in 1942)
3) _____ (29 in 1942)   7) _____ (20 in 1976)
4) _____ (27 in 1907)

74. NATIONAL LEAGUE BATTING CHAMPS

Five diamondmen who once played for the Yankees won batting titles in the National League. How many of them can you name and match up with the respective years and clubs?

1) _____ (1916 Reds)
2) _____ (1927, 1934, and 1936 Pirates)
3) _____ (1929 Phillies and 1932 Dodgers)
4) _____ (1939 Cardinals)
5) _____ (1966 Pirates)

75. STANDOUT SWISHERS

Ten of the Yankees listed below have struck out 100 or more times in a season. Can you pick them out from among the following 25 players? Check the correct names.

Wally Pipp
Babe Ruth
Bob Meusel
Tony Lazzeri
Frankie Crosetti
Joe Gordon
George Stirnweiss
Charlie Keller
Joe DiMaggio
Johnny Mize
Mickey Mantle
Joe Collins
Norm Siebern

Bill Skowron
Clete Boyer
Roger Maris
Tom Tresh
Charley Smith
Steve Whitaker
Gene Michael
Bobby Murcer
Graig Nettles
Bobby Bonds
Roy White
Reggie Jackson

Answers

63. Stepping into the Box

1) R	16) R
2) L	17) R
3) L	18) L
4) R	19) R
5) L	20) L
6) S	21) R
7) S	22) L
8) S (1967)	23) L
9) L	24) R
10) S	25) S
11) R	26) L
12) L	27) R
13) S	28) S
14) S	29) L
15) R	30) R

64. The Year They Hit the Heights, Part I

1) Earle Combs (1927)
2) Bob Meusel (1927)
3) Charlie Keller (1939)
4) Wally Pipp (1922)
5) Mark Koenig (1928) or Wally Schang (1922)
6) Mark Koenig or Wally Schang
7) Ben Chapman (1930)
8) George Selkirk (1935)
9) Jake Powell (1936)
10) Joe Dugan (1924)

65. The Year They Hit the Heights, Part II

1) Mickey Mantle (1957)
2) Ellie Howard (1961)
3) Bobby Murcer (1971)
4) Mickey Rivers (1977)
5) Yogi Berra (1950)
6) Bill Skowron (1955)
7) Thurman Munson (1975)

8) Lou Piniella (1978)
9) Tommy Henrich (1948)
10) Bobby Richardson (1962)

66. Highest Single-Season Average per Position

1) b
2) d
3) c
4) a
5) b
6) a
7) c
8) d
9) c

67. Batting Champions

1) Babe Ruth (1924)
2) Lou Gehrig (1934)
3) Joe DiMaggio (1939–40)
4) George Stirnweiss (1945)
5) Mickey Mantle (1956)
6) Don Mattingly (1984)

68. Highest Lifetime Average per Position

1) c
2) d
3) b
4) d
5) a
6) a, b
7) c
8) b
9) c

69. Two-Base Hits

1) Don Mattingly (1986)
2) Lou Gehrig (1927)
3) Bob Meusel (1927)
4) Red Rolfe (1939)
5) Babe Ruth (1923)
6) Joe DiMaggio (1936)

70. Three-Base Hits

1) Earle Combs (1927)
2) George Stirnweiss (1945)
3) Birdie Cree (1911)
4) Lou Gehrig (1926)
5) Wally Pipp (1924)

71. Single-Season RBI Leaders

1) b (1931)
2) c (1926)
3) d (1931)
4) d (1977)
5) b (1921)

6) c (1937)
7) a (1921)
8) d (1937)
9) a (1936 and 1941)

72. Joe DiMaggio's Batting Streak

1) d
2) b
3) c
4) a
5) a

6) d
7) d
8) b
9) c
10) c

73. Batting Streaks

1) Roger Peckinpaugh
2) Earle Combs
3) Joe Gordon
4) Hal Chase

5) Babe Ruth
6) Buddy Hassett
7) Mickey Rivers

74. National League Batting Champs

1) Hal Chase
2) Paul Waner
3) Lefty O'Doul

4) Johnny Mize
5) Matty Alou

75. Standout Swishers

1) Frank Crosetti
2) Charlie Keller
3) Mickey Mantle (eight times)
4) Bill Skowron
5) Clete Boyer
6) Tommy Tresh

7) Charley Smith
8) Bobby Murcer (two times)
9) Bobby Bonds
10) Reggie Jackson (four times)

117

Historical Interlude Number Twelve

Thurman Munson, like many other great Yankees of the past, was consistent.

A .292 lifetime batter, he hit .300 and drove home 100 runs from 1975 to 1977. The last player to do that was Bill White (1962–64), now a Yankee broadcaster.

In the 1976 World Series he batted a torrid .529. In 1977–78 he hit .320 in each Fall Classic. Lifetime, he batted .379 in the World Series.

Munson connected safely in his last six official at bats of the 1976 Series to tie the record that had been set by Goose Goslin of the 1924 Senators. In his first at bat of the 1977 Series, he hit safely to set a record of seven consecutive hits in Fall Classic play.

In post-season play (playoffs and World Series) he hit safely in 27 of 30 contests. The first ten games Munson played in the World Series, he hit safely. In the first game of 1978, his streak was ended; but then he started another one by hitting safely in the last five games of the Series.

When it came to clutch performances, Munson was c-o-n-s-i-s-t-e-n-t. Much like Roberto Clemente, who hit safely in all 14 World Series games in which he played, and another Yankee, who hit safely in a record 17 games.

Who was that other Yankee, who played the game just as hard as Munson—in the clutch—and just as consistently?

Answer: Hank Bauer

CHAPTER THIRTEEN

The Home-Run Hitters

76. ROOKIE ROCKETS

Six Yankees have hit 20 or more home runs in their rookie year in the major leagues. (From the standpoint of this quiz, a rookie had to have more than 100 at bats in a season before he outgrew the name.) Can you name them? You might be surprised to learn some of the names that are not included in this elite group.

1) _____ (20 in 1925)   4) _____ (21 in 1961)
2) _____ (29 in 1936)   5) _____ (20 in 1962)
3) _____ (25 in 1938)   6) _____ (26 in 1969)

77. HOME-RUN CROWN WINNERS

Ten Yankees have won home-run crowns. The dates when they did it are provided. Can you provide the sluggers?

1) _____ (1916–17)   5) _____ (1937, 1948)
2) _____ (1920–21, 1923–24, 1926–31)   6) _____ (1944)
                          7) _____ (1955–56, 1958, 1960)
3) _____ (1925)
4) _____ (1931, 1934, 1936)   8) _____ (1961)
                          9) _____ (1976)
                         10) _____ (1980)

78. THE 30-HOME-RUN CLUB

Eighteen Yankees have hit 30 or more home runs in one season. Can you name them? Their season's high, in addition to the year in which they reached it, is provided.

1)	_____ (61) 1961	10)	_____ (33) 1925
2)	_____ (60) 1927	11)	_____ (33) 1941
3)	_____ (54) 1961	12)	_____ (33) 1972
4)	_____ (49) 1934, 1936	13)	_____ (32) 1975
		14)	_____ (32) 1987
5)	_____ (46) 1937	15)	_____ (31) 1941
6)	_____ (41) 1980	16)	_____ (31) 1966
7)	_____ (37) 1976	17)	_____ (30) 1940
8)	_____ (37) 1982	18)	_____ (30) 1952, 1956
9)	_____ (35) 1985		

79. HOME-RUN HITTERS WITH OTHER CLUBS

Seven players who once performed for the Yankees won home-run titles for other teams. (Five of them did it in the American League; two of them did it in the National League.) Can you name them?

1) _____ (1910 Red Sox)
2) _____ (1911–14 Athletics)
3) _____ (1915 White Sox-Indians)
4) _____ (1959 Indians)
5) _____ (1973, 1975 A's, and 1982 Angels)
6) _____ (1939–40 Cardinals, 1947–48 Giants)
7) _____ (1979 Cubs and 1982 Mets)

80. HIGHEST SINGLE-SEASON HOME-RUN TOTAL PER POSITION

Select the player with the highest single-season home-run total from the following multiple-choice groups.

1) 1B __ (49): a. Lou Gehrig b. Joe Pepitone c. Bill Skowron d. Wally Pipp
2) 2B __ (30): a. Tony Lazzeri b. Joe Gordon c. Aaron Ward d. Gil McDougald*
3) SS __ (20): a. Frankie Crosetti b. Lyn Lary c. Tony Kubek d. Tommy Tresh**
4) 3B __ (37): a. "Home Run" Baker b. Clete Boyer c. Graig Nettles d. Billy Johnson
5) LF __ (33): a. Bob Meusel b. Charlie Keller c. Gene Woodling d. Tommy Tresh***
6) CF __ (54): a. Joe DiMaggio b. Joe Pepitone c. Earle Combs d. Mickey Mantle
7) RF __ (61): a. Tommy Henrich b. Babe Ruth c. Roger Maris d. Reggie Jackson
8) C __ (30): a. Bill Dickey b. Yogi Berra c. Thurman Munson d. Elston Howard
9) P __ (5): a. Ray Caldwell b. Red Ruffing c. Don Larsen d. Tommy Byrne

*He hit 32 home runs for the Indians in 1948.
**He played 43 games in the outfield that season.
***Two answers are correct here. You need both of them to score.

81. HIGHEST CAREER HOME-RUN TOTAL PER POSITION

Select the player, from the multiple-choice groups for each position, who hit the most home runs in his career.

Most of them played more than one position, but they are recognized mainly at the position at which they are listed. Some of them played for more than one team, but they are remembered as Yankees.

1) 1B __ (493): a. Wally Pipp b. Bill Skowron c. Joe Pepitone d. Lou Gehrig
2) 2B __ (253): a. Joe Gordon b. Billy Martin c. Tony Lazzeri d. Aaron Ward
3) SS __ (98): a. Lyn Lary b. Phil Rizzuto c. Frankie Crosetti d. Mark Koenig
4) 3B __ (319): a. "Home Run" Baker b. Red Rolfe c. Graig Nettles d. Clete Boyer
5) LF __ (189): a. Charlie Keller b. Roy White c. Bob Meusel d. Gene Woodling
6) CF __ (536): a. Joe DiMaggio b. Mickey Mantle c. Cliff Mapes d. Earle Combs
7) RF __ (714): a. Roger Maris b. Reggie Jackson c. Tommy Henrich d. Babe Ruth
8) C __ (358): a. Ellie Howard b. Bill Dickey c. Thurman Munson d. Yogi Berra
9) P __ (36): a. Tommy Byrne b. Don Larsen c. Ray Caldwell d. Red Ruffing

82. TRIPLE THREATS

Can you identify the 12 players from the following list of 30 who hit three home runs in one game for the Yankees? Check the correct names. Two players did it three times and two players did it twice. Which ones?

Tom Tresh	Graig Nettles
Roger Maris	Cliff Johnson
Yogi Berra	Charlie Keller
Bill Skowron	Tommy Henrich
Ben Chapman	Joe Gordon
Thurman Munson	Babe Ruth

Bob Meusel	Billy Johnson
Ellie Howard	Johnny Mize
Bill Dickey	Mickey Mantle
Bobby Murcer	Joe Pepitone
Chris Chambliss	Hank Bauer
Joe DiMaggio	Bob Cerv
Gene Woodling	Johnny Blanchard
Lou Gehrig	Tony Lazzeri
Red Rolfe	Wally Pipp

83. GRAND SLAMMERS

Nine Yankees have hit seven or more grand slams during their careers. How many of them can you name? Can you put them in their proper order?

1) _____ (23)   6) _____ (8)
2) _____ (16)   7) _____ (8)
3) _____ (13)   8) _____ (7)
4) _____ (9)   9) _____ (7)
5) _____ (9)

84. POTPOURRI POSERS

Take the following players and place them in their proper categories below: Lou Gehrig, Ray Caldwell, Earle Combs, Joe DiMaggio, Ray Barker, Bobby Murcer, Cliff Johnson, Mickey Mantle, Charlie Keller, and Johnny Blanchard. (One of them should be used twice.)

Two Home Runs in One Inning
1) _____
2) _____

Four Consecutive Home Runs

3) _____

4) _____

5) _____

6) _____

Two Consecutive Pinch-hit Home Runs

7) _____

8) _____

9) _____

10) _____

Answers

76. Rookie Rockets

1) Lou Gehrig
2) Joe DiMaggio
3) Joe Gordon
4) Johnny Blanchard
5) Tommy Tresh
6) Bobby Murcer

77. Home-Run Crown Winners

1) Wally Pipp
2) Babe Ruth
3) Bob Meusel
4) Lou Gehrig
5) Joe DiMaggio
6) Nick Etten
7) Mickey Mantle
8) Roger Maris
9) Graig Nettles
10) Reggie Jackson

78. The 30-Home-Run Club

1) Roger Maris
2) Babe Ruth
3) Mickey Mantle
4) Lou Gehrig
5) Joe DiMaggio
6) Reggie Jackson
7) Graig Nettles
8) Dave Winfield
9) Don Mattingly
10) Bob Meusel
11) Charlie Keller
12) Bobby Murcer
13) Bobby Bonds
14) Mike Pagliarilo
15) Tommy Henrich
16) Joe Pepitone
17) Joe Gordon
18) Yogi Berra

79. Home-Run Hitters with Other Clubs

1) Jake Stahl
2) Frank Baker
3) Braggo Roth
4) Rocky Colavito
5) Reggie Jackson
6) Johnny Mize
7) Dave Kingman

80. Highest Single-Season Home-Run Total per Position

1) a (1934 and 1936)
2) b (1940)
3) d (1962)
4) c (1977)
5) a, b (1925, 1941)

6) d (1961)
7) c (1961)
8) b (1952, 1956)
9) b (1936)

81. Highest Career Home-Run Total per Position

1) d
2) a
3) c
4) c
5) a

6) b
7) d
8) d
9) d

82. Triple Threats

1) Tommy Tresh (1965)
2) Ben Chapman (1932)
3) Cliff Johnson (1977)
4) Charlie Keller (1940)
5) Babe Ruth (1930)
6) Bill Dickey (1939)
7) Bobby Murcer (1970 and 1973)

8) Joe DiMaggio (1937, 1948, and 1950)
9) Lou Gehrig (1927 twice and 1930)
10) Johnny Mize (1950)
11) Mickey Mantle (1955)
12) Tony Lazzeri (1927 and 1936)

83. Grand Slammers

1) Lou Gehrig
2) Babe Ruth
3) Joe DiMaggio
4) Yogi Berra
5) Mickey Mantle
6) Bill Dickey
7) Tony Lazzeri
8) Charlie Keller
9) Joe Pepitone

84. Potpourri Posers

Two Home Runs in One Inning

Joe DiMaggio (1936)

Cliff Johnson (1977)
Joe Pepitone (1962)

Four Consecutive Home Runs

Lou Gehrig (1932)
Johnny Blanchard (1961)

Mickey Mantle (1962)
Bobby Murcer (1970)

Two Consecutive Pinch-Hit Home Runs

Ray Caldwell (1915)
Charlie Keller (1948)

Johnny Blanchard (1961)
Ray Barker (1965)

Historical Interlude
Number Thirteen

The greatest one-man comeback in the history of baseball took place, I believe, midway through the 1949 season.

Joe DiMaggio, the Yankees' big run producer, had been sidelined for the first 65 games of the season because of a painful heel that had not responded favorably to off-season surgery on a bone spur. The Yankees, who were in first place, were fading fast to the streaking Red Sox, who had reeled off nine victories in their last ten games.

On June 29–July 1 a pivotal weekend series was set between the Yankees and the host Red Sox. Yankee fans were worried. If only we had DiMaggio, we thought. Then, miraculously, the pain in DiMaggio's heel suddenly disappeared. He decided to test it in game play against the Red Sox.

In Game One he had to swing against the serves of one of the hardest-throwing young lefties in the American League. That would be the major test. Ellis Kinder and Mel Parnell, who were scheduled to pitch Game Two and Game Three, respectively, were cuties. (Kinder won 23 games and Parnell 25, that year.) DiMaggio survived the test. He hit a single and a home run, which provided the game-winning run.

In Game Two the Red Sox staked Kinder to a 7–1 lead. But DiMaggio's three-run homer and three follow-up counters knotted the score at 7–7. DiMaggio then hit his second game-winning home run in two days, and the Yankees won, 9–7.

The Yankees were ecstatic. They once again had the momentum. DiMaggio was *back*.

In Game Three, with Vic Raschi clinging tenaciously to a 3–2 lead, DiMaggio lifted a home run, with two men on base, into the light tower in left. The Yankees won, 6–3.

For the third time, in as many days, DiMaggio had hit a game-winning home run.

In that series DiMaggio got five hits in 11 at bats and drove home nine clutch runs. Four of his hits were home runs.

I'll always remember the first, though. It was hit against a pitcher who would turn in a 2–6 record for the 1956 Yankees. Do you remember *him*?

Answer: Mickey McDermott

CHAPTER FOURTEEN

The Pitchers

---

85. WINDING UP

Mark in the provided spaces *L* for the pitchers who threw left-handed and *R* for the hurlers who threw right-handed. There are equal numbers of southpaws and portsiders in the list.

1) __ Bob Kuzava		16) __ Bill Wight
2) __ Bob Grim		17) __ Lindy McDaniel
3) __ Eddie Lopat		18) __ Bud Daley
4) __ Luis Arroyo		19) __ Jim Coates
5) __ Steve Hamilton		20) __ Duke Maas
6) __ Allie Reynolds		21) __ Harry Byrd
7) __ Marius Russo		22) __ Joe Ostrowski
8) __ Jim McDonald		23) __ Karl Drews
9) __ Jack Chesbro		24) __ Herb Pennock
10) __ Tom Morgan		25) __ Allen Gettel
11) __ Joe Page		26) __ Vernon Gomez
12) __ Roland Sheldon		27) __ Bump Hadley
13) __ Pete Mikkelsen		28) __ Monte Pearson
14) __ Fritz Peterson		29) __ Stubby Overmire
15) __ Steve Barber		30) __ Ron Guidry

86. 20-GAME WINNERS

From the 14 names that follow, place the Yankees' one-time 20-game winners in the left-hand column and the Yankees' two-time* 20-game winners in the right-hand column: Ron Guidry, Tommy John, Whitey Ford, Catfish

*or more than two-time

Hunter, Spud Chandler, Fritz Peterson, Jim Bouton, Ralph Terry, Waite Hoyt, Herb Pennock, Bob Turley, Carl Mays, Bob Grim, and Russ Ford. (The order within each column does not matter.)

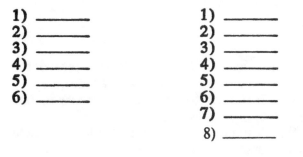

One-Time

1) ———
2) ———
3) ———
4) ———
5) ———
6) ———

Two-Time or More

1) ———
2) ———
3) ———
4) ———
5) ———
6) ———
7) ———
8) ———

87. BACK-TO-BACK 20-GAME WINNERS

Ten Yankee pitchers have won 20 or more games in back-to-back years. The dates are provided. Can you provide the pitchers?

1) ——— (1903–04)
2) ——— (1910–11)
3) ——— (1919–20)
4) ——— (1920–21)
5) ——— (1927–28)
6) ——— (1931–32)
7) ——— (1936–39)
8) ——— (1949–51)
9) ——— (1968–69)
10) ——— (1979–80)

88. SEASON SHUTOUTS

Pick the six of the following 15 pitchers who hurled at least seven shutouts in a season: Red Ruffing, Lefty Gomez, Catfish Hunter, Vic Raschi, Jack Chesbro, Mel Stottlemyre, Monte Pearson, Allie Reynolds, Al Downing,

Bob Shawkey, Whitey Ford, Carl Mays, Russ Ford, Spud Chandler, and Ron Guidry. (The order does not matter.)

1) _____   4) _____
2) _____   5) _____
3) _____   6) _____

Flash Followup

7) _____ Which one of them holds the record for shutouts by a left-hander in the American League?
8) _____ Which pitcher tossed eight shutouts in one year and seven blankings in another?
9) _____ Which pitcher hurled seven shutouts in each of back-to-back years?

89. CLUB SHUTOUTS

Match the following pitchers with the number of Yankee shutouts that they spun: Vic Raschi, Herb Pennock, Whitey Ford, Hank Borowy, Allie Reynolds, Mel Stottlemyre, Bob Turley, Red Ruffing, Ralph Terry, and George Pipgras.

1) _____ (45)   6) _____ (21)
2) _____ (40)   7) _____ (19)
3) _____ (37)   8) _____ (16)
4) _____ (27)   9) _____ (13)
5) _____ (24)   10) _____ (11)

90. PRIME PITCHERS: PRE-1930

Match the following "Old-Timers" (pre-1930) with their highest number of victories in a season: George Pipgras, Jack Chesbro, Joe Bush, Al Orth, Bob Shawkey, Carl Mays, and Russ Ford.

1) _____ (41)   5) _____ (26)
2) _____ (27)   6) _____ (24)
3) _____ (27)   7) _____ (24)
4) _____ (26)

91. PRIME PITCHERS: POST-1960

Match the following "New-Timers" (post-1960) with their highest number of victories in a season: Ed Figueroa, Ron Guidry, Tommy John, Mel Stottlemyre, Whitey Ford, Catfish Hunter, Jim Bouton, and Fritz Peterson.

1) _____ (25)   5) _____ (21)
2) _____ (25)   6) _____ (21)
3) _____ (23)   7) _____ (20)
4) _____ (22)   8) _____ (20)

92. CAREER WINS

Match the following pitchers with their respective total of wins with the Yankees: Fritz Peterson, Ralph Terry, Whitey Ford, Waite Hoyt, Vic Raschi, Bob Turley, Lefty Gomez, Allie Reynolds, Mel Stottlemyre, and Johnny Murphy.

1) _____ (236)   6) _____ (120)
2) _____ (189)   7) _____ (109)
3) _____ (164)   8) _____ (93)
4) _____ (157)   9) _____ (82)
5) _____ (131)   10) _____ (78)

93. YANKEE CAREER WINNING PERCENTAGE

Match the following pitchers with their respective career winning percentages with the Yankees: Al Downing, Vic Raschi, Tommy Byrne, Spud Chandler, Ralph Terry, Allie Reynolds, Ernie Bonham, Eddie Lopat, Whitey Ford, and Carl Mays.

1) _____ (.717)   6) _____ (.657)
2) _____ (.706)   7) _____ (.643)
3) _____ (.690)   8) _____ (.612)
4) _____ (.686)   9) _____ (.569)
5) _____ (.670)   10) _____ (.559)

94. SINGLE-SEASON LOW ERA MARKS

Ten Yankee starting pitchers have recorded earned run averages of 2.06 or less in one season. Can you single them out from among the 25 hurlers listed below and match them with their ERA?

Vic Raschi
Ray Caldwell
Herb Pennock
Waite Hoyt
Stan Bahnsen
Tom Zachary
Urban Shocker
Joe Bush
Spud Chandler
Ron Guidry
Eddie Lopat
Bump Hadley
Carl Mays

George Pipgras
Lefty Gomez
Russ Ford
Marius Russo
Ernie Bonham
Hank Borowy
Jack Chesbro
Whitey Ford
Nick Cullop
Hippo Vaughn
Joe Lake
Red Ruffing

1) _____ (1.64)
2) _____ (1.65)
3) _____ (1.74)
4) _____ (1.82)
5) _____ (1.83)

6) _____ (1.88)
7) _____ (1.94)
8) _____ (2.01)
9) _____ (2.05)
10) _____ (2.06)

95. SUB-3.00 ERA MARKS

Pick the eight of the following 20 pitchers who weaved ERA's of less than 3.00 in their careers with the Yankees:

Ed Lopat	Russ Ford
Ralph Terry	Whitey Ford
Ernie Bonham	Lefty Gomez
Carl Mays	Al Downing
Allie Reynolds	Stan Bahnsen
Jack Chesbro	Spud Chandler
Jim Bouton	Bob Shawkey
Jack Quinn	Ray Caldwell
Al Orth	Jack Warhop
Fritz Peterson	Mel Stottlemyre

1) _____ (2.54)		5) _____ (2.74)
2) _____ (2.58)		6) _____ (2.84)
3) _____ (2.72)		7) _____ (2.97)
4) _____ (2.73)		8) _____ (2.99)

96. STRIKEOUT ARTISTS

Six of the 15 pitchers listed below struck out more than 1,000 batters while they were members of the Yankees. Which ones?

Whitey Ford	Lefty Gomez
Allie Reynolds	Bob Turley
Vic Raschi	Herb Pennock
Jim Bouton	Red Ruffing

Jack Chesbro
Al Downing
Bob Shawkey
Fritz Peterson

Tommy Byrne
Mel Stottlemyre
Waite Hoyt

1) _____ (1,956)
2) _____ (1,526)
3) _____ (1,468)

4) _____ (1,257)
5) _____ (1,163)
6) _____ (1,028)

97. DEAD-BALL IRON MEN

Before 1920, five Yankee pitchers hurled 300 or more innings in a season. Can you turn back the pages of the Yankees' pitching calendar and come up with at least three correct answers?

1) _____
2) _____
3) _____

4) _____
5) _____

98. LIVE-BALL IRON MEN

Since 1920 the Yankees have had five pitchers who threw 300 or more innings in a season. Can you name them?

1) _____
2) _____
3) _____

4) _____
5) _____

99. GOOD-HITTING PITCHERS

Fourteen of the 30 pitchers listed below compiled .200-plus lifetime averages. Which ones? The respective batting averages are posted. See if you can match them up with their respective averages.

Jack Chesbro	Monte Pearson
Al Orth	Joe Page
Jack Powell	Allie Reynolds
Jack Warhop	Vic Raschi
Russ Ford	Eddie Lopat
Ray Caldwell	Whitey Ford
Bob Shawkey	Tommy Byrne
Carl Mays	Johnny Sain
Waite Hoyt	Don Larsen
Joe Bush	Bob Turley
Sam Jones	Ralph Terry
Herb Pennock	Bobby Shantz
Urban Shocker	Mel Stottlemyre
Rosy Ryan	Pedro Ramos
Red Ruffing	Al Downing

1)	_____	(.273)	8)	_____	(.238)
2)	_____	(.269)	9)	_____	(.228)
3)	_____	(.268)	10)	_____	(.214)
4)	_____	(.253)	11)	_____	(.211)
5)	_____	(.248)	12)	_____	(.209)
6)	_____	(.245)	13)	_____	(.208)
7)	_____	(.242)	14)	_____	(.205)

100. .300-HITTING PITCHERS

Ten of the 25 pitchers listed below hit .300 in a season with the Yankees. Who are they? Check the correct names.

Al Orth
Vic Raschi
Allie Reynolds
Red Ruffing
Herb Pennock
Jack Chesbro
Bob Shawkey
Whitey Ford
Tom Morgan
Tom Gorman
Carl Mays
Joe Bush
Ralph Terry

Frank Shea
Marius Russo
Waite Hoyt
Joe Page
Spud Chandler
Tommy Byrne
Don Larsen
Johnny Sain
Eddie Lopat
Tom Sturdivant
Monte Pearson
Bill Donovan

101. PINCH-HITTING PITCHERS

Five of the pitchers listed in Quiz 100 had career pinch-hitting averages that were better than .200, also. (One of them pinch-hit 228 times.) They needed at least 19 substitute plate appearances in order to qualify. Once again the averages will be posted from the highest to the lowest marks.

1) _____ (.316)   4) _____ (.234)
2) _____ (.254)*   5) _____ (.218)
3) _____ (.234)

*228 at bats

102. HOME-RUN-HITTING PITCHERS

Five of the moundsmen listed in Quiz 99, "Good-Hitting Pitchers," smacked more than *ten* career homers. Which ones?

1) _____   4) _____
2) _____   5) _____
3) _____

Answers

85. Winding Up

1) L		16) L	
2) R		17) R	
3) L		18) L	
4) L		19) R	
5) L		20) R	
6) R		21) R	
7) L		22) L	
8) R		23) R	
9) R		24) L	
10) R		25) R	
11) L		26) L	
12) R		27) R	
13) R		28) R	
14) L		29) L	
15) L		30) L	

86. 20-Game Winners

One-Time

1) Catfish Hunter (1975)
2) Fritz Peterson (1970)
3) Jim Bouton (1963)
4) Ralph Terry (1962)
5) Bob Turley (1958)
6) Bob Grim (1954)

Two-Time

1) Tommy John (1979–80)
2) Whitey Ford (1961, 1963)
3) Spud Chandler (1943, 1946)
4) Waite Hoyt (1927–28)
5) Herb Pennock (1924, 1926)
6) Carl Mays (1920–21)
7) Russ Ford (1910–11)
8) Ron Guidry (1978, 1983, and 1985)

87. Back-to-Back 20-Game Winners

1) Jack Chesbro
2) Russ Ford
3) Bob Shawkey
4) Carl Mays
5) Waite Hoyt
6) Lefty Gomez
7) Red Ruffing
8) Vic Raschi
9) Mel Stottlemyre
10) Tommy John

88. Season Shutouts

1) Catfish Hunter
2) Mel Stottlemyre
3) Allie Reynolds
4) Whitey Ford
5) Russ Ford
6) Ron Guidry

Flash Followup

7) Ron Guidry
8) Whitey Ford (1964, 1958)
9) Mel Stottlemyre (1971–72)

89. Club Shutouts

1) Whitey Ford
2) Mel Stottlemyre
3) Red Ruffing
4) Allie Reynolds
5) Vic Raschi
6) Bob Turley
7) Herb Pennock
8) Ralph Terry
9) George Pipgras
10) Hank Borowy

90. Prime Pitchers: Pre-1930

1) Jack Chesbro (1904)
2) Al Orth (1906)
3) Carl Mays (1921)
4) Russ Ford (1910)
5) Joe Bush (1922)
6) Bob Shawkey (1916)
7) George Pipgras (1928)

91. Prime Pitchers: Post-1960

1) Whitey Ford (1961)
2) Ron Guidry (1978)
3) Catfish Hunter (1975)
4) Tommy John (1980)
5) Jim Bouton (1963)
6) Mel Stottlemyre (1968)
7) Fritz Peterson (1970)
8) Ed Figueroa (1978)

92. Career Wins

1) Whitey Ford
2) Lefty Gomez
3) Mel Stottlemyre
4) Waite Hoyt
5) Allie Reynolds
6) Vic Raschi
7) Fritz Peterson
8) Johnny Murphy
9) Bob Turley
10) Ralph Terry

93. Yankee Career Winning Percentage

1) Spud Chandler
2) Vic Raschi
3) Whitey Ford
4) Allie Reynolds
5) Carl Mays
6) Eddie Lopat
7) Tommy Byrne
8) Ernie Bonham
9) Ralph Terry
10) Al Downing

94. Single-Season Low ERA Marks

1) Spud Chandler (1943)
2) Russ Ford (1910)
3) Ron Guidry (1978)
4) Jack Chesbro (1904)
5) Hippo Vaughn (1910)
6) Joe Lake (1909)
7) Ray Caldwell (1914)
8) Whitey Ford (1958)
9) Nick Cullop (1916
10) Stan Bahnsen (1968)

95. Sub-3.00 ERA Marks

1) Russ Ford
2) Jack Chesbro
3) Al Orth
4) Ernie Bonham

143

5) Whitey Ford
6) Spud Chandler

7) Mel Stottlemyre
8) Ray Caldwell

96. Strikeout Artists

1) Whitey Ford
2) Red Ruffing
3) Lefty Gomez

4) Mel Stottlemyre
5) Bob Shawkey
6) Al Downing

97. Dead-Ball Iron Men

1) Jack Chesbro (four times in succession: 1903–06)
2) Jack Powell (1904)

3) Al Orth (1905)
4) Russ Ford (1910)
5) Ray Caldwell (1915)

98. Live-Ball Iron Men

1) Carl Mays (1920–21)
2) Bob Shawkey (1922)
3) George Pipgras (1928)

4) Mel Stottlemyre (1969)
5) Catfish Hunter (1975)

99. Good-Hitting Pitchers

1) Al Orth
2) Red Ruffing
3) Carl Mays
4) Joe Bush
5) Ray Caldwell
6) Johnny Sain
7) Don Larsen

8) Tommy Byrne
9) Monte Pearson
10) Bob Shawkey
11) Eddie Lopat
12) Russ Ford
13) Urban Shocker
14) Joe Page

100. .300-Hitting Pitchers

1) Al Orth
2) Red Ruffing (eight times)
3) Bob Shawkey (twice)
4) Carl Mays
5) Joe Bush
6) Waite Hoyt
7) Tommy Byrne (twice)
8) Don Larsen
9) Tom Sturdivant
10) Monte Pearson

101. Pinch-Hitting Pitchers

1) Johnny Sain
2) Red Ruffing
3) Ray Caldwell
4) Joe Bush
5) Al Orth

102. Home-Run-Hitting Pitchers

1) Red Ruffing (36)
2) Pedro Ramos (15)
3) Tommy Byrne (14)
4) Don Larsen (14)
5) Al Orth (12)

Historical Interlude
Number Fourteen

The name Cookie Lavagetto still prompts nightmares for followers of the 1947 Yankees.

In Game Four of the 1947 World Series, Bill Bevens of the Yankees entered the bottom half of the ninth inning with a no-hitter and a 2–1 lead. All day long the 7–13 pitcher had stifled the Brooklyn batters while he battled his control. Wildness had cost him in the fifth inning. (He walked a World Series record ten batters that day.) Two free passes, in addition to a sacrifice and an infield out, had led to the Dodgers' only run up to that point.

Bevens got the first two hitters in the ninth, but once again wildness got him in trouble. He passed Carl Furillo, who gave way to pinch-runner Al Gionfriddo, who promptly stole second base. That left first base open, and Yankee manager Bucky Harris decided to fill it by walking Pete Reiser, who was batting for Hugh Casey. Brooklyn manager Burt Shotton decided to go to his bench again. He sent up his second straight pinch hitter, Cookie Lavagetto, who promptly broke up the no-hitter and the game (3–2) with a double off the right field wall. It was Lavagetto's second double of the year and his last hit in the majors.

There was a lot of maneuvering in the ninth inning by Shotton. The key move, of course, was the insertion of Lavagetto in the lineup. He batted for a player who was to perform on three different pennant winners over a five-year span and a player who was to be the future manager of three different major-league teams.

Who was that lifted batter?

Answer: Eddie Stanky

CHAPTER FIFTEEN

The World Series

103. WORLD SERIES WINS

Can you name the Yankee opponents in the years in which they won the World Series? Every initial franchise in the National League is involved.

1) _____ (1923)
2) _____ (1927)
3) _____ (1928)
4) _____ (1932)
5) _____ (1936)
6) _____ (1937)
7) _____ (1938)
8) _____ (1939)
9) _____ (1941)
10) _____ (1943)
11) _____ (1947)
12) _____ (1949)
13) _____ (1950)
14) _____ (1951)
15) _____ (1952)
16) _____ (1953)
17) _____ (1956)
18) _____ (1958)
19) _____ (1961)
20) _____ (1962)
21) _____ (1977)
22) _____ (1978)

104. WORLD SERIES DEFEATS

Can you name the Yankee opponents in the years in which they lost the World Series? Teams that are involved include the Dodgers, the Reds, the Cardinals, the Pirates, the Braves, and the Giants.

1) _____ (1921)
2) _____ (1922)
3) _____ (1926)
4) _____ (1942)
5) _____ (1955)
6) _____ (1957)
7) _____ (1960)
8) _____ (1963)
9) _____ (1964)
10) _____ (1976)
11) _____ (1981)

105. BABE RUTH AWARD

Eleven Yankees, beginning in 1949, have been named the top player in a World Series. Do you recognize them in the list below? Match them with the proper years.

Joe DiMaggio
Charlie Keller
Tommy Henrich
Joe Page
Bobby Brown
Jerry Coleman
Phil Rizzuto
Yogi Berra
Allie Reynolds
Vic Raschi
Johnny Mize
Bill Skowron
Billy Martin
Gil McDougald
Bobby Richardson

Don Larsen
Tony Kubek
Roger Maris
Mickey Mantle
Thurman Munson
Ellie Howard
Clete Boyer
Graig Nettles
Whitey Ford
Ralph Terry
Bob Turley
Reggie Jackson
Sparky Lyle
Luis Arroyo
Bucky Dent

1) _____ (1949)
2) _____ (1950)
3) _____ (1951)
4) _____ (1952)
5) _____ (1953)
6) _____ (1956)

7) _____ (1958)
8) _____ (1961)
9) _____ (1962)
10) _____ (1977)
11) _____ (1978)

106. .400 HITTERS

Twenty-five players who had (or have had) ten or more at bats in a World Series hit (or have hit) .400 or better. (Most of them have batted well over 15 times.) How many of them can you pick out of the following list of 72 names? Check the correct names. (Six of them did it twice.)

Aaron Ward	Irv Noren
Bob Meusel	Ralph Houk
Babe Ruth	Gene Woodling
Wally Schang	Bob Cerv
Joe Dugan	Bill Skowron
Everett Scott	Andy Carey
Lou Gehrig	Billy Martin
Mark Koenig	Enos Slaughter
Joe Sewell	Norm Siebern
Ben Chapman	Mickey Mantle
Tony Lazzeri	Jerry Lumpe
Earle Combs	Tony Kubek
Frank Crosetti	Harry Simpson
George Selkirk	Ellie Howard
Joe DiMaggio	Bobby Richardson
Red Rolfe	Roger Maris
Tommy Henrich	Clete Boyer
Jake Powell	Hector Lopez
Joe Gordon	Johnny Blanchard
Johnny Sturm	Tommy Tresh
Phil Rizzuto	Dale Long
Charlie Keller	Phil Linz
Tuck Stainback	Joe Pepitone
Buddy Hassett	Chris Chambliss
Nick Etten	Willie Randolph
Billy Johnson	Graig Nettles
Johnny Lindell	Thurman Munson
George McQuinn	Lou Piniella
George Stirnweiss	Mickey Rivers
Bobby Brown	Roy White
Jerry Coleman	Bobby Murcer
Yogi Berra	Bucky Dent
Joe Collins	Oscar Gamble
Gil McDougald	Brian Doyle
Hank Bauer	Bill Dickey
Johnny Mize	Reggie Jackson

107. SERIES STARTERS

Match the pitchers of the Yankees and their opposing moundsmen listed below in the left-hand column with the years in the right-hand column in which they started the opening game of the World Series.

1) __ Ford-Sadecki		a)	1932
2) __ Reynolds-Newcombe		b)	1947
3) __ Ruffing-Davis		c)	1936
4) __ Ruffing-Bush		d)	1963
5) __ Hoyt-Watson		e)	1964
6) __ Ruffing-Hubbell		f)	1921
7) __ Ruffing-Derringer		g)	1943
8) __ Shea-Branca		h)	1937
9) __ Reynolds-Koslo		i)	1957
10) __ Ford-Koufax		j)	1949
11) __ Ditmar-Law		k)	1952
12) __ Raschi-Konstanty		l)	1961
13) __ Mays-Douglas		m)	1923
14) __ Pennock-Sherdel		n)	1941
15) __ Gomez-Hubbell		o)	1951
16) __ Reynolds-Black		p)	1939
17) __ Ford-Maglie		q)	1950
18) __ Ford-O'Toole		r)	1926
19) __ Ford-Spahn		s)	1956
20) __ Chandler-Lanier		t)	1960

108. TWO-GAME WINNERS

Thirteen of the 41 Yankee pitchers listed below won two games in a World Series. The number of times they did it is placed in parentheses. Which ones?

Waite Hoyt
Carl Mays
Bob Shawkey
Bullet Joe Bush
Sad Sam Jones
Herb Pennock
Urban Shocker
George Pipgras
Tom Zachary
Red Ruffing
Lefty Gomez
Wilcy Moore
Monte Pearson
Bump Hadley
Johnny Murphy
Ernie Bonham
Marius Russo
Spud Chandler
Atley Donald
Hank Borowy
Jim Turner

Frank Shea
Joe Page
Allie Reynolds
Vic Raschi
Eddie Lopat
Tommy Byrne
Johnny Sain
Whitey Ford
Bob Grim
Bob Turley
Don Larsen
Art Ditmar
Ralph Terry
Jim Bouton
Al Downing
Mel Stottlemyre
Catfish Hunter
Ron Guidry
Sparky Lyle
Mike Torrez

1) _____ (1)
2) _____ (1)
3) _____ (1)
4) _____ (1)
5) _____ (1)
6) _____ (1)
7) _____ (1)

8) _____ (1)
9) _____ (1)
10) _____ (2)
11) _____ (2)
12) _____ (2)
13) _____ (3)

109. OPPOSING MOUND MASTERPIECES

Eleven opposing pitchers have spun shutouts against the Yankees. Select them from the following multiple-choice groups:

1) __ (1921) a. Art Nehf b. Phil Douglas c. Jesse Barnes d. Fred Toney

2) __ (1922) a. Jack Scott b. Hugh McQuillan c. Rosy Ryan d. Jack Bentley

3) __ (1926) a. Pete Alexander b. Bill Sherdel c. Jesse Haines d. Flint Rhem

4) __ (1942) a. Johnny Beazley b. Mort Cooper c. Ernie White d. Max Lanier

5) __ (1949) a. Don Newcombe b. Preacher Roe c. Ralph Branca d. Rex Barney

6) __ (1955) a. Roger Craig b. Russ Meyer c. Billy Loes d. Johnny Podres

7) __ (1956) a. Sal Maglie b. Carl Erskine c. Don Bessent d. Clem Labine

8) __ (1957) a. Lew Burdette b. Ernie Johnson c. Don McMahon d. Bob Buhl

9) __ (1958) a. Bob Rush b. Juan Pizzaro c. Warren Spahn d. Gene Conley

10) __ (1962) a. Billy Pierce b. Jack Sanford c. Billy O'Dell d. Juan Marichal

11) __ (1963) a. Sandy Koufax b. Ron Perranoski c. Pete Richert d. Don Drysdale

Flash Followup

12) _____ Which one of them shut out the Yankees twice by 1–0 scores? (He has been the only pitcher in history to twice win 1–0 games.)

152

13) _____ Which one of them was the only one to twice blank the Yankees in the same Series?

14) _____ Which one of them shut out the Yankees 1–0 on the day following Allie Reynolds' 1–0 blanking of his team? (It has been the only time that teams have posted reverse 1–0 wins in back-to-back games.)

15) _____ Which one of them lost a 1–0 seventh game decision to Ralph Terry?

16) _____ Which one of them halted Hank Bauer's 17-game hitting streak?

17) _____ Which one of them pitched the only extra-inning shutout win over the Yankees, a 1–0 game that was decided on Jackie Robinson's tenth-inning single?

18) _____ Which one of them halted a 42-game scoring streak by the Yankees?

19) _____ Which one of them defeated the Yankees in the final game two years in a row, then turned around and dropped the final to the Bombers the following year?

20) _____ Which one of them posted a 4–1 record in Series play?

110. PITCHING RECORDS

Match the following pitchers with their World Series records: Babe Ruth, Whitey Ford, Vic Raschi, Allie Reynolds, Eddie Lopat, Red Ruffing, Ron Guidry, Lefty Gomez, Don Larsen, Bob Turley, Herb Pennock, Waite Hoyt, Monte Pearson, Tom Zachary, and George Pipgras. (They are listed in order of the number of wins they posted; Nos. 2 and 3 and 12–14 are interchangeable.)

1) _____ (10–8)	**9)** _____ (4–1)
2) _____ (7–2)	**10)** _____ (4–2)
3) _____ (7–2)	**11)** _____ (4–3)
4) _____ (6–0)	**12)** _____ (3–0)
5) _____ (6–4)	**13)** _____ (3–0)
6) _____ (5–0)	**14)** _____ (3–0)
7) _____ (5–3)	**15)** _____ (3–1)
8) _____ (4–0)	

Flash Followup

1) _____ Which one, of them got all of his wins with a team other than the Yankees?

2) _____ Which one of them won two games for the Senators in 1924?

3) _____ Which one of them picked up his final win in relief—against the Yankees?

4) _____ Which one of them has been the only pitcher—he was not with the Yankees at the time—to split four decisions in one Series?

5) _____ Which one of them picked up two wins and one save in the last three games of a seven-game Series?

6) _____ Which one of them umpired in the 1944 Series?

7) _____ Which one of them picked up four saves?

8) _____ Which one of them picked up three saves?

9) _____ Which one of them lost a no-hitter when Ernie Lombardi singled with one out in the eighth?

10) _____ Which one of them lost his no-hitter when Terry Moore singled with two out in the eighth?

111. SERIES SHUTOUTS

Referring to the list in Quiz 108, see if you can pick out the pitchers who spun at least one shutout. (The number of times that they did it is provided in parentheses.)

1) _____ (1)   7) _____ (1)
2) _____ (1)   8) _____ (1)
3) _____ (1)   9) _____ (1)
4) _____ (1)   10) _____ (2)
5) _____ (1)   11) _____ (3)
6) _____ (1)

112. TWO-GAME LOSERS

Which of the pitchers in the list in Quiz 108 lost two games in a World Series? (The years in which they did it are provided in parentheses.)

1) _____ (1921)   4) _____ (1960)
2) _____ (1922)   5) _____ (1963)
3) _____ (1960)

113. HOW TO WEIGH AN ERA

Below you will find the names of 30 pitchers with career ERA marks that range from 0.50 to 4.97. Place those with marks of 1.99 or under in the left-hand column, those with averages between 2.00 and 2.99 in the middle column, and those with stats of 3.00 or over in the right-hand column. (The pitchers had to participate in at least two fall get-togethers in order to be considered.)

Red Ruffing
Luis Arroyo
Vic Raschi
Tom Sturdivant
Johnny Murphy
Bob Grim
Joe Page
Marius Russo
Johnny Kucks
Art Ditmar
Jim Bouton
Bobby Shantz
Allie Reynolds
Bob Turley
Hank Borowy

Don Larsen
Whitey Ford
Ernie Bonham
Tommy Byrne
Bob Shawkey
Eddie Lopat
Ralph Terry
Herb Pennock
Monte Pearson
Carl Mays
Spud Chandler
Lefty Gomez
Waite Hoyt
Wiley Moore
Sparky Lyle

Under 2.00

1) _____ (0.50)
2) _____ (0.56)
3) _____ (1.01)
4) _____ (1.10)
5) _____ (1.29)
6) _____ (1.48)
7) _____ (1.62)
8) _____ (1.83)
9) _____ (1.89)
10) _____ (1.95)

2.00 to 2.99

1) _____ (2.20)
2) _____ (2.24)
3) _____ (2.53)
4) _____ (2.60)
5) _____ (2.63)
6) _____ (2.71)
7) _____ (2.75)
8) _____ (2.79)
9) _____ (2.86)
10) _____ (2.93)

Over 3.00

1) _____ (3.18)
2) _____ (3.19)
3) _____ (3.21)
4) _____ (3.27)
5) _____ (3.86)
6) _____ (4.15)
7) _____ (4.34)
8) _____ (4.75)
9) _____ (4.91)
10) _____ (4.97)

114. WORLD SERIES WRAPUPS

In this quiz you'll be presented with the starting pitchers of the final game of each World Series in which the Yankees have played. You must name the winning pitcher and losing pitcher of each Classic finale. You can choose either the Yankees' starter or the opponent's starter. Or you may decide that it's neither one of them. In that case you'll refer to the four pitchers listed next for each game, two of whom are Yankees and two of whom are opposing pitchers of that respective year. Put the names of the winning pitcher to the left of the date and that of the losing pitcher to the right of the date.

1) _____ 1921 _____ Art Nehf (Giants) vs. Waite Hoyt (Yankees)
(Jesse Barnes, Phil Douglas, Carl Mays, or Bob Shawkey)

2) _____ 1922 _____ Joe Bush (Yankees) vs. Art Nehf (Giants)
(Sam Jones, Lefty O'Doul, Jack Scott, or Rosy Ryan)

3) _____ 1923 _____ Herb Pennock (Yankees) vs. Art Nehf (Giants)
(Joe Bush, Sam Jones, Jack Bentley, or Virgil Barnes)

4) _____ 1926 _____ Jesse Haines (Cardinals) vs. Waite Hoyt (Yankees)
(Pete Alexander, Wild Bill Hallahan, Urban Shocker, or Dutch Ruether)

5) _____ 1927 _____ Carmen Hill (Pirates) vs. Wilcy Moore (Yankees)
(Johnny Miljus, Lee Meadows, George Pipgras, or Waite Hoyt)

6) _____ 1928 _____ Waite Hoyt (Yankees) vs. Bill Sherdel (Cardinals)
(George Pipgras, Tom Zachary, Clarence Mitchell, or Flint Rhem)

7) _____ 1932 _____ Johnny Allen (Yankees) vs. Guy Bush (Cubs)

(Wilcy Moore, George Pipgras, Burleigh Grimes, or Jakie May)

8) _____ 1936 _____ Lefty Gomez (Yankees) vs. Freddie Fitzsimmons (Giants)

(Bump Hadley, Pat Malone, Hal Schumacher, or Harry Gumbert)

9) _____ 1937 _____ Lefty Gomez (Yankees) vs. Cliff Melton (Giants)

(Monte Pearson, Johnny Murphy, Al Smith, or Dick Coffman)

10) _____ 1938 _____ Bill Lee (Cubs) vs. Red Ruffing (Yankees)

(Charlie Root, Larry French, Monte Pearson, or Johnny Murphy)

11) _____ 1939 _____ Oral Hildebrand (Yankees) vs. Paul Derringer (Reds)

(Steve Sundra, Johnny Murphy, Bucky Walters, or Lee Grissom)

12) _____ 1941 _____ Ernie Bonham (Yankees) vs. Whit Wyatt (Dodgers)

(Marius Russo, Atley Donald, Hugh Casey, or Johnny Allen)

13) _____ 1942 _____ Johnny Beazley (Cardinals) vs. Red Ruffing (Yankees)

(Mort Cooper, Max Lanier, Hank Borowy, or Jim Turner)

14) _____ 1943 _____ Spud Chandler (Yankees) vs. Mort Cooper (Cardinals)

(Hank Borowy, Ernie Bonham, Max Lanier, or Murry Dickson)

15) _____ 1947 _____ Hal Gregg (Dodgers) vs. Frank Shea (Yankees)

(Joe Hatten, Rex Barney, Bill Bevens, or Joe Page)

16) _____ 1949 _____ Vic Raschi (Yankees) vs. Rex Barney (Dodgers)

(Tommy Byrne, Joe Page, Jack Banta, or Erv Palica)

17) _____ 1950 _____ Bob Miller (Phillies) vs. Whitey Ford (Yankees)

(Jim Konstanty, Robin Roberts, Allie Reynolds, or Joe Page)

18) _____ 1951 _____ Dave Koslo (Giants) vs.

Vic Raschi (Yankees)
(Jim Hearn, Larry Jansen, Johnny Sain, or Bob Kuzava)
19) _____ 1952 _____ Eddie Lopat (Yankees) vs.
Joe Black (Dodgers)
(Allie Reynolds, Bob Kuzava, Preacher Roe, or Carl Erskine)
20) _____ 1953 _____ Carl Erskine (Dodgers) vs.
Whitey Ford (Yankees)
(Bob Milliken, Clem Labine, Allie Reynolds, or Tom Gorman)
21) _____ 1955 _____ Johnny Podres (Dodgers)
vs. Tommy Byrne (Yankees)
(Don Bessent, Karl Spooner, Whitey Ford, or Bob Grim)
22) _____ 1956 _____ Johnny Kucks (Yankees)
vs. Don Newcombe (Dodgers)
(Don Larsen, Tom Sturdivant, Roger Craig, or Ed Roebuck)
23) _____ 1957 _____ Lew Burdette (Braves) vs.
Don Larsen (Yankees)
(Warren Spahn, Don McMahon, Bobby Shantz, or Art Ditmar)
24) _____ 1958 _____ Don Larsen (Yankees) vs.
Lew Burdette (Braves)
(Bob Turley, Ryne Duren, Bob Rush, or Warren Spahn)
25) _____ 1960 _____ Bob Turley (Yankees) vs.
Vernon Law (Pirates)
(Bobby Shantz, Ralph Terry, Roy Face, or Harvey Haddix)
26) _____ 1961 _____ Ralph Terry (Yankees) vs.
Joey Jay (Reds)
(Bud Daley, Bill Stafford, Jim Maloney, or Jim Brosnan)
27) _____ 1962 _____ Ralph Terry (Yankees) vs.
Jack Sanford (Giants)
(Marshall Bridges, Jim Coates, Billy Pierce, or Billy O'Dell)
28) _____ 1963 _____ Whitey Ford (Yankees) vs.
Sandy Koufax (Dodgers)
(Jim Bouton, Al Downing, Johnny Podres, or Ron Perranoski)
29) _____ 1964 _____ Mel Stottlemyre (Yankees)
vs. Bob Gibson (Cardinals)

(Pete Mikkelsen, Rollie Sheldon, Ray Sadecki, or Barney Schultz)

30) _____ 1976 _____ Gary Nolan (Reds) vs. Ed Figueroa (Yankees)

(Will McEnaney, Jack Billingham, Sparky Lyle, or Grant Jackson)

31) _____ 1977 _____ Burt Hooton (Dodgers) vs. Mike Torrez (Yankees)

(Tommy John, Charlie Hough, Dick Tidrow, or Sparky Lyle)

32) _____ 1978 _____ Catfish Hunter (Yankees) vs. Don Sutton (Dodgers)

(Jim Beattie, Goose Gossage, Bob Welch, or Doug Rau)

33) _____ 1981 _____ Burt Hooton (Dodgers) vs. Tommy John (Yankees)

(Jerry Reuss, Fernando Valenzuela, Ron Davis, or George Frazier)

115. FALL CLASSIC FINALES

Who are the four Yankee pitchers to twice win the final game of a World Series?

1) _____
2) _____
3) _____
4) _____
5) _____ Which one of them won one game as a starter and one game as a reliever?
6) _____ Which one of them won both games in relief?
7) _____ Who was the one Yankee pitcher to twice lose the final game of a Fall Classic?

Who are the three Yankee pitchers below who both won and lost the final game of a World Series?

8) _____
9) _____
10) _____

Answers

103. World Series Wins

1) Giants	12) Dodgers
2) Pirates	13) Phillies
3) Cardinals	14) Giants
4) Cubs	15) Dodgers
5) Giants	16) Dodgers
6) Giants	17) Dodgers
7) Cubs	18) Braves
8) Reds	19) Reds
9) Dodgers	20) Giants
10) Cardinals	21) Dodgers
11) Dodgers	22) Dodgers

104. World Series Defeats

1) Giants	7) Pirates
2) Giants	8) Dodgers
3) Cardinals	9) Cardinals
4) Cardinals	10) Reds
5) Dodgers	11) Dodgers
6) Braves	

105. Babe Ruth Award

1) Joe Page	7) Hank Bauer
2) Jerry Coleman	8) Whitey Ford
3) Phil Rizzuto	9) Ralph Terry
4) Johnny Mize	10) Reggie Jackson
5) Billy Martin	11) Bucky Dent
6) Don Larsen	

106. .400 Hitters

1) Aaron Ward (.417 in 1923)

2) Babe Ruth (.400 in 1927 and .625 in 1928)
3) Lou Gehrig (.545 in 1928 and .529 in 1932)
4) Mark Koenig (.500 in 1927)
5) Tony Lazzeri (.400 in 1937)
6) Red Rolfe (.400 in 1936)
7) Jake Powell (.455 in 1936)
8) Joe Gordon (.500 in 1941 and .400 in 1938)
9) Charlie Keller (.438 in 1939)
10) Johnny Lindell (.500 in 1947)
11) Bobby Brown (.500 in 1949)
12) Yogi Berra (.429 in 1953 and .417 in 1955)
13) Hank Bauer (.429 in 1955)
14) Johnny Mize (.400 in 1952)
15) Gene Woodling (.429 in 1950)
16) Billy Martin (.500 in 1953)
17) Mickey Mantle (.400 in 1960)
18) Ellie Howard (.462 in 1960)
19) Bobby Richardson (.406 in 1964)
20) Johnny Blanchard (.455 in 1960 and .400 in 1961)
21) Thurman Munson (.529 in 1976)
22) Bucky Dent (.417 in 1978)
23) Brian Doyle (.438 in 1978)
24) Bill Dickey (.438 in 1932 and .400 in 1938)
25) Reggie Jackson (.450 in 1977)

107. Series Starters

1) e
2) j
3) n
4) a
5) m
6) c
7) p
8) b
9) o
10) d
11) t
12) q
13) f
14) r
15) h
16) k
17) s
18) l
19) i
20) g

108. Two-Game Winners

1) Red Ruffing
2) Spud Chandler
3) Frank Shea
4) Allie Reynolds
5) Vic Raschi
6) Eddie Lopat
7) Bob Turley
8) Ralph Terry
9) Mike Torrez
10) Waite Hoyt
11) Herb Pennock
12) Lefty Gomez
13) Whitey Ford

109. Opposing Mound Masterpieces

1) a
2) a
3) c
4) c
5) b
6) d
7) d
8) a
9) c
10) b
11) d

Flash Followup

12) Art Nehf
13) Lew Burdette
14) Preacher Roe
15) Jack Sanford
16) Warren Spahn
17) Clem Labine
18) Ernie White
19) Art Nehf
20) Johnny Podres

110. Pitching Records

1) Whitey Ford
2) Red Ruffing
3) Allie Reynolds
4) Lefty Gomez
5) Waite Hoyt
6) Herb Pennock
7) Vic Raschi
8) Monte Pearson
9) Eddie Lopat
10) Don Larsen
11) Bob Turley
12) Babe Ruth or Tom Zachary or George Pipgras
13) Babe Ruth or Tom Zachary or George Pipgras
14) Babe Ruth or Tom Zachary or George Pipgras
15) Ron Guidry

Flash Followup

1) Babe Ruth (Red Sox)
2) Tom Zachary
3) Don Larsen (1962 Giants)
4) Hank Borowy (1945 Cubs)
5) Bob Turley (1958)
6) George Pipgras
7) Allie Reynolds
8) Herb Pennock
9) Monte Pearson
10) Red Ruffing

111. Series Shutouts

1) Carl Mays (1921)
2) Waite Hoyt (1921)
3) Monte Pearson (1939)
4) Spud Chandler (1943)
5) Vic Raschi (1950)
6) Don Larsen (1956)
7) Johnny Kucks (1956)
8) Bob Turley (1958)
9) Ralph Terry (1962)
10) Allie Reynolds (1949, 1952)
11) Whitey Ford (1960, twice, and 1961)

112. Two-Game Losers

1) Carl Mays (1921)
2) Joe Bush (1922)
3) Ralph Terry (1960)
4) Art Ditmar (1960)
5) Whitey Ford (1963)

113. How to Weigh an ERA

1) Marius Russo
2) Wilcy Moore
3) Monte Pearson
4) Johnny Murphy
5) Sparky Lyle
6) Jim Bouton
7) Spud Chandler
8) Waite Hoyt
9) Johnny Kucks
10) Herb Pennock

1) Carl Mays
2) Vic Raschi
3) Tommy Byrne
4) Eddie Lopat
5) Red Ruffing
6) Whitey Ford
7) Don Larsen
8) Allie Reynolds
9) Lefty Gomez
10) Ralph Terry

1) Art Ditmar
2) Bob Turley
3) Ernie Bonham
4) Joe Page
5) Luis Arroyo
6) Bobby Shantz
7) Tom Sturdivant
8) Bob Shawkey
9) Bob Grim
10) Hank Borowy

114. World Series Wrapups

1) Art Nehf—1921—Waite Hoyt
2) Art Nehf—1922—Joe Bush
3) Herb Pennock—1923—Art Nehf
4) Jesse Haines—1926—Waite Hoyt
5) Wilcy Moore—1927—Johnny Miljus
6) Waite Hoyt—1928—Bill Sherdel
7) Wilcy Moore—1932—Jakie May
8) Lefty Gomez—1936—Freddie Fitzsimmons
9) Lefty Gomez—1937—Cliff Melton
10) Red Ruffing—1938—Bill Lee
11) John Murphy—1939—Bucky Walters
12) Ernie Bonham—1941—Whit Wyatt
13) Johnny Beazley—1942—Red Ruffing

14) Spud Chandler—
1943—Mort Cooper
15) Joe Page—1947—
Hal Gregg
16) Vic Raschi—1949—
Rex Barney
17) Whitey Ford—1950
—Bob Miller
18) Vic Raschi—1951—
Dave Koslo
19) Allie Reynolds—
1952—Joe Black
20) Allie Reynolds—
1953—Clem Labine
21) Johnny Podres—1955
—Tommy Byrne
22) Johnny Kucks—1956
—Don Newcombe
23) Lew Burdette—1957
—Don Larsen

24) Bob Turley—1958—
Lew Burdette
25) Harvey Haddix—
1960—Ralph Terry
26) Bud Daley—1961—
Joey Jay
27) Ralph Terry—1962—
Jack Sanford
28) Sandy Koufax—
1963—Whitey Ford
29) Bob Gibson—1964—
Mel Stottlemyre
30) Gary Nolan—1976—
Ed Figueroa
31) Mike Torrez—1977
—Burt Hooton
32) Catfish Hunter—
1978—Don Sutton
33) Burt Hooton—1981
—George Frazier

115. Fall Classic Finales

1) Wilcy Moore (1927, 1932)
2) Lefty Gomez (1936–37)
3) Vic Raschi (1949, 1951)
4) Allie Reynolds (1952–53)
5) Wilcy Moore

6) Allie Reynolds
7) Waite Hoyt (1921, 1926)
8) Waite Hoyt (1928 winner)
9) Red Ruffing (1938 winner, 1942 loser)
10) Ralph Terry (1960 loser, 1962 winner)

Historical Interlude
Number Fifteen

Perhaps the blackest moment in Dodger World Series history—and there have been many of them—occurred on October 5, 1941. Hugh Casey struck out Tommy Henrich for the final out of the game, but the Yankees ended up winning the contest, 7–4.

Let's reconstruct the scenario. In Game Four, with the Yankees having won two games and lost one, Hugh Casey was trying to protect a 4–3 Dodger lead in the ninth inning. When the first two hitters for the Yankees, Johnny Sturm and Red Rolfe, rolled out easily, Casey breathed more easily. But he still had to retire the dangerous Tommy Henrich. "Old Reliable" swung and missed a sharp-breaking third-strike curveball—or spitball, depending upon the source—and the game appeared to be over. But the Dodger catcher could not handle the pitch, and the ball rolled to the screen, allowing Henrich to reach first base safely.

Then the roof fell in on Casey. Joe DiMaggio lined a hard single to left, Henrich stopping at second. Charlie Keller then drove the game-winning hit, a two-run double off the wall in right. Bill Dickey then walked and Joe Gordon doubled over Jimmy Wasdell's head in left for two insurance runs.

Instead of tying the Series at two games apiece, the Dodgers fell behind the Yankees, three games to one. The Yankees wrapped up the Series the following day, behind Ernie Bonham, with a 3–1 win.

But the Series might have turned out differently if the Dodger catcher, who had committed only two passed balls and three errors all season long, had handled that swinging strike to Henrich.

Can you recall that catcher, whom the Dodgers obtained from the Cardinals before the 1941 season?

Answer: Mickey Owen

168

CHAPTER SIXTEEN

World Series Chronology

---

116. WORLD SERIES CHRONOLOGY

In this section we shall proceed chronologically from the first year in which the Yankees appeared in a World Series (1921) to the last year (1981). The questions will be presented in multiple-choice fashion. Let's see if you're a Yankee expert from start to finish.

-1921-
Yankees vs. Giants

1) ___ Whose bunt single gave Waite Hoyt a 3–1 win in Game Five? a. Wally Pipp b. Bob Meusel c. Babe Ruth d. Frank Baker

2) ___ Who stole home in the Yankees' first World Series game? a. Mike McNally b. Aaron Ward c. Roger Peckinpaugh d. Elmer Miller

3) ___ Who pitched the first shutout for the Yankees in Series history? a. Waite Hoyt b. Carl Mays c. Joe Bush d. Bob Shawkey

4) ___ In Game One, who was deprived of a triple—he didn't even get a hit on the play—when he failed to touch first base? a. Wally Schang b. Chick Fewster c. Bob Meusel d. Babe Ruth

5) ___ Who grounded into a 4-3-5 double play to end the Series? a. Aaron Ward b. Wally Pipp c. Roger Peckinpaugh d. Frank Baker

-1922-
Yankees vs. Giants

6) __ Who got two homers, his only two hits of the Series? a. Aaron Ward b. Everett Scott c. Joe Dugan d. Whitey Witt

7) __ Who was the umpire who called Game Two—a 3–3 tie—because of darkness, even though there were "45 minutes" of daylight left? a. Bill Klem b. George Hildebrand c. Brick Owens d. Bill McCormick

8) __ Who was the Yankee pitcher who went all the way in that game, the Bombers' only tie in history? a. Joe Bush b. Carl Mays c. Waite Hoyt d. Bob Shawkey

9) __ Which one of the following pitchers did not lose a game in this Series? a. Joe Bush b. Waite Hoyt c. Carl Mays d. Sam Jones

10) __ In Game Three, what Giant outfielder made a sensational snatch of Babe Ruth's 475-foot blast, one of the really great catches of World Series history? a. Casey Stengel b. Billy Cunningham c. Ross Youngs d. Irish Meusel

-1923-
Yankees vs. Giants

11) __ Who hit the first home run—an inside-the-parker—in Yankee Stadium? a. Babe Ruth b. Bob Meusel c. Wally Pipp d. Casey Stengel

12) __ Who led the Yankees with a .417 average? a. Aaron Ward b. Babe Ruth c. Bob Meusel d. Whitey Witt

13) __ Who hit the first home run that cleared the fence at Yankee Stadium? a. Babe Ruth b. Bob Meusel c. Wally Pipp d. Casey Stengel

14) __ Who became the first player to hit three home runs in one game? a. Bob Meusel b. Joe Dugan c. Babe Ruth d. Wally Pipp

15) __ Whose three-run single—he drove home eight runs in the Series—accounted for the tying and the winning runs in the 6–4 finale to give the Yankees their first championship? a. Babe Ruth b. Bob Meusel c. Aaron Ward d. Wally Schang

-1926-
Yankees vs. Cardinals

16) __ Who struck out on a quick pitch, got another chance, and hit a home run? a. Babe Ruth b. Mark Koenig c. Earle Combs d. Tony Lazzeri

17) __ Who had three home runs in Game Four, a second for him in World Series play? a. Lou Gehrig b. Tony Lazzeri c. Bob Meusel d. Babe Ruth

18) __ . Whom did Pete Alexander strike out with the bases loaded and two outs in Game Seven to set up a 3–2 win for the Cardinals? a. Mark Koenig b. Tony Lazzeri c. Ben Paschal d. Lou Gehrig

19) __ Who was the player-manager of the Cardinals? a. Bob O'Farrell b. Jim Bottomley c. Rogers Hornsby d. Billy Southworth

20) __ Who became the oldest pitcher (39 years, 7 months, and 13 days) to throw a complete game when he defeated the Yankees 10–2 in Game Six? a. Flint Rhem b. Jesse Haines c. Bill Sherdel d. Pete Alexander

-1927-
Yankees vs. Pirates

21) __ Who hit the only two home runs of the Series? a. Babe Ruth b. Joe Harris c. Pie Traynor d. Lou Gehrig

22) __ What infielder became the first Yankee to hit .500 in the Series? a. Mark Koenig b. Lou Gehrig c. Tony Lazzeri d. Joe Dugan

23) __ Who broke up Herb Pennock's perfect game

171

with one out in the eighth? a. Paul Waner b. Lloyd Waner c. Pie Traynor d. Glenn Wright

24) __ Who was the Pirate star who sat out the Series because of an altercation with manager Donie Bush? a. Pie Traynor b. Johnny Gooch c. George Grantham d. Kiki Cuyler

25) __ Who scored the winning run of the four-game sweep on a wild pitch? a. Mark Koenig b. Joe Dugan c. Earle Combs d. Tony Lazzeri

-1928-
Yankees vs. Cardinals

26) __ Who was the Cardinal manager who was demoted to Rochester of the International League because the Yankees swept his team in four games? a. Bill McKechnie b. Rogers Hornsby c. Bob O'Farrell d. Frankie Frisch

27) __ Who took the place of Earle Combs, out with a broken finger, in center field? a. Gene Robertson b. Ben Paschal c. Cedric Durst d. Mike Gazella

28) __ Who finished all four games at second base for Tony Lazzeri, who had a sore arm? a. Joe Dugan b. Gene Robertson c. Leo Durocher d. Mike Gazella

29) __ Who hit .625, the World Series high? a. Lou Gehrig b. Mark Koenig c. Babe Ruth d. Bob Meusel

30) __ Who hit four home runs in four games? a. Lou Gehrig b. Babe Ruth c. Frankie Frisch d. Bob Meusel

-1932-
Yankees vs. Cubs

31) __ Who was the Yankee manager, relieved by the Cubs two years earlier, who gained vengeance via the Yankees' four-game sweep over his former club? a. Bob Shawkey b. Miller Huggins c. Art Fletcher d. Joe McCarthy

32) __ Who was the Cub manager who took over the

172

Bruins during the season and led them into the Series? a. Rogers Hornsby b. Charlie Grimm c. Gabby Hartnett d. Billy Jurges

33) __ Against whom did Babe Ruth hit his last Series home run? a. Charlie Root b. Don Warneke c. Guy Bush d. Burleigh Grimes

34) __ Who connected for nine hits—three of them homers—scored nine runs, and drove in eight? a. Babe Ruth b. Ben Chapman c. Lou Gehrig d. Tony Lazzeri

35) __ Who was the Yankee great of the 1920s who played for the Cubs in this Series? a. Bob Meusel b. Everett Scott c. Joe Dugan d. Mark Koenig

-1936-
Yankees vs. Giants

36) __ What Giant pitcher ended the Yankees' streak of 12 straight victories with his 6–1 win in the opener? a. Hal Schumacher b. Carl Hubbell c. Freddie Fitzsimmons d. Slick Castleman

37) __ Who, in addition to the above pitcher, was the only moundsman to defeat the Yankees in the 1930s? a. Hal Schumacher b. Randy Gumpert c. Freddie Fitzsimmons d. Frank Gablerman

38) __ Who was the second player—and the first Yankee—to hit a grand slam in Series play? a. Lou Gehrig b. Joe DiMaggio c. Bill Dickey d. Tony Lazzeri

39) __ What Bronx Bomber pitcher was the recipient of 31 runs in two games? a. Red Ruffing b. Lefty Gomez c. Monte Pearson d. Bump Hadley

40) __ Who was the .455 hitter, picked up in a trade for Ben Chapman, who drove home the winning run of the Series with a two-run single in Game Six? a. George Selkirk b. Myril Hoag c. Jake Powell d. Joe Glenn

-1937-
Yankees vs. Giants

41) __ Who closed out 12 seasons with the Yankees by hitting .400, the highest mark in the Series? a. Tony Lazzeri b. Joe Sewell c. Lyn Lary d. George Selkirk

42) __ Who was the notoriously weak hitter who singled home the winning run of the Series? a. Monte Pearson b. Bump Hadley c. Johnny Murphy d. Lefty Gomez

43) __ Who substituted for the injured Tommy Henrich and batted .300? a. Jake Powell b. Myril Hoag c. George Selkirk d. Don Heffner

44) __ Who hit his tenth-and-last home run, against Carl Hubbell? a. Mel Ott b. Lou Gehrig c. Babe Ruth d. Bill Dickey

45) __ Who was the Yankee pitcher who hit .500? a. Lefty Gomez b. Ivy Andrews c. Kemp Wicker d. Red Ruffing

-1938-
Yankees vs. Cubs

46) __ Who was the rookie second baseman who hit .400? a. George Stirnweiss b. Joe Gordon c. Gerry Priddy d. Bill Knickerbocker

47) __ Who hit .500 for the Cubs? a. Stan Hack b. Joe Marty c. Phil Cavarretta d. Gabby Hartnett

48) __ Who was the .250-hitting infielder who banged a game-winning homer in Game Two and a three-run triple in Game Four? a. Lou Gehrig b. Joe Gordon c. Frankie Crosetti d. Red Rolfe

49) __ Who hit .438 against the Cubs in 1932 and .400 against the Bruins in 1938? a. Bill Dickey b. Tony Lazzeri c. Red Rolfe d. Joe DiMaggio

50) __ Who won his sixth career game without a defeat? a. Red Ruffing b. Lefty Gomez c. Monte Pearson d. Johnny Murphy

-1939-
Yankees vs. Reds

51) __ Who was the rookie who batted .438 on seven hits, which included three homers, a triple, and a double? a. Tommy Henrich b. Charlie Keller c. Phil Rizzuto d. Joe Gordon

52) __ Who had to retire from a start after one inning because of a lame arm? a. Red Ruffing b. Bump Hadley c. Lefty Gomez d. Oral Hildebrand

53) __ Whose ninth-inning error cost the Reds a win in Game Four? a. Lonny Frey b. Billy Myers c. Billy Werber d. Ival Goodman

54) __ Who took Lou Gehrig's place in the lineup? a. George Selkirk b. Tommy Henrich c. Jack Saltzgaver d. Babe Dahlgren

55) __ Who was the Red outfielder—he hit .250—who once hit two home runs in each of three successive Series for an American League team? a. Jimmie Foxx b. Al Simmons c. Goose Goslin d. Frank McCormick

-1941-
Yankees vs. Dodgers

56) __ Who was the Dodger rookie who ruined his team's late-inning chance to tie the game in Contest One when he was thrown out at third, trying to advance on Jimmy Wasdell's foul pop to Bill Dickey? a. Cookie Lavagetto b. Pee Wee Reese c. Dixie Walker d. Pete Reiser

57) __ Who was the Dodger pitcher, in Game Two, who stopped the Yankees' consecutive win streak at ten games? a. Freddie Fitzsimmons b. Whit Wyatt c. Curt Davis d. Kirbe Higbe

58) __ Who was the Dodger pitcher, in Game Three, who had to leave the contest after seven scoreless innings because he was hit with a line drive that caromed off his leg? (The Dodgers lost, 2–1.) a. Hugh Casey b. Johnny Allen c. Larry French d. Freddie Fitzsimmons

175

59) ___ Who was the Yankee pitcher who hit the liner? a. Red Ruffing b. Spud Chandler c. Marius Russo d. Atley Donald

60) ___ Name the second Yankee (non-first baseman) infielder to hit .500 in a Series. a. Johnny Sturm b. Joe Gordon c. Phil Rizzuto d. Red Rolfe

-1942-
Yankees vs. Cardinals

61) ___ Who, in Game One, became the first pitcher to win seven games? a. Lefty Gomez b. Spud Chandler c. Red Ruffing d. Johnny Murphy

62) ___ Enos Slaughter's great throw cut down what Yankee outfielder at third base in the pivotal play of the Cardinals' 4–3 win in Game Two? a. Roy Cullenbine b. Charlie Keller c. Joe DiMaggio d. Tuck Stainback

63) ___ Who was the Redbird righty who hit a game-winning triple in Game Two and a game-winning homer in Game Five? a. Whitey Kurowski b. Terry Moore c. Marty Marion d. Walker Cooper

64) ___ Who was the MVP player—he batted only .095 in the Series—who got picked off second by Walker Cooper in the ninth inning of the final game? a. Phil Rizzuto b. Red Rolfe c. Joe Gordon d. Johnny Lindell

65) ___ Who allowed only one run, and only four Cardinals to reach first base in Game Three, yet finished on the bottom side of a 2–0 score? a. Ernie Bonham b. Hank Borowy c. Marius Russo d. Spud Chandler

-1943-
Yankees vs. Cardinals

66) ___ Whose three-run triple was decisive in Game Three? a. Nick Etten b. Billy Johnson c. Johnny Lindell d. Charlie Keller

67) ___ Who, in Game Four, allowed one unearned run and scored the winning run—he had doubled—on a long

fly ball by Frankie Crosetti? a. Spud Chandler b. Hank
Borowy c. Marius Russo d. Ernie Bonham

68) __ Whose two-run homer accounted for the only
two markers in the final game? a. Joe Gordon b. Bill
Dickey c. Charlie Keller d. Johnny Lindell

69) __ Who allowed only one earned run in 18 innings
of pitching? a. Spud Chandler b. Marius Russo c. Ernie
Bonham d. Hank Borowy

70) __ Whose football block on Whitey Kurowski at
third base in Game Three turned the Series around in the
Yankees' favor? a. Charlie Keller b. Joe Gordon c. Tuck
Stainback d. Johnny Lindell

-1947-
Yankees vs. Dodgers

71) __ Who retired the first 12 Yankees that he faced
in Game One before being hammered from the box in the
fifth inning with a five-run barrage? a. Hal Gregg
b. Ralph Branca c. Rex Barney d. Vic Lombardi

72) __ Who was the pinch runner who scored the winning run in Game Four on Cookie Lavagetto's pinch hit
double? a. Pete Reiser b. Eddie Miksis c. Bruce Edwards d. Cookie Lavagetto

73) __ Whose home run in the fifth inning of Game
Five gave the Yankees a 2–1 win? a. Joe DiMaggio
b. Yogi Berra c. Tommy Henrich d. George McQuinn

74) __ Whose great catch of Joe DiMaggio's 415-foot
blast in Game Six sent the Series to Game Seven? a. Dixie
Walker b. Carl Furillo c. Al Gionfriddo d. Gene Her-
manski

75) __ Who, in his last 11 and one-third innings of
pitching in the majors, allowed only three hits? a. Spud
Chandler b. Bobo Newsom c. Butch Wensloff d. Bill
Bevens

-1949-
Yankees vs. Dodgers

76) ___ Who was the Dodger pitcher who struck out 11 batters in the opener but lost, 1–0? a. Don Newcombe b. Rex Barney c. Preacher Roe d. Ralph Branca

77) ___ Whose two-run pinch single in the ninth inning of Game Three proved decisive for the Yankees? a. Yogi Berra b. Billy Johnson c. Johnny Mize d. Johnny Lindell

78) ___ Who was the starter who relieved in Game Four and retired the last ten batters to preserve a 6–4 Yankee win? a. Vic Raschi b. Eddie Lopat c. Allie Reynolds d. Tommy Byrne

79) ___ Who came on in relief to blank the Brooks for two and one-third innings in the final game and save the Series for the Yankees? a. Fred Sanford b. Allie Reynolds c. Cuddles Marshall d. Joe Page

80) ___ Who was the part-time player who led the Yankees in runs scored (4), hits (6), triples (2), RBI (5), and batting average (.500)? a. Hank Bauer b. Bobby Brown c. Cliff Mapes d. Gene Woodling

-1950-
Yankees vs. Phillies

81) ___ Who was the Phillie pitcher who did not start one of the 74 games in which he appeared during the regular season, but started the opener of the Series and lost a heartbreaker, 1–0? a. Ken Heintzelman b. Jim Konstanty c. Bob Miller d. Blix Donnelly

82) ___ Who was the Yankee contact hitter whose sacrifice fly won Game One and whose single in the ninth inning decided Game Three? a. Jerry Coleman b. Phil Rizzuto c. Bobby Brown d. Johnny Hopp

83) ___ Whose home run in the tenth inning downed Robin Roberts, 2–1? a. Joe DiMaggio b. Yogi Berra c. Johnny Mize d. Hank Bauer

84) __ Whose error on a fly ball with one out remaining in the Series deprived rookie Whitey Ford of a shutout? a. Hank Bauer b. Johnny Lindell c. Gene Woodling d. Jackie Jensen

85) __ Who got one victory and one save in the four-game set? a. Vic Raschi b. Whitey Ford c. Eddie Lopat d. Allie Reynolds

-1951-
Yankees vs. Giants

86) __ Who was the Giant surprise starter who snapped a Yankee nine-game winning streak in opening games? a. Jim Hearn b. Sheldon Jones c. Dave Koslo d. George Spencer

87) __ Who was the Giant star who got four hits and stole home in the opener? a. Monte Irvin b. Bobby Thomson c. Willie Mays d. Whitey Lockman

88) __ Who kicked the ball out of Phil Rizzuto's glove, setting up a five-run inning, in Game Three? a. Al Dark b. Eddie Stanky c. Hank Thompson d. Don Mueller

89) __ Who made a sensational sliding catch to save Game Six and the Series? a. Hank Bauer b. Joe DiMaggio c. Gene Woodling d. Mickey Mantle

90) __ Who, held hitless in the first three games, broke out with six hits, including two doubles and a homer, in the final three games? a. Yogi Berra b. Johnny Mize c. Joe DiMaggio d. Phil Rizzuto

-1952-
Yankees vs. Dodgers

91) __ Who started only two games during the regular season but outdueled Allie Reynolds in the opener, 4-2? a. Billy Loes b. Ken Lehman c. Johnny Rutherford d. Joe Black

92) __ Whose passed ball in the ninth inning of Game

Three cost his team the game? a. Yogi Berra b. Charlie Silvera c. Roy Campanella d. Bruce Edwards

93) __ Who struck out ten batters en route to a 2–0 shutout in Game Four? a. Vic Raschi b. Allie Reynolds c. Eddie Lopat d. Johnny Sain

94) __ Whose shoestring catch with the bases loaded and two outs in the seventh inning saved the game and the Series for the Yankees? a. Joe Collins b. Phil Rizzuto c. Billy Martin d. Gil McDougald

95) __ Who retired the final eight batters in Game Seven to get the Series-deciding save? a. Tom Gorman b. Ray Scarborough c. Bob Kuzava d. Ewell Blackwell

-1953-
Yankees vs. Dodgers

96) __ Whose three-run triple in the first inning of the opener set the Series tone in the Yankees' favor? a. Mickey Mantle b. Gene Woodling c. Yogi Berra d. Billy Martin

97) __ Whose eighth-inning home run decided Game Two in the Yankees' favor? a. Yogi Berra b. Johnny Mize c. Joe Collins d. Mickey Mantle

98) __ Who set a Series record by striking out 14 batters in Game Three? a. Preacher Roe b. Carl Erskine c. Billy Loes d. Clem Labine

99) __ Whose grand slam was the dramatic blow of Game Five? a. Mickey Mantle b. Gene Woodling c. Gil McDougald d. Hank Bauer

100) __ Who stroked a record 12 hits, including two home runs, in a six-game Series? a. Hank Bauer b. Billy Martin c. Gil McDougald d. Mickey Mantle

-1955-
Yankees vs. Dodgers

101) __ Who stole home against Whitey Ford in the first game? a. Pee Wee Reese b. Carl Furillo c. Sandy Amoros d. Jackie Robinson

102) __ Who became the first lefty to pitch a complete-game victory over the Dodgers in 1955? a. Whitey Ford b. Eddie Lopat c. Tommy Byrne d. Rip Coleman

103) __ Who hit four Series homers for the Dodgers? a. Duke Snider b. Gil Hodges c. Roy Campanella d. Jackie Robinson

104) __ Who four-hit the Dodgers to get the Yankees even in Game Six? a. Whitey Ford b. Bob Turley c. Don Larsen d. Bob Grim

105) __ Who drove in both Brooklyn runs in the Dodgers' 2–0 clincher? a. Jackie Robinson b. Gil Hodges c. Duke Snider d. Carl Furillo

-1956-
Yankees vs. Dodgers

106) __ Whose grand slam home run in Game Two was neutralized by Brooklyn's 13-run outburst? a. Mickey Mantle b. Ellie Howard c. Yogi Berra d. Bill Skowron

107) __ Who was the 40-year-old who turned the Series around in the Yankees' favor with a three-run homer in Game Three? a. Hank Bauer b. Enos Slaughter c. Bob Cerv d. George Wilson

108) __ Whom did Don Larsen strike out to finalize his perfect game? a. Sandy Amoros b. Jim Gilliam c. Rube Walker d. Dale Mitchell

109) __ Whose misplay of Jackie Robinson's line drive in the tenth inning of Game Six permitted Clem Labine to outpitch Bob Turley, 1–0? a. Hank Bauer b. Ellie Howard c. Mickey Mantle d. Enos Slaughter

110) __ In Games Three through Seven, five Yankee pitchers—Whitey Ford, another pitcher, Don Larsen, Bob Turley, and Johnny Kucks—set a record by hurling five straight complete games by five different moundsmen. Who was left out? a. Tom Sturdivant b. Tom Morgan c. Mickey McDermott d. Bob Grim

Yankees vs. Braves

111) __ Who was the Yankee rookie who hit two home runs in one game in front of his home-town fans? a. Jerry Lumpe b. Andy Carey c. Tony Kubek d. Bobby Richardson

112) __ Who was the Brave left fielder, not known for his defensive ability, who made a great catch and also threw out Yogi Berra at the plate in Game Two? a. Hank Aaron b. Wes Covington c. Andy Pafko d. Bob Hazle

113) __ Who was the "shoe polish" batter who, in getting hit by a pitch in the tenth inning of Game Four, enabled Johnny Logan to double home the tying run and Eddie Mathews to homer over the winning runs? a. Del Crandall b. Frank Torre c. Del Rice d. Nippy Jones

114) __ Whose indecision on a slow ground ball by Eddie Mathews cost Whitey Ford a 1–0 decision to Lew Burdette? a. Jerry Coleman b. Gil McDougald c. Andy Carey d. Jerry Lumpe

115) __ Whose throwing error with the bases loaded in the first inning of the final game paved the way for Lew Burdette's 5–0 shutout over Don Larsen? a. Jerry Lumpe b. Tony Kubek c. Bill Skowron d. Jerry Coleman

-1958-
Yankees vs. Braves

116) __ In Game Three, who got four ribbies en route to batting safely in his record 17th consecutive game? a. Bill Skowron b. Gil McDougald c. Hank Bauer d. Mickey Mantle

117) __ Who hurt Whitey Ford in his 3–0 loss to Warren Spahn by losing two fly balls in the sun? a. Hank Bauer b. Norm Siebern c. Ellie Howard d. Yogi Berra

118) __ Who won the fifth game via a shutout and the

seventh game via a strong relief outing? a. Bob Turley
b. Don Larsen c. Johnny Kucks d. Bobby Shantz

119) __ Who hit four home runs in the Series for the
Yankees? a. Mickey Mantle b. Bill Skowron c. Hank
Bauer d. Yogi Berra

120) __ Whose three-run homer in the eighth inning of
Game Seven ensured the Yankees' sixth world title of the
decade? a. Yogi Berra b. Mickey Mantle c. Ellie Howard
d. Bill Skowron

-1960-
Yankees vs. Pirates

121) __ Who hit home runs in Game One and Game
Seven for the Pirates? a. Roberto Clemente b. Dick Groat
c. Dick Stuart d. Bill Mazeroski

122) __ Who hit three home runs—two of them in one
game—and batted .400? a. Roger Maris b. Mickey Mantle
c. Yogi Berra d. Elston Howard

123) __ Who drove home a record six runs in one
game? a. Mickey Mantle b. Roberto Clemente c. Bobby
Richardson d. Bill Mazeroski

124) __ Who, in Game Four and Game Five, picked up
two saves by pitching two and two-thirds innings of hitless
ball in each contest? a. Roy Face b. Harvey Haddix
c. Luis Arroyo d. Ryne Duren

125) __ Who threw the pitch that Bill Mazeroski hit for
the Series-ending homer? a. Ralph Terry b. Whitey Ford
c. Bob Turley d. Art Ditmar

-1961-
Yankees vs. Reds

126) __ Who was limited to six at bats because of an
abscessed hip? a. Roger Maris b. Tony Kubek c. Bill
Skowron d. Mickey Mantle

127) __ Who got a record nine hits in this five-game

Series? a. Yogi Berra b. Clete Boyer c. Bobby Richardson d. Hector Lopez

128) ___ In Game Three who delivered the key pinch-hit home run that tied the score in the eighth inning? (Roger Maris' home run in the ninth inning decided the game.) a. Hector Lopez b. Johnny Blanchard c. Jack Reed d. Billy Gardner

129) ___ Who was the seventh-game substitute who drove home five runs, three of them on a home run? a. Johnny Blanchard b. Hector Lopez c. Tommy Tresh d. Joe Pepitone

130) ___ Who was the other Yankee substitute who batted .400, hit two home runs, and drove home four runs? a. Hector Lopez b. Johnny Blanchard c. Dale Long d. Phil Linz

-1962-
Yankees vs. Giants

131) ___ Who was the Giant pitcher who defeated the Yankees 2–0 and lost to them 1–0? (He also dropped a 5–3 decision in a game in which he struck out ten batters.) a. Billy Pierce b. Billy O'Dell c. Jack Sanford d. Juan Marichal

132) ___ In Game Four, who hit the first grand slam homer in National League history? a. Willie McCovey b. Willie Mays c. Orlando Cepeda d. Chuck Hiller

133) ___ Who was the son of a former major leaguer— he was also a rookie—whose three-run homer downed Jack Sanford in Game Five? a. Tommy Tresh b. Clete Boyer c. Jack Reed d. Dale Long

134) ___ Who was the Yankee outfielder whose great cut-off and return throw on Willie Mays's ninth-inning double prevented a tie in Game Seven? a. Roger Maris b. Mickey Mantle c. Tommy Tresh d. Yogi Berra

135) ___ Who grounded into a double play to score the only run of Game Seven? a. Bobby Richardson b. Bill Skowron c. Yogi Berra d. Tony Kubek

-1963-
Yankees vs. Dodgers

136) ___ Who struck out a record 15 Yankees in Game One? a. Johnny Podres b. Don Drysdale c. Roger Craig d. Sandy Koufax

137) ___ Whose three-run "Chinese" home run cost Whitey Ford that first game? a. Maury Wills b. Johnny Roseboro c. Tommy Davis d. Jim Gilliam

138) ___ Who was the former Yankee star who homered in Game Two and batted .385 for the Series? a. Dick Tracewski b. Frank Howard c. Bill Skowron d. Johnny Podres

139) ___ Who pitched a three-hit 1–0 shutout against the Yankees in Game Three? a. Sandy Koufax b. Roger Craig c. Don Drysdale d. Johnny Podres

140) ___ Who hit a sacrifice fly to drive home the winning run of the game and the Series? a. Tommy Davis b. Jim Gilliam c. Frank Howard d. Willie Davis

-1964-
Yankees vs. Cardinals

141) ___ Who got a record-tying three-pinch-hits for St. Louis? a. Lou Brock b. Carl Warwick c. Dal Maxvill d. Bob Skinner

142) ___ Who was the "bulldog" who picked up two wins for the Yankees? a. Mel Stottlemyre b. Jim Bouton c. Al Downing d. Whitey Ford

143) ___ Who was the Redbird who hit the second—and last—grand slam homer in National League history? a. Curt Flood b. Mike Shannon c. Bill White d. Ken Boyer

144) ___ Whose three-run homer in the tenth inning won Game Five for the Cardinals? a. Dick Groat b. Mike Shannon c. Tim McCarver d. Bill White

145) ___ Who hit three home runs for the Yankees? a. Mickey Mantle b. Roger Maris c. Ellie Howard d. Joe Pepitone

-1976-
Yankees vs. Reds

146) ___ Who was the National League's first designated hitter—he batted .357— in World Series history? a. Dan Driessen b. Ed Armbrister c. Bob Bailey d. Doug Flynn

147) ___ Who picked up two saves for Cincinnati, including one in the final game for the second consecutive year? a. Pedro Borbon b. Rawley Eastwick c. Gary Nolan d. Will McEnaney

148) ___ Who hit two home runs and collected six ribbies for the Reds? a. Joe Morgan b. Tony Perez c. Johnny Bench d. Ken Griffey

149) ___ Who collected a Series-high nine hits? a. Johnny Bench b. Thurman Munson c. George Foster d. Lou Piniella

150) ___ Who did third baseman Pete Rose neutralize by playing far up on the infield grass? a. Willie Randolph b. Roy White c. Mickey Rivers d. Fred Stanley

-1977-
Yankees vs. Dodgers

151) ___ In Game One, who singled home the winning run in the twelfth inning? a. Paul Blair b. Roy White c. Mickey Rivers d. Thurman Munson

152) ___ In Game Four, who four-hit the Dodgers en route to a 4–2 win? a. Mike Torrez b. Catfish Hunter c. Ron Guidry d. Don Gullett

153) ___ Who was the hitting hero of the final game? a. Steve Garvey b. Davey Lopes c. Thurman Munson d. Reggie Jackson

154) ___ In Game Six, who pitched his second complete-game victory of the Series? a. Catfish Hunter b. Mike Torrez c. Don Gullett d. Ron Guidry

155) ___ Who batted .450 for the Yankees? a. Thurman Munson b. Lou Piniella c. Reggie Jackson d. Mickey Rivers

-1978-
Yankees vs. Dodgers

156) __ Whose five fielding gems in Game Three got the Yankees back in the Series? a. Bucky Dent b. Brian Doyle c. Chris Chambliss d. Graig Nettles

157) __ Who won a game—without a loss—for the second consecutive year? a. Catfish Hunter b. Ed Figueroa c. Jim Beattie d. Ron Guidry

158) __ In Game Four, whom did the Dodgers claim "interfered" with Bill Russell's attempt to throw out Lou Piniella for a double play? a. Reggie Jackson b. Bucky Dent c. Thurman Munson d. Paul Blair

159) __ Who was the Yankee rookie who pitched his first complete game in the majors—a 12–2 win—in Game Five? a. Ken Clay b. Jim Beattie c. Goose Gossage d. Dick Tidrow

160) __ Who copped his fifth World Series win in the final game? a. Ron Guidry b. Mike Torrez c. Catfish Hunter d. Don Gullett

-1981-
Yankees vs. Dodgers

161) __ Who became the first pitcher to lose three games in a seven-game World Series? a. Ron Davis b. Goose Gossage c. George Frazier d. Ron Guidry

162) __ Who got only one hit in 22 official at-bats? a. Rick Cerone b. Graig Nettles c. Dave Winfield d. Jerry Mumphrey

163) __ Who, in his first official World Series at bat, bunted into a double play to kill a Yankee threat in Game Three? a. Bobby Murcer b. Larry Milbourne c. Bob Watson d. Jerry Mumphrey

164) Who inexplicably got doubled off first base on the preceding play? a. Willie Randolph b. Reggie Jackson c. Dave Winfield d. Larry Milbourne

165) __ Who hit two home runs and a triple for the Yankees? a. Bob Watson b. Willie Randolph c. Dave Winfield d. Reggie Jackson

Answers

116. World Series Chronology

1) c	34) c	67) c	100) b	133) a
2) a	35) d	68) b	101) d	134) a
3) b	36) b	69) a	102) c	135) d
4) c	37) a	70) d	103) a	136) d
5) d	38) d	71) b	104) a	137) b
6) a	39) b	72) b	105) b	138) c
7) b	40) c	73) a	106) c	139) c
8) d	41) a	74) c	107) b	140) d
9) d	42) d	75) d	108) d	141) b
10) b	43) b	76) a	109) d	142) b
11) d	44) b	77) c	110) a	143) d
12) a	45) d	78) c	111) c	144) c
13) d	46) b	79) d	112) b	145) a
14) c	47) b	80) b	113) d	146) a
15) b	48) c	81) b	114) a	147) d
16) a	49) a	82) a	115) b	148) c
17) d	50) b	83) a	116) c	149) b
18) b	51) b	84) c	117) b	150) c
19) c	52) c	85) d	118) a	151) a
20) d	53) b	86) c	119) c	152) c
21) a	54) d	87) a	120) d	153) d
22) a	55) b	88) b	121) d	154) b
23) c	56) b	89) a	122) b	155) c
24) d	57) b	90) c	123) c	156) d
25) c	58) d	91) d	124) a	157) d
26) a	59) c	92) a	125) a	158) a
27) b	60) b	93) b	126) d	159) b
28) c	61) c	94) c	127) c	160) c
29) c	62) d	95) c	128) b	161) c
30) a	63) a	96) d	129) b	162) c
31) d	64) c	97) d	130) b	163) a
32) b	65) d	98) b	131) c	164) d
33) a	66) b	99) a	132) d	165) b

Historical Interlude
Number Sixteen

Thirty-three years have rolled by since Don Larsen became the first and only pitcher to spin a no-hitter in the World Series. What fixed the feat indelibly in the minds of those who saw the game or heard the broadcast was the fact that the no-hitter was a perfect one.

There are certain aspects of trivia about that game that stand out. Two defensive plays, for example. In the second inning, Jackie Robinson lashed a one-hopper toward left field, but third baseman Andy Carey got a glove on the ball and deflected it to Gil McDougald, and the Dodger runner was gunned down, by a step, at first base. In the sixth inning, Mickey Mantle made a sensational backhand catch of Gil Hodges' long fly ball in left center field.

Other things stand out, too. Sandy Amoros hit a wicked line drive that hooked foul before it reached the right-field foul pole, and Mickey Mantle hit a wicked line drive that didn't hook foul before it reached the foul pole. Mantle's blast was the only run of the 2–0 game that Larsen would need to win.

Suddenly it was the ninth inning and Larsen needed *only* three outs to remain perfect. Carl Furillo flied out, Roy Campanella bounced out, and pinch hitter Dale Mitchell struck out.

On a bad pitch, the .312 lifetime hitter claimed afterward. But no one argued. The plate umpire had called a beautiful game. It just happened to be a coincidence that in the last plate assignment of his illustrious career, he got a chance to work his first perfect game.

Who was that National League arbiter who retired from umpiring in that inimitable fashion?

Answer: Babe Pinelli

189

CHAPTER SEVENTEEN

World Series Who's Who

117. WHO'S WHO

You can use the following list as a guide to the answers in this quiz:

George Pipgras
Tony Kubek
Bob Meusel
Charlie Keller
Lou Gehrig
Babe Ruth
Bud Metheny
Joe Bush
Johnny Blanchard
Charlie Silvera
Ewell Blackwell
Tony Lazzeri
Russ Ford
Vic Raschi
Marshall Bridges
Hank Bauer
Mike Torrez
Bill Dickey
Billy Martin
Art Jorgens
Phil Rizzuto
Mickey Mantle
Johnny Murphy
Herb Pennock

Johnny Mize
Frankie Crosetti
Reggie Jackson
Wally Schang
Joe Gordon
Whitey Ford
Al Downing
Joe DiMaggio
Bobby Richardson
Lefty Gomez
Irv Noren
Gene Woodling
Billy Johnson
Johnny Kucks
Yogi Berra
Ellie Howard
Enos Slaughter
Gil McDougald
Bob Kuzava
Johnny Sain
Art Ditmar
Hank Bauer
Jim Mason

1) _____ Who was the last Yankee pitcher to throw two complete-game victories in a Series?

2) _____ Who hit into a career-record seven double plays?

3) _____ Who hit into a record five double plays in one Series?

4) _____ Who was the pitcher of the 1930s who struck out a record five times in one game?

5) _____ Who drove home all of the Yankees' four runs—to set a major-league record—in a 4–0 victory over the Braves?

6) _____ Who was the Yankee catcher who got a record-tying four singles in one game?

7) _____ Who was the former Yankee infielder who stroked a record-tying two triples in one game?

8) _____ Who set the record of most home runs—two—in one game by a rookie?

9) _____ Who is the former infielder who tied it?

10) _____ Who has been the only Yankee right-handed lead-off batter to start a game with a home run?

11) _____ Who has been the only Yankee lefty to repeat the feat?

12) _____ Who was the Yankee batsman who walked four times in one game?

13) _____ Who was the anemic-hitting Yankee pitcher who walked a record-setting two times in one inning?

14) _____ Who received a record five consecutive walks in a Series?

15) _____ Who was the Yankee outfielder who twice stole home during his Series career?

16) _____ Who has been the only Yankee to steal two bases in one inning?

17) _____ Who was the former Yankee manager who got caught stealing a record-tying two times in one game?

18) _____ Who got hit by pitches a record-tying two times in one game?

19) _____ Who has been the only Yankee to be awarded first base on catcher's interference?

20) _____ Who was eligible for the most Series—five—without appearing in one of them?

21) _____ Who did not miss a single game of the ten World Series in which he played?

22) _____ Who appeared as an active player on the most winning teams?

23) _____ Who appeared on the most losing teams in American League history?

24) _____ Who became the first—and only—player to perform for four world titlists his first four years in the majors?

25) _____ Who was the only other regular to play on pennant winners his first four years in the majors?

26) _____ Who was the only pitcher to play on four pennant winners his first four years in the majors?

27) _____ Who played in a career-record 75 Series games?

28) _____ Who played in a record 30 consecutive Series games?

29) _____ Who hit .300 or over for the Series a record six times?

30) _____ Who averaged .361 in 34 career Series games?

31) _____ Who was the Yankee infielder who hit a league record-tying three triples in one Series and a major-league record-tying four triples in his career?

32) _____ Who scored a record 42 runs in 65 Series games?

33) _____ Who walked a record 43 times and struck out a record 54 times in Series games?

34) _____ Who was the strong-armed left fielder who whiffed a record seven times in a four-game Series?

35) _____ Who, in back-to-back Series, did not strike out in 52 official at bats?

36) _____ Who pinch-hit a record ten times in Series games?

37) _____ Who was the pitcher for three different pennant winners who had a record gap of 18 years between his first Series and his last?

38) _____ Who has been the oldest regular player to appear in a Series game?

39) _____ Who played shortstop, third base, left field, and center field in Series action?

40) _____ Who was the relief pitcher who appeared in a record six Series?

41) _____ Who was the onetime Yankee pitcher who, in a career span that included stays with three different pennant winners, lost five consecutive games?

42) _____ Who was eligible to play in seven Series, but came to bat only twice?

43) _____ Who was the only major leaguer to play on five winners his last five years in the majors?

44) _____ Who was the first rookie to hit a grand slam in the October get-togethers?

45) _____ Who was the .284 lifetime hitter who caught for the Yankees in the 1920s and played in six World Series for three different teams?

46) _____ Who was the light-hitting infielder whose two-run homer turned back an "over-the-hill" but valiant Dizzy Dean in Game Two of 1938?

47) _____ Who was the Highlander who won a rookie league-record 26 games?

48) _____ Who was the Yankee relief pitcher of the 1950s who saved the final game of two consecutive World Series?

49) _____ Who called time out during a Series in order to watch a plane fly overhead?

50) _____ Who was the versatile infielder who played seven-game Series, at three different positions, on world-title teams?

51) _____ Who was the former Brave great who played on three Yankee world-title teams?

52) _____ Who was the onetime "Whip" who started the fifth game of the 1952 Series for the Yankees?

53) _____ Who was the well-muscled outfielder who "introduced" himself to Ernie Lombardi in the 1939 Series?

54) _____ Who was the onetime MVP winner who turned the 1958 Series around with a great diving catch in left field?

55) _____ Who was the slugger who in four consecutive official at bats hit a record four home runs?

56) _____ Who was the infielder who hit .400 for the Yankees in his last American League Series, but .000 for

a National League team against the Bronx Bombers the following year?

57) _____ Who was the infielder who replaced the preceding player in the lineup the following season and matched his predecessor's .400 of the previous year?

58) _____ Who was the only Yankee pitcher in history to both win and lose a 1–0 decision?

59) _____ Who was the first baseman who set a record by homering in three consecutive games?

60) _____ Who was the pitcher whose only World Series victory was a seventh-game shutout?

61) _____ Who was the southpaw chucker who threw two shutouts in the same Series?

62) _____ Who was the right-hander who lost two starts in the same Series even though he pitched a total of only one and two-thirds innings?

63) _____ Who was the only Yankee right-handed hitter to belt four home runs in one Series?

64) _____ Who was the first black pitcher to appear in a World Series game for the Yankees?

65) _____ Who was the first black pitcher to start a game for an American League team?

66) _____ Who was the light-hitting substitute infielder who hit the only Yankee home run against the Reds in 1976?

67) _____ Who was the Yankee infielder who was suspended for 30 days at the beginning of the 1943 season for shoving umpire Bill Summers in the 1942 Classic?

68) _____ Who was the outfield star who later managed the only non-Yankee team, in the American League, to a World Series sweep?

Answers

117. Who's Who

1) Mike Torrez (1977)
2) Joe DiMaggio
3) Irv Noren (1955)
4) George Pipgras (1932)
5) Hank Bauer (1958)
6) Bill Dickey (1938)
7) Bobby Richardson (1960)
8) Charlie Keller (1939)
9) Tony Kubek (1957)
10) Phil Rizzuto (1942)
11) Gene Woodling (1953)
12) Babe Ruth (1926)
13) Lefty Gomez (1937)
14) Lou Gehrig (1928)
15) Bob Meusel (1921 and 1928)
16) Babe Ruth (1921)
17) Billy Martin (1955)
18) Yogi Berra (1953)
19) Bud Metheny (1943)
20) Art Jorgens
21) Joe DiMaggio
22) Yogi Berra (10)
23) Elston Howard (6)
24) Joe DiMaggio (1936-39)
25) Ellie Howard (1955-58)
26) Johnny Kucks (1955-58)
27) Yogi Berra
28) Bobby Richardson (1960-64)

29) Babe Ruth
30) Lou Gehrig
31) Billy Johnson
32) Mickey Mantle
33) Mickey Mantle
34) Bob Meusel (1927)
35) Yogi Berra (1957-58)
36) Johnny Blanchard
37) Herb Pennock (Athletics, '14-Yankees, '32)
38) Enos Slaughter (42 in 1958)
39) Tony Kubek.
40) Johnny Murphy
41) Joe Bush (Athletics, Red Sox, Yankees)
42) Charlie Silvera
43) Johnny Mize (1949-53)
44) Gil McDougald (1951)
45) Wally Schang (Athletics, Red Sox, and Yankees)
46) Frankie Crosetti
47) Russ Ford (1910)
48) Bob Kuzava (1951-52)
49) Lefty Gomez (1937)
50) Gil McDougald (third, short, and second)
51) Johnny Sain (1951-53)

52) Ewell Blackwell
53) Charlie Keller (in a home-plate collision)
54) Ellie Howard
55) Reggie Jackson (1977)
56) Tony Lazzeri (1937 and 1938)
57) Joe Gordon (1938)
58) Vic Raschi (He won in 1950 and lost in 1949)
59) Johnny Mize (1952)
60) Johnny Kucks (1956)
61) Whitey Ford (1960)
62) Art Ditmar (1960)
63) Hank Bauer (1958)
64) Marshall Bridges (1962)
65) Al Downing (1963)
66) Jim Mason
67) Frankie Crosetti
68) Hank Bauer (1966 Orioles)

Historical Interlude Number Seventeen

"Next year" finally came on October 4, 1955. It could have waited at least until "next year," Yankee diehards said.

Johnny Podres of the Dodgers and Tommy Byrne of the Yankees were in seventh-game form that afternoon. Podres pitched an eight-hit shutout. Byrne allowed only three safeties in five and one-third innings. But during that time Gil Hodges singled home one run and drove another across the plate with a sacrifice fly. Bob Grim and Bob Turley mopped up.

The big play of the game occurred in the home half of the sixth. With one out, Billy Martin walked and Gil McDougald beat out a bunt. That brought to the plate the dangerous Yogi Berra, a notorious pull hitter. The Dodger outfield swung to right field with substitute left fielder Sandy Amoros defending against the slice. Berra proceeded to slice one of Podres' wicked curves in front of the left-field foul pole. Amoros, racing toward the line, reached out his glove and made a sensational snatch of the ball. The Yankee runners, sure that the ball was going to drop safely, were off with the crack of the bat. Without hesitating, Amoros wheeled and threw to the relay man, Pee Wee Reese, who fired to Hodges to double off the surprised McDougald.

Podres, bailed out of his biggest jam, settled down and blanked the Yankees the rest of the way to bring the first world championship to Brooklyn.

Much has been written about this thrilling game, but not much has been noted about the move that set up Amoros' play of the day. In the top half of the sixth, George Shuba was sent up to pinch-hit for Don Zimmer, the second baseman. Dodger manager Walt Alston then moved his regular left fielder to second base in the bottom half of the inning and inserted Amoros in left.

Whose place in the sun field did Amoros take?

Answer: Jim Gilliam's

CHAPTER EIGHTEEN

The Managers

118. WHO'S WHO

You can use the following list as a guide to the answers in this quiz:

Bob Lemon
Casey Stengel
Roger Peckinpaugh
Art Fletcher
Frank Chance
Miller Huggins
Harry Wolverton
Johnny Neun
Bucky Harris
Bob Shawkey
George Stallings

Joe McCarthy
Kid Elberfeld
Wild Bill Donovan
Yogi Berra
Billy Martin
Bill Virdon
Ralph Houk
Clark Griffith
Hal Chase
Johnny Keane

1) _____ Who, in addition to Bill Dickey, served as an interim manager in 1946?

2) _____ Who was the Yankee manager who once singled home the winning run of a World Series?

3) _____ Who was the Yankee manager who once pitched his team—not the Yankees—to victory in the final game of a World Series?

4) _____ Who was the Yankee manager who once hit two two-run homers in the seventh and deciding game of a World Series?

5) _____ Who was the Yankee manager who once got 11 hits, including two home runs, in a seven-game Series?

6) _____ Who was the Yankee manager who once provided the winning run for the Giants in two games in

the same Series with home runs *against* the Bronx Bombers?

7) _____ Who managed the Yankees between Ralph Houk (second tenure) and Billy Martin (first tenure)?

8) _____ Who had the shortest term as a Yankee manager?

9) _____ Who was the Yankee manager who won his first pennant in his tenth year as a pilot? (That's a record.)

10) _____ Who was the only Yankee manager between 1918 and 1973 who led the Bronx Bombers for one full year but failed to lead a major-league team to a pennant?

11) _____ Who was the Yankee manager who guided the Bronx Bombers during a period in which they scored in a record 308 consecutive games?

12) _____ Who was the Yankee manager who played eight years in the major leagues without hitting a home run or stealing a base?

13) _____ Who won ten pennants and seven world titles?

14) _____ Who skippered eight Yankee pennant winners and seven New York world-title teams?

15) _____ Who was the Yankee pilot who's been the youngest skipper to lead a big-league club?

16) _____ Who was the Yankee manager who later led a National League team to the first World Series sweep? (The Cubs and Tigers tied one game in 1907.)

17) _____ Who was the Yankee manager who became the first skipper to win pennants in both leagues?

18) _____ Who was the Yankee manager who became the second skipper to do so?

19) _____ Who was the manager who won world titles a record 23 years apart for two different American League teams?

20) _____ Who was the manager who, in 24 years of directing major-league teams, never wound up in the second division?

21) _____ Who was the manager who, in 13 years of guiding National League teams, never wound up in the first division?

22) _____ Who was the former pennant-winning skipper of the White Sox who led the Yankees?

23) _____ Who was the Yankee manager who once guided a National League team to four pennants and two world titles?

24) _____ Who was the Yankee manager who once pitched in three consecutive World Series for another American League team?

25) _____ Who took the place of Miller Huggins after the "Mighty Mite" died in 1929?

26) _____ Who was the Yankee who became player-manager after he carped about the club's skipper to the team owner?

27) _____ Who was the Yankee manager who won a record three pennants in his first three years at the helm?

28) _____ Who has been the only Yankee manager to be ejected from a World Series game?

29) _____ Who was the only rookie Yankee manager to lead his team to a world title?

30) _____ Who was the only other rookie manager to guide the Yankees to a pennant?

31) _____ Who was the only Yankee manager to take the team over during the season—when the club was not in first place—and lead it to a pennant and world title?

32) _____ Who was the last Yankee manager to guide the Bombers to back-to-back pennants?

33) _____ Who was the first manager to guide the Yankees to four straight world titles?

34) _____ Who was the first manager to lead the Yankees to five consecutive world titles?

35) _____ Who was the only Yankee manager to lose World Series to three National League teams?

36) _____ Who was the only manager in history to win world titles in his first two years as a team leader?

37) _____ Who was the first Yankee manager to lead his team to back-to-back World Series sweeps?

38) _____ Who was the only other Yankee manager to repeat the feat?

39) _____ Who was the World Series opponent of a Yankee manager one year and his replacement at the helm of the Bombers the following year?

40) _____ Who was the manager who led the Yankees to a team-high 110 wins in one season?

41) _____ Who was the Yankee manager who played a pivotal role for a National League team whose victory forced the "retirement" of Casey Stengel?

42) _____ Who was the Yankee manager who was later barred from baseball for life?

43) _____ What Highlander combination pitcher and manager is in the Hall of Fame?

44) _____ What Highlander combination first baseman and manager is in the Hall of Fame?

45) _____ Who was the Yankee manager whose final game errors cost two American League teams world titles?

46) _____ Who was the Yankee manager who was called the "Tabasco Kid"?

47) _____ Who was the Yankee manager who lost more games in one season—102—than any other Pinstripe skipper?

48) _____ Who was the only Yankee pennant-winning manager who never played in the major leagues?

49) _____ Who was the Yankee playing manager who, in his one season with the club, had a pinch-hitting average (10–26) of .385?

50) _____ Who was the Yankee manager who once made an unassisted triple play?

119. MATCHING MANAGERS, PART I

Take the following managers of more than one year and match them up with their Yankee winning percentages listed below: Bill Virdon, Johnny Keane, Joe McCarthy, Wild Bill Donovan, Bucky Harris, George Stallings, Miller Huggins, Frank Chance, Casey Stengel, Clark Griffith, and Ralph Houk.

1) _____ (.627)   2) _____ (.620)

3) _____ (.619)	8) _____ (.524)
4) _____ (.597)	9) _____ (.521)
5) _____ (.539)	10) _____ (.480)
6) _____ (.536)	11) _____ (.445)
7) _____ (.531)	

Flash Followup

Here's an easy chance to make up for any possible lost ground in the preceding quiz. Five of the above won more than 400 games with the Yankees. Which ones?

1) _____ (1,460)	4) _____ (944)
2) _____ (1,149)	5) _____ (419)
3) _____ (1,067)	

120. MATCHING MANAGERS, PART II

Take the following seven managers of one year or less and match them up with their Yankee winning percentages listed below: Art Fletcher, Kid Elberfeld, Johnny Neun, Bill Dickey, Harry Wolverton, Bob Shawkey, and Roger Peckinpaugh.

1) _____ (.571)	5) _____ (.529)
2) _____ (.558)	6) _____ (.328)
3) _____ (.545)	7) _____ (.276)
4) _____ (.543)	

Flash Followup

Which three managers won fewer than ten games with the Yankees?

8) _____ (9)	10) _____ (6)
9) _____ (8)	

121. MATCHING MANAGERS, PART III

Match the Yankee managers listed in the left-hand column with the statements in the right-hand column that relate to them.

1) __ Clark Griffith

2) __ Kid Elberfeld

3) __ George Stallings

4) __ Hal Chase

5) __ Harry Wolverton

6) __ Frank Chance

7) __ Roger Peckin-
   paugh

8) __ William Donovan

9) __ Miller Huggins

10) __ Art Fletcher

11) __ Bob Shawkey

12) __ Joe McCarthy

13) __ Bill Dickey

14) __ Johnny Neun

15) __ Bucky Harris

a) He led the Astros to a divisional title.

b) He's a coach for a National League team.

c) He was called "Marse Joe."

d) He ended up his managerial career with more wins (1,491) than any of the other managers listed.

e) He threw out the ceremonial pitch at the unveiling of New Yankee Stadium.

f) He resigned his job after a 4–16 season start.

g) After he was fired by the Yankees, he managed a National League club for eight consecutive years.

h) He played shortstop for eight summers with New York.

i) He played with or managed all four New York franchises.

j) He was a switch (.229) hitter.

k) He managed in the major leagues for 29 years.

16) ___ Casey Stengel

17) ___ Ralph Houk

18) ___ Yogi Berra

19) ___ Johnny Keane

20) ___ Bill Virdon

21) ___ Billy Martin

22) ___ Dick Howser

23) ___ Bob Lemon

24) ___ Gene Michael

25) ___ Dallas Green

l) He split six World Series decisions.

m) He won 207 major league games.

n) He was both a manager and a general manager.

o) He died an outcast.

p) After a 17-year career—during which he served a short stint as manager—he led Cleveland for seven years.

q) He played in eight World Series.

r) He played shortstop for the Giants in four World Series.

s) He finished first in his first full season of managing and last in his last full season of managing.

t) In World Series play he threw five complete games in five starts, with a 2.70 ERA, but he lost four of his five decisions.

u) This switch-hitting .289 batter managed the Reds for two years following his short stint with the Yankees.

v) He got fired after winning 103 games in his first full season as a manager.

w) He won a world title with the 1980 Phillies.

x) He batted .333 in five World Series.

y) With the exception of 59 games with the Senators, he spent his entire career in the National League before finishing up as playing manager of New York in 1912.

Answers

118. Who's Who

1) Johnny Neun
2) Billy Martin (1953)
3) Bob Lemon (1948 Indians)
4) Yogi Berra (1956)
5) Bucky Harris (1924 Senators)
6) Casey Stengel (1923)
7) Bill Virdon (1974–75)
8) Art Fletcher (11 games)
9) Casey Stengel (1949)
10) Bob Shawkey (1930)
11) Joe McCarthy (1931–33)
12) Ralph Houk
13) Casey Stengel (1949–60)
14) Joe McCarthy (1931–46)
15) Roger Peckinpaugh (23)
16) George Stallings (1914 Braves)
17) Joe McCarthy (1929 Cubs)
18) Yogi Berra (1973 Mets)
19) Bucky Harris (1924 Senators-1947 Yankees)
20) Joe McCarthy
21) Casey Stengel
22) Clark Griffith (1903–08)
23) Frank Chance (1905–12 Cubs)
24) Wild Bill Donovan (1907–09)
25) Art Fletcher
26) Hal Chase (1910–11)
27) Ralph Houk (1961–63)
28) Billy Martin (1976)
29) Ralph Houk (1961)
30) Yogi Berra (1964)
31) Bob Lemon (1978)
32) Billy Martin (1976–77)
33) Joe McCarthy (1936–39)
34) Casey Stengel (1949–53)
35) Casey Stengel (Dodgers, Braves, Pirates)
36) Ralph Houk (1961–62)
37) Miller Huggins (1927–28)
38) Joe McCarthy (1938–39)
39) Johnny Keane (Yogi Berra) 1964–65
40) Miller Huggins (1927)
41) Bill Virdon (1960 Pirates)
42) Hal Chase
43) Clark Griffith
44) Frank Chance

45) Roger Peckinpaugh
(1921 Yankees-1925
Senators)
46) Kid Elberfeld
47) Harry Wolverton
(1912)

48) Joe McCarthy
49) Harry Wolverton
(1912)
50) Johnny Neun (1927)

119. Matching Managers, Part I

1) Joe McCarthy (.627)
2) Bucky Harris (.620)
3) Casey Stengel (.619)
4) Miller Huggins (.597)
5) Ralph Houk (.539)
6) Bill Virdon (.536)
7) Clark Griffith (.531)

8) George Stallings
(.524)
9) Frank Chance (.521)
10) Wild Bill Donovan
(.480)
11) Johnny Keane (.445)

Flash Followup

1) Joe McCarthy
2) Casey Stengel
3) Miller Huggins

4) Ralph Houk
5) Wild Bill Donovan

120. Matching Managers, Part II

1) Johnny Neun
2) Bob Shawkey
3) Art Fletcher
4) Bill Dickey

5) Roger Peckinpaugh
6) Harry Wolverton
7) Kid Elberfeld

Flash Followup

8) Roger Peckinpaugh

9) Johnny Neun
10) Art Fletcher

121. Matching Managers, Part III

1) d		14) u
2) h		15) k
3) g		16) i
4) o		17) n
5) y		18) b
6) s		19) f
7) p		20) a
8) t		21) x
9) l		22) v
10) r		23) m
11) e		24) j
12) c		25) w
13) q		

Historical Interlude Number Eighteen

Casey Stengel had a checkered career as a manager.

In nine years of leading major-league teams in the National League, he never brought one of his clubs home in the first division. The best finishes that he ever posted were fifth-place windups with the 1935 Dodgers and the 1938 Braves.

Then, after a minor-league interlude, George Weiss hand-picked Casey to lead the 1949 Yankees. At the age of 59, he became the oldest manager to win his first pennant. He also set a record by becoming the manager with the most experience—ten years—to win his first pennant.

Casey never stopped setting records after that first year in New York. His 1949–53 clubs became the first group of players to win five consecutive world titles. That made him the first manager to guide five consecutive title winners.

After a one-year hiatus (1954) from winning pennants, Casey and his boys got back on the winning track in 1955 and continued on that victory path for three more years. (It was ironic, by the way, that Casey failed to win the pennant in 1954, for that was the first—and last—year in which one of his teams won 100 games. The Yankees, as a matter of fact, won 103 games that year. But the Indians won an American League record 111 games.)

The Yankees dropped to third place in 1959, but in 1960 they rebounded to win their last pennant under Casey. That was his tenth pennant. The only other manager to win ten pennants was John McGraw. But McGraw could claim only three world titles. Casey won seven world championships. The only other manager to equal that total was Joe McCarthy.

Overall, Casey won ten pennants—and seven world titles—in his 12-year stay with the Yankees, quite a reversal from his previous National League form. In order to unify his story, we might suppose, Casey went back to the National League, with the Mets, and finished off his career with four tenth-place finishes.

He even had a checkered career as a manager in New York.

When Yankee fans think of Casey, they like to think of him as a Yankee; with the Yankees he finished off the lead only two times. To the same manager, by the way.

Who was that American League skipper who beat Casey to the wire in both 1954 and 1959? This hint might help: he caught for Casey with both the Dodgers and the Braves.

Answer: Al Lopez

CHAPTER NINETEEN

The Hall-of-Famers

122. CLUES TO COOPERSTOWN

There are 35 former Yankees in the Hall of Fame. That includes players, managers, general managers, owners, and broadcasters. Some of them earned their niche in Cooperstown through their exploits with the Yankees; others gained it through their feats elsewhere. But all of them, in one way or another, contributed to the Yankee success story. Below you will find a list of the Yankee Hall-of-Famers. You may want to refer to it as you challenge the 102 pitches that follow.

Babe Ruth	Branch Rickey
Lou Gehrig	Waite Hoyt
Willie Keeler	Stan Coveleski
Clark Griffith	Earle Combs
Frank Chance	George Weiss
Jack Chesbro	Yogi Berra
Herb Pennock	Lefty Gomez
Paul Waner	Mickey Mantle
Ed Barrow	Whitey Ford
Bill Dickey	Bucky Harris
Frank Baker	Joe Sewell
Dazzy Vance	Larry McPhail
Joe DiMaggio	Mel Allen
Joe McCarthy	Red Barber
Miller Huggins	Johnny Mize
Casey Stengel	Enos Slaughter
Bill McKechnie	Catfish Hunter
Red Ruffing	

1) _____ Which one of them had a 5–0 pitching record with the Yankees?

2) _____ Which one of them sprayed a club-record* 231 hits in one year?

3) _____ Which one of them won three games—but not with the Yankees—in a World Series?

4) _____ Which one of them took the place of Ray Chapman, who was killed by a Carl Mays fastball?

5) _____ Which one of them, as a player and a manager, performed for four New York teams?

6) _____ Which one of them managed three different teams in the World Series?

7) _____ Which one of them won three batting titles in the National League?

8) _____ Which one of them won four home-run titles in the National League?

9) _____ Which one of them had a 1.83 ERA for 12 World Series appearances?

10) _____ Which one of them managed five different teams over 29 years?

11) _____ Which one of them subscribed to the motto of "hitting them where they ain't"?

12) _____ Which one of them split six decisions as a World Series manager?

13) _____ Which one of them was the subject of a famous poem?

14) _____ Which one of them served as a coach under Casey Stengel?

15) _____ Which one of them discovered Honus Wagner?

16) _____ Which one of them twice hit ten home runs with the Yankees of the 1910s?

17) _____ Which one of them set a National League record, since broken by Pete Rose, by stroking 200 or more hits eight times?

18) _____ Who was sold to New York after he was a holdout for a full year?

19) _____ Which one of them was a 20-game winner for six consecutive years?

20) _____ Who, as a manager, never finished below

third place in the National League or above sixth place in the American League?

21) _____ Who was the Highlander pitcher who hit four career home runs? (It was quite a feat in those days.)

22) _____ Who later became general manager of the Phillies?

23) _____ Who "guided" the Yankees to 14 pennants and 10 world titles?

24) _____ Who was the GM of 11 pennant winners and eight world titlists?

25) _____ Who was the onetime Yankee pitcher who won 28 games for a poor 1924 Dodger club while the Pinstripers were being edged by the Senators?

26) _____ Who was the Yankee righthander who hit for the highest average in a season?

27) _____ Who was the only Yankee manager to die while he was still leading the club?

28) _____ Who twice hit .400 in World Series play for another American League team?

29) _____ Who broke into the majors with nine consecutive .300 seasons—and one batting title—before he dipped to .289 with the 1948 Giants?

30) _____ Who twice hit .400 *against* the Yankees in Series play?

31) _____ Who guided two different losing teams in World Series action against the Yankees?

32) _____ Who was the Yankee pitcher who logged the most career wins? (Wins with other teams count, too.)

33) _____ Who instituted team-owned farm teams?

34) _____ Who later became a broadcaster for Cincinnati?

35) _____ Who chalked up 214 career wins, posted four 20-win seasons, and weaved a 2.88 lifetime ERA? (He pitched for two teams other than the Yankees in Series play. He was the hero in one, the goat in the other.)

36) _____ Who led the American League in triples three times and batted .340 in four World Series?

37) _____ Who was the GM who ended his executive career with the Mets?

38) _____ Who was the great clutch hitter whom Paul Richards called the "best late-inning hitter in baseball"?

39) _____ Who was 9–1 in World Series and All Star game action?

40) _____ Who was the manager who ranks third in wins and second in losses?

41) _____ Who broke into the majors with a .900 winning percentage in an abbreviated season?

42) _____ Who was selected for 20 All-Star games?

43) _____ Who didn't start pitching in the American League until he was 26 years old—he played the outfield earlier—but won 20 or more games in seven seasons?

44) _____ Who coined nicknames such as "The Yankee Clipper," "Old Reliable," and "The Super Chief"?

45) _____ Who gleefully said, "Oh, Doctor!" when Al Gionfriddo made the great catch of Joe DiMaggio's long drive in the 1947 World Series?

46) _____ Who owned two New York teams?

47) _____ Who hurled more shutouts in one season than any other pitcher who is listed above?

48) _____ Who averaged only four strikeouts per year in his three years with the Yankees?

49) _____ Who walked only two batters in 27 innings of pitching in a World Series?

50) _____ Who was the pitcher who twice lost more than 20 games in a season?

51) _____ Who was the manager who led a team that lost the first pennant playoff game in American League history?

52) _____ Who led the league in slugging in his next-to-last year in the majors?

53) _____ Who was the 240-game winner who pitched in ten World Series games, posted a 1.000 point winning percentage, weaved a 1.95 ERA, and recorded three saves?

54) _____ Who drove home 100 or more runs for 13 consecutive seasons?

55) _____ Who led the National League one season with 28 wins?

56) _____ Who was the Yankee who compiled a 2.28 ERA over a ten-year pitching career?

57) _____ Who hit World Series home runs against Dizzy Dean, Robin Roberts, and Sal Maglie?

58) _____ Who had a .311 average for 61 pinch-hit attempts in 1953?

59) _____ Which one of the Yankee managers was a lawyer?

60) _____ Who was the onetime Yankee who would never manage his team on a Sunday? (Jimmy Austin would fill in for him.)

61) _____ Who won six of nine decisions for the Yankees in World Series play? (Two of the games that he lost were by shutouts—1-0 and 3-0—and one of them was by a 3-2 score.)

62) _____ Who averaged 202 hits a season over a five-year span for the Yankees?

63) _____ Who led the league in triples and homers in the same season?

64) _____ Who posted his all-time high in hits (206), doubles (44), and triples (15) in his rookie season?

65) _____ Who, in three World Series wins, limited the opposition to five hits in each game?

66) _____ Who won his first six starts in World Series play?

67) _____ Who didn't win his first World Series game away from home until the seventh Fall Classic in which he pitched?

68) _____ Who hit a ninth-inning game-winning home run against the Cardinals?

69) _____ Who was the youngest manager to guide his team—not the Yankees—to a world title?

70) _____ Who broke the color line in major-league baseball?

71) _____ Who was the Yankee announcer whose voice trademark was "How about that"?

72) _____ Who authored a book called *In the Catbird Seat*?

216

73) _____ Who had a book written about him that was titled *Lucky to Be a Yankee*?

74) _____ Who had a book written about him—and others—called *The Quality of Courage*?

75) _____ Who wrote a book that was titled *It Takes Heart*?

76) _____ Who was known for the number of times that he fired Leo Durocher?

77) _____ Who was the pitcher who hit 36 career home runs?

78) _____ Who guided teams that lost back-to-back pennants on the last day of the season?

79) _____ Who got 200 or more hits eight times in his career with the Yankees?

80) _____ Who, at age 39, led his league in shutouts?

81) _____ Who was only five feet four and a half inches tall?

82) _____ Who hit for the highest single-season mark of any major leaguer who played his position?

83) _____ Who led his league in strikeouts seven years in a row?

84) _____ Who left the highest lifetime average (.307) at his position?

85) _____ Who was the first player to hit a World Series home run at Yankee Stadium?

86) _____ Who was the Yankee manager who later owned a big-league team?

87) _____ Who was the listed player who ended his career with the highest average of any Yankee Hall-of-Famer?

88) _____ Who finished his career with a lifetime average of .313 and 202 home runs?

89) _____ Who pitched for four years with two major-league teams after he managed the Yankees?

90) _____ Who was the listed name who once managed the Red Sox to a pennant and a world title?

91) _____ Who, in his second season in the majors, won a batting title with a .380 average?

92) _____ Who was the Yankee manager who two times led his league in stolen bases and pilfered a career total of 401?

93) _____ Who was the former Pirate pitcher who won 62 games in his first two years in New York?

94) _____ Who was the Yankee pitcher who twice won two games in a World Series and once registered two saves in a Fall Classic?

95) _____ Who was the pitcher who didn't win his first major-league game until he was 31 but won 197 games before he hung up his spikes?

96) _____ Who guided a team that won 20 of 23 World Series games in one decade?

97) _____ Who was the catcher who hit 20 or more home runs in ten consecutive seasons?

98) _____ Who was the pitcher whom the Yankees supported with nine runs per game in seven World Series outings?

99) _____ Who hurled three World Series shutouts?

100) _____ Who was responsible for getting rid of Billy Martin shortly after the "Copacabana incident" in 1957?

101) _____ Who won the final game of the Yankees' last World Championship?

102) _____ Who finished his career with a batting average of .300?

Answers

122. Clues to Cooperstown

1) Babe Ruth
2) Earle Combs (1927)
3) Stan Coveleski (1920 Indians)
4) Joe Sewell (1920)
5) Casey Stengel (player with the Dodgers and Giants, manager of the Dodgers, Yankees, and Mets)
6) Bill McKechnie (1925 Pirates, 1928 Cardinals, 1939–40 Reds)
7) Paul Waner (1927, 1934, 1936 Pirates)
8) Johnny Mize (1939–40 Cardinals and 1947–48 Giants)
9) Waite Hoyt
10) Bucky Harris
11) Willie Keeler
12) Miller Huggins
13) Frank Chance ("Tinkers to Evers to Chance")
14) Bill Dickey
15) Ed Barrow
16) Frank Baker (1916, 1919)
17) Paul Waner
18) Frank Baker
19) Clark Griffith (1894–99 Chicago Cubs)
20) Frank Chance
21) Jack Chesbro
22) Herb Pennock
23) Ed Barrow
24) George Weiss
25) Dazzy Vance
26) Joe DiMaggio (.381 in 1937)
27) Miller Huggins (1929)
28) Frank Baker (.409 in 1910 and .455 in 1913)
29) Johnny Mize
30) Casey Stengel (.400 in 1922 and .417 in 1923)
31) Bill McKechnie (1928 Cardinals and 1939 Reds)
32) Red Ruffing (273)
33) Branch Rickey
34) Waite Hoyt
35) Stan Coveleski (3–0 with 1920 Indians and 0–2 with 1925 Senators)
36) Earle Combs
37) George Weiss
38) Yogi Berra
39) Lefty Gomez

40) Bucky Harris (2159–2219)
41) Whitey Ford (1950)
42) Mickey Mantle
43) Bob Lemon
44) Mel Allen
45) Red Barber
46) Larry McPhail (Dodgers and Yankees)
47) Bob Lemon (10 in 1948)
48) Joe Sewell (1931–33)
49) Stan Coveleski (1920 Indians)
50) Red Ruffing (10–25 and 9–22 for the 1928–29 Red Sox)
51) Joe McCarthy (1948 Red Sox)
52) Joe DiMaggio (.585 in 1950)
53) Herb Pennock
54) Lou Gehrig (1926–28)
55) Jack Chesbro (1902 Pirates)
56) Babe Ruth
57) Joe DiMaggio
58) Johnny Mize
59) Miller Huggins
60) Branch Rickey
61) Waite Hoyt
62) Earle Combs (1925–29)
63) Mickey Mantle (1955)
64) Joe DiMaggio (1936)

65) Stan Coveleski (1920 Indians)
66) Lefty Gomez
67) Whitey Ford (1960)
68) Mickey Mantle (1964)
69) Bucky Harris (27 with the 1924 Senators)
70) Branch Rickey (1947 Dodgers)
71) Mel Allen
72) Red Barber
73) Joe DiMaggio
74) Mickey Mantle
75) Mel Allen
76) Larry McPhail
77) Red Ruffing
78) Joe McCarthy (1948–49)
79) Lou Gehrig
80) Dazzy Vance (4 in 1930 with the Dodgers)
81) Willie Keeler
82) Bill Dickey (.362 in 1936)
83) Dazzy Vance
84) Frank Baker
85) Casey Stengel (1923)
86) Clark Griffith (Senators)
87) Willie Keeler (.345)
88) Bill Dickey
89) Clark Griffith (Reds and Senators)
90) Ed Barrow (1918)
91) Paul Waner (1927)
92) Frank Chance

93) Jack Chesbro
   (1903–04)
94) Herb Pennock
95) Dazzy Vance
96) Joe McCarthy
   (1930s)

97) Yogi Berra
   (1949–58)
98) Lefty Gomez
99) Whitey Ford
100) George Weiss
101) Catfish Hunter
102) Enos Slaughter

Historical Interlude Number Nineteen

As the Yankees came to bat, in the top of the first inning of the fifth game of the 1977 playoffs against host Kansas City, the oddsmakers were not betting that New York would duplicate its final-game theatrics of the preceding year.

Ron Guidry had to start with just two days' rest. Paul Splittorff, "The Yankee Killer," had plenty of rest. And Reggie Jackson, the Yankees' controversial slugger, had been benched by Yankee manager Billy Martin.

The Royals seemed bound to take advantage of their edge. In the first inning they scored two runs; in the third inning they tallied one more. And, what was more important, in that third inning they got rid of Ron Guidry, who had given up three runs on six hits. He was replaced, though, by a veteran right-hander, working on just one day's rest, who silenced the KC bats for five and one-third innings before giving way to Sparky Lyle in the eighth inning.

The Yankees, in the meantime, scored single runs in both the third and eighth innings, the latter coming on a pinch-hit single by Jackson.

Coming to the ninth inning, once again, the Yankees were in a do-or-die situation. Could history repeat?

Paul Blair led off the inning with a single to center and moved to second on a walk, by reliever Dennis Leonard, to Roy White. Mickey Rivers' game-tying single struck an ominous chord in the hearts of Kansas City fans. Willie Randolph's sacrifice fly rang the death knell, and a throwing error by George Brett, on a ground ball, paved the funeral cortege.

The Yankees won 5–3.

Obscured by the Yankees' dramatic comeback was the valiant relief effort by that unnamed right-hander who went on to greater glory in the World Series. Can you recall his name?

Answer: Mike Torrez

222

CHAPTER TWENTY

Touching All the Bases

123. MOST VALUABLE PLAYERS

Eleven Yankees have won the Most Valuable Player Award. Can you pick them out of the following 26 names? Check the correct names. If you can name the three players who won it three times and the one player who copped it twice, add one tough point to your total.

Bill Dickey	Whitey Ford
Tony Lazzeri	Bob Turley
Babe Ruth	Yogi Berra
Red Ruffing	Mickey Mantle
Lou Gehrig	Bobby Richardson
Bob Meusel	Roger Maris
Joe DiMaggio	Bill Skowron
Joe Gordon	Ellie Howard
Red Rolfe	Thurman Munson
Lefty Gomez	Graig Nettles
Spud Chandler	Sparky Lyle
Tommy Henrich	Reggie Jackson
Phil Rizzuto	Don Mattingly

124. SINGLE-SEASON STOLEN BASES

Match the following eleven players with their highest total of stolen bases in a season: Birdie Cree, Willie Randolph, Fred Maisel, Mickey Rivers, Wid Conroy, Ben

Chapman, George Stirnweiss, Charlie Hemphill, Bert Daniels, Rickey Henderson, and Dave Fultz.

1) _____ (130) 7) _____ (43)
2) _____ (74)   8) _____ (42)
3) _____ (61)   9) _____ (41)
4) _____ (55)   10) _____ (41)
5) _____ (48)   11) _____ (37)
6) _____ (44)

125. YANKEE PLAYERS AND MANAGERS

Ten players who were Yankees at one time or another went on to lead teams that they later managed to pennants. How many of them can you name and match up with the respective pennant-winning teams listed below?

1) _____ (1912 Red Sox)
2) _____ (1925 Pirates, 1928 Cardinals, 1939–40 Reds)
3) _____ (1930–31 Cardinals)
4) _____ (1941 Dodgers, 1951 and 1954 Giants)
5) _____ (1945 Tigers)
6) _____ (1961–63 Yankees)
7) _____ (1964 Yankees and 1973 Mets)
8) _____ (1966 Orioles)
9) _____ (1976–77 Yankees)
10) _____ (1985 Royals)

126. KEY TRADES

The players listed below in the left-hand column were traded by the Yankees in either even-up swaps or multiple-player deals; the players listed in the right-hand column were the principal parties, from the Bronx Bombers' point of view, in the respective exchanges. Match the principal player the Yankees traded in the left-hand column with the chief player in the right-hand column whom they acquired.

1) __ Oscar Gamble	a)	Bob Cerv
2) __ Roger Maris	b)	Chris Chambliss
3) __ Bill Skowron	c)	Jay Johnstone
4) __ Fritz Peterson	d)	Sparky Lyle
5) __ Doc Medich	e)	Fran Healy
6) __ John Ellis	f)	Lou Piniella
7) __ Bobby Bonds	g)	Oscar Gamble
8) __ Rawley Eastwick	h)	Bucky Dent
9) __ Elliott Maddox	i)	Rich McKinney
10) __ Bobby Murcer	j)	Mickey Rivers
11) __ Ryne Duren	k)	Bill Robinson
12) __ Danny Cater	l)	Eddie Lopat
13) __ Hank Bauer	m)	Marty Perez
14) __ Joe Gordon	n)	Graig Nettles
15) __ Larry Gura	o)	Mike Torrez
16) __ Ken Brett	p)	Charlie Smith
17) __ Pat Dobson	q)	Paul Blair
18) __ Lindy McDaniel	r)	Ryne Ruren
19) __ Terry Whitfield	s)	Stan Williams
20) __ Stan Bahnsen	t)	Gary Thomasson
21) __ Doc Ellis	u)	Carlos May
22) __ Clete Boyer	v)	Willie Randolph
23) __ Del Alston	w)	Allie Reynolds
24) __ Billy Martin	x)	Roger Maris
25) __ Aaron Robinson	y)	Bobby Bonds

127. THE MISSING INFIELDER

Supply the missing infielder for the designated years.

1) _____ (1909–10) Hal Chase, Frank LaPorte, Jack Knight, and 3B?

2) _____ (1918–19) Wally Pipp, Roger Peckinpaugh, Frank Baker, and 2B?

3) _____ (1922–24) Wally Pipp, Aaron Ward, Joe Dugan, and SS?

4) _____ (1926–28) Tony Lazzeri, Mark Koenig, Joe Dugan, and 1B?

5) _____ (1932–33) Lou Gehrig, Tonny Lazzeri, Joe Sewell, and SS?

6) _____ (1935–37) Lou Gehrig, Tony Lazzeri, Frankie Crosetti, and 3B?

7) _____ (1939–40) Joe Gordon, Frankie Crosetti, Red Rolfe, and 1B?

8) _____ (1947–48) George McQuinn, Phil Rizzuto, Billy Johnson, and 2B?

9) _____ (1950–51) Jerry Coleman, Phil Rizzuto, Bobby Brown, and 1B?

10) _____ (1952–53) Joe Collins, Phil Rizzuto, Gil McDougald, and 2B?

11) _____ (1960–61) Bill Skowron, Bobby Richardson, Clete Boyer, and SS?

12) _____ (1963–65) Bobby Richardson, Tony Kubek, Clete Boyer, and 1B?

13) _____ (1970–71) Danny Cater, Horace Clarke, Gene Michael, and 3B?

14) _____ (1977–78) Chris Chambliss, Willie Randolph, Graig Nettles, and SS?

15) _____ (1980–81) Willie Randolph, Bucky Dent, Graig Nettles, and 1B (right-handed hitter)?

128. SIX TO FOUR TO THREE

Match the double-play combinations (short to second to first) in the left-hand column with the respective years in the right-hand column that they teamed up together.

1) ___ Kubek to Richard-   a) 1968
son to Skowron

2) __ Tresh to Clarke to Mantle	b)	1953
3) __ Crosetti to Lazzeri to Gehrig	c)	1971
4) __ Koenig to Lazzeri to Gehrig	d)	1972
5) __ Lary to Lazzeri to Gehrig	e)	1977
6) __ McDougald to Martin to Skowron	f)	1927
7) __ Rizzuto to Martin to Collins	g)	1956
8) __ Rizzuto to Coleman to Henrich	h)	1960
9) __ Crosetti to Stirnweiss to Etten	i)	1947
10) __ Rizzuto to Stirnweiss to McQuinn	j)	1949
11) __ Michael to Clarke to Cater	k)	1921
12) __ Michael to Clarke to Blomberg	l)	1931
13) __ Crosetti to Gordon to Dahlgren	m)	1940
14) __ Dent to Randolph to Chambliss	n)	1945
15) __ Peckinpaugh to Ward to Pipp	o)	1935

129. THE MISSING LINK

Supply the third starting outfielder for the respective years (placed in parentheses) from the names that follow: Hector Lopez, Johnny Lindell, Norm Siebern, Bobby Murcer, Irv Noren, Whitey Witt, Matty Alou, Tuck Stainback, Gene Woodling, Joe DiMaggio, Roger Maris, Bobby Bonds, Yogi Berra, George Selkirk, Joe

Pepitone, Tommy Henrich, Earle Combs, Ben Chapman, Lou Piniella, and Jake Powell.

1) Bob Meusel, _____, and Babe Ruth (1922)
2) _____, Mickey Mantle, and Hank Bauer (1952)
3) _____, Mickey Mantle, and Roger Maris (1960)
4) Joe DiMaggio, _____,* and George Selkirk (1936)
5) Bob Meusel, _____, and Babe Ruth (1927)
6) _____, Mickey Rivers, and Reggie Jackson (1977)
7) _____, Earle Combs, and Babe Ruth (1932)
8) Roy White, Elliott Maddox, and _____ (1975)
9) Roy White, Bobby Murcer, and _____ (1973)
10) Charlie Keller, Joe DiMaggio, and _____ (1941)
11) _____, Joe DiMaggio, and Tommy Henrich (1947)
12) Hersh Martin, _____, and Bud Metheny (1945)
13) _____, Mickey Mantle, and Roger Maris (1961)
14) Tom Tresh, _____, and Steve Whitaker (1967)
15) Tom Tresh, Mickey Mantle, and _____ (1964)
16) _____, Mickey Mantle, and Hank Bauer (1958)
17) _____, Mickey Mantle, and Hank Bauer (1954)
18) Gene Woodling, _____, and Hank Bauer (1951)
19) _____, Joe DiMaggio, and Charlie Keller (1939)
20) Lou Piniella, Elliott Maddox, and _____ (1974)

*Late season, after Ben Chapman was traded.

130. MATCHING NUMBERS

Match the following 20 players with their uniform numbers: Gene Woodling, Mel Stottlemyre, Gil McDougald, Frankie Crosetti, Joe Page, Don Larsen, Joe DiMaggio, Babe Ruth, Bob Turley, Lou Gehrig, Hank Bauer, Vic Raschi, Tommy Henrich, Clete Boyer, Mickey Mantle, Whitey Ford, Phil Rizzuto, Bobby Richardson, Yogi Berra, and Allie Reynolds.

1) _____ (1)		11) _____ (11)
2) _____ (2)		12) _____ (12)
3) _____ (3)		13) _____ (14)
4) _____ (4)		14) _____ (15)
5) _____ (5)		15) _____ (16)
6) _____ (6)		16) _____ (17)
7) _____ (7)		17) _____ (18)
8) _____ (8)		18) _____ (19)
9) _____ (9)		19) _____ (22)
10) _____ (10)		20) _____ (23)

131. RETIRED NUMBERS

Thirteen Yankee numbers have been retired. One number—8—was retired in honor of two players; either order is correct for them. Place the names of the players who made the numbers ultra-recognizable in their respective places.

1) _____ (1)		8) _____ (9)
2) _____ (3)		9) _____ (10)
3) _____ (4)		10) _____ (15)
4) _____ (5)		11) _____ (16)
5) _____ (7)		12) _____ (32)
6) _____ (8)		13) _____ (37)
7) _____ (8)		

14) Which of these Yankees had the very same number retired by another club?

132. THE BABE'S NUMBER

Five Yankees wore Babe Ruth's number, 3, after he left the Bronx Bombers and before it was retired. How many of the players can you name? All of them, like

Babe Ruth, played right field at one time or another with the Yankees. (One of them wore it during spring training.)

1) ———   4) ———
2) ———   5) ———
3) ———

133. POST-PLAYING-DAY PURSUITS

Match the players in the left-hand column with the pursuits in the right-hand column that they took up in their post-playing days.

1) __ Joe DiMaggio
2) __ Roger Maris
3) __ Bobby Richardson
4) __ Charlie Keller
5) __ Bobby Brown
6) __ Ralph Terry
7) __ Red Rolfe
8) __ Clark Griffith
9) __ Jim Bouton
10) __ Yogi Berra
11) __ Tony Kubek
12) __ Phil Rizzuto
13) __ Lefty Gomez
14) __ Frankie Crosetti
15) __ Johnny Murphy
16) __ Atley Donald
17) __ Jim Turner
18) __ Ryne Duren
19) __ Phil Linz
20) __ Steve Hamilton

a) Nightclub owner
b) Yankee scout
c) Game of Week announcer
d) Pro golfer
e) TV commercial celebrity
f) College professor
g) Yankee pitching coach
h) Yankee third-base coach
i) Major-league club owner
j) Heart specialist
k) College baseball coach
l) Beer-distributor executive
m) Horse breeder
n) Director of alcoholic rehabilitation center
o) Athletic director at Dartmouth College
p) Author-announcer

q) Two-time pennant-win-
ning manager
r) Yankee announcer
s) General manager of the
Mets
t) Sporting-goods sales-
man

134. THE NATIONAL PASTIME

Match the players in the left-hand column with the cities and the states in the right-hand column in which they
were born.

1) __ Babe Ruth	a)	Newark, N.J.
2) __ Lou Gehrig	b)	Trenton, N.J.
3) __ Bill Dickey	c)	San Francisco, Cal.
4) __ Joe DiMaggio	d)	East St. Louis, Ill.
5) __ Joe Gordon	e)	Baltimore, Md.
6) __ Tommy Henrich	f)	Spavinaw, Okla.
7) __ Charlie Keller	g)	New York, N.Y.
8) __ Yogi Berra	h)	Sumter, S.C.
9) __ Allie Reynolds	i)	Akron, Ohio
10) __ Hank Bauer	j)	Massilon, Ohio
11) __ Mickey Mantle	k)	Berkley, Cal.
12) __ Frank Shea	l)	Los Angeles, Cal.
13) __ Tony Kubek	m)	Martinez, Cal.
14) __ Bobby Richardson	n)	Bastrop, La.
15) __ Thurman Munson	o)	Naugatuck, Conn.
16) __ Frankie Crosetti	p)	Bethany, Okla.
17) __ Billy Martin	q)	Milwaukee, Wis.
18) __ Vic Raschi	r)	Middletown, Md.
19) __ Jim Bouton	s)	St. Louis, Mo.
20) __ Al Downing	t)	West Springfield, Mass.

135. YANKEE KILLERS

Ten of the 24 pitchers listed below defeated the Yankees 30 or more times during their careers. Which ones? The number of times appears in parentheses; when two or more pitchers did it the same number of times, the order is not important.

Lefty Grove
Bob Lemon
Dizzy Trout
Hooks Dauss
Mel Parnell
Catfish Hunter
Luis Tiant
Walter Johnson
George Earnshaw
Bobo Newsom
Bob Feller
Ted Lyons

Dean Chance
Chief Bender
Eldon Auker
Mel Harder
Ed Cicotte
Stan Coveleski
Billy Pierce
Early Wynn
Jim Bunning
Red Faber
Camilo Pascual
Hal Newhouser

1) _____ (60)
2) _____ (35)
3) _____ (35)
4) _____ (33)
5) _____ (33)

6) _____ (32)
7) _____ (32)
8) _____ (30)
9) _____ (30)
10) _____ (30)

136. YANKEES AT THE MET

Twenty of the 50 players listed below played for both the Yankees and the Mets. How many of them can you identify? Check the correct names.

Yogi Berra
Charlie Neal

Elliott Maddox
Pedro Gonzalez

Elio Chacon
Rod Kanehl
Duke Carmel
Jim Hickman
Choo Choo Coleman
Bob Friend
Frank Thomas
Jay Hook
Frank Lary
Phil Linz
Jack Reed
Dale Long
Hal Reniff
Jesse Gonder
Bud Daley
Rollie Sheldon
Tom Sturdivant
Jim Coates
Marv Throneberry
Charlie Smith
Harry Bright
Steve Hamilton
Ruben Amaro

Pete Mikkelsen
Jack Aker
Celerino Sanchez
Ron Swoboda
Jim Fregosi
Jim Ray Hart
Ralph Terry
Jim McAndrew
Otto Velez
Gene Woodling
Doc Medich
Benny Ayala
Billy Cowan
Don Hahn
Dave Kingman
Dave Pagan
Billy Gardner
Bill Sudakis
Ellie Hendricks
Bob Apodaca
Sandy Alomar
Tug McGraw
Rusty Staub

137. WHERE DID THEY PLAY?

Below you'll find a list of 25 players who performed for at least three years with the Yankees. All you have to do is to name the primary positions—outfield, infield, catcher, pitcher—that they played. Seems easy, right? Don't be so sure.

1) _____ Bill Drescher
2) _____ Cedric Durst
3) _____ Frank Fernandez
4) _____ Mike Gazella
5) _____ Joe Glenn
6) _____ Pedro Gonzalez

7) _____	Oscar Grimes	18) _____	Jack Reed
8) _____	Don Heffner	19) _____	Jack Saltz-
9) _____	Art Jorgens		gaver
10) _____	Bill Knicker-	20) _____	Harry Wolter
	bocker	21) _____	Myril Hoag
11) _____	Jerry Lumpe	22) _____	Aaron Robin-
12) _____	Jim Lyttle		son
13) _____	Fritz Maisel	23) _____	Tuck Stain-
14) _____	Mike McNally		back
15) _____	Lefty O'Doul	24) _____	Roy Hartzell
16) _____	Ben Paschal	25) _____	George Mur-
17) _____	Jack Phillips		ray

138. HIGH AVERAGE

Match the players in the left-hand column with their
season's-high batting average in the right-hand column. (It
doesn't have to be with the Yankees.)

1) __	Bob Watson	a)	.276
2) __	Willie Randolph	b)	.308
3) __	Bucky Dent	c)	.330
4) __	Graig Nettles	d)	.288
5) __	Rick Cerone	e)	.274
6) __	Dave Winfield	f)	.333
7) __	Lou Piniella	g)	.337
8) __	Mickey Rivers	h)	.307
9) __	Jim Spencer	i)	.277
10) __	Elliott Maddox	j)	.305

139. HOME RUN HIGH

Match the players in the left-hand column with their season's-high home run totals in the right-hand column. (This quiz pertains only to Yankee stats.)

1) __ Graig Nettles   a) 8
2) __ Rick Cerone   b) 23
3) __ Jim Spencer   c) 18
4) __ Willie Randolph   d) 14
5) __ Bucky Dent   e) 13
6) __ Lou Piniella   f) 9
7) __ Bob Watson   g) 37
8) __ Oscar Gamble   h) 12
9) __ Ruppert Jones   i) 11
10) __ Eric Soderholm   j) 7

140. YANKS WITH 100 RIBBIES

Babe Ruth, Lou Gehrig, Joe DiMaggio, Yogi Berra, Mickey Mantle, Roger Maris, and Reggie Jackson have each driven in 100 or more runs at least one time with the Yankees. So have 17 other Pinstripers. How many of them can you name?

141. 100 RUN MEN

Babe Ruth, Lou Gehrig, Joe DiMaggio, Charlie Keller, Yogi Berra, and Mickey Mantle have each scored 100 or more runs at least once with the Yankees. So have 23 other Bronx Bombers. How many of them can you name?

142. .300 HITTERS

Since 1940 Joe DiMaggio, Yogi Berra, Mickey Mantle, Bill Skowron, Ellie Howard, Thurman Munson, Lou Piniella, and Mickey Rivers have hit .300 in at least one season. So have 27 other Yankees. How many of them can you name?

143. PLAYERS IN THE BIG APPLE

Next to the players listed below write "Y–G–D" if they played with all three New York teams, "Y–G" if they played with the Yankees and Giants, or "Y–D" if they played with the Yankees and Dodgers.

1) _____ Lefty O'Doul
2) _____ Bobo Newsom
3) _____ Joe Beggs
4) _____ Paul Waner
5) _____ Johnny Mize
6) _____ Tony Lazzeri
7) _____ Sal Maglie
8) _____ Johnny Allen
9) _____ Frenchy Bordagaray
10) _____ Ben Chapman
11) _____ Hal Chase
12) _____ Lonny Frey
13) _____ Mark Koenig
14) _____ Jumbo Brown
15) _____ Willie Keeler
16) _____ Hugh Casey
17) _____ Babe Dahlgren

18) _____ Bill McKechnie
19) _____ Fred Merkle
20) _____ Rosy Ryan
21) _____ Buddy Hassett
22) _____ Tuck Stainback
23) _____ Burleigh Grimes
24) _____ Wes Ferrell
25) _____ Johnny Hopp

Answers

123. Most Valuable Players

1) Lou Gehrig (1936)
2) Joe DiMaggio (1939, 1941, 1947)
3) Joe Gordon (1942)
4) Spud Chandler (1943)
5) Phil Rizzuto (1950)
6) Yogi Berra (1951, 1954, 1955)
7) Mickey Mantle (1956–57, 1962)
8) Roger Maris (1960–61)
9) Ellie Howard (1963)
10) Thurman Munson (1976)
11) Don Mattingly (1985)

124. Single-Season Stolen Bases

1) Rickey Henderson
2) Fred "Fritz" Maisel
3) Ben Chapman
4) George Stirnweiss
5) Birdie Cree
6) Dave Fultz
7) Mickey Rivers
8) Charlie Hemphill
9) Wid Conroy or Bert Daniels
10) Wid Conroy or Bert Daniels
11) Willie Randolph

125. Yankee Players and Managers

1) Jake Stahl
2) Bill McKechnie
3) Gabby Street
4) Leo Durocher
5) Steve O'Neill
6) Ralph Houk
7) Yogi Berra
8) Hank Bauer
9) Billy Martin
10) Dick Howser

126. Key Trades

1) h
2) p
3) s
4) b
5) v
6) n

7) j	17) g
8) c	18) f
9) q	19) m
10) y	20) i
11) a	21) o
12) d	22) k
13) x	23) t
14) w	24) r
15) e	25) l
16) u	

127. The Missing Infielder

1) Jimmy Austin	9) Johnny Mize
2) Del Pratt	10) Billy Martin
3) Everett Scott	11) Tony Kubek
4) Lou Gehrig	12) Joe Pepitone
5) Frankie Crosetti	13) Jerry Kenney
6) Red Rolfe	14) Bucky Dent
7) Babe Dahlgren	15) Bob Watson
8) George Stirnweiss	

128. Six to Four to Three

1) h	9) n
2) a	10) i
3) o	11) c
4) f	12) d
5) l	13) m
6) g	14) e
7) b	15) k
8) j	

129. The Missing Link

1) Whitey Witt	4) Jake Powell
2) Gene Woodling	5) Earle Combs
3) Hector Lopez	6) Lou Piniella

7) Ben Chapman
8) Bobby Bonds
9) Matty Alou
10) Tommy Henrich
11) Johnny Lindell
12) Tuck Stainback
13) Yogi Berra

14) Joe Pepitone
15) Roger Maris
16) Norm Siebern
17) Irv Noren
18) Joe DiMaggio
19) George Selkirk
20) Bobby Murcer

130. Matching Numbers

1) Bobby Richardson
2) Frankie Crosetti
3) Babe Ruth
4) Lou Gehrig
5) Joe DiMaggio
6) Clete Boyer
7) Mickey Mantle
8) Yogi Berra
9) Hank Bauer
10) Phil Rizzuto

11) Joe Page
12) Gil McDougald
13) Gene Woodling
14) Tommy Henrich
15) Whitey Ford
16) Vic Raschi
17) Don Larsen
18) Bob Turley
19) Allie Reynolds
20) Mel Stottlemyre

131. Retired Numbers

1) Billy Martin
2) Babe Ruth
3) Lou Gehrig
4) Joe DiMaggio
5) Mickey Mantle
6) Bill Dickey or
   Yogi Berra
7) Yogi Berra or
   Bill Dickey

8) Roger Maris
9) Phil Rizzuto
10) Thurman Munson
11) Whitey Ford
12) Elston Howard
13) Casey Stengel
14) Casey Stengel (Mets)

132. The Babe's Number

1) George Selkirk
2) Allie Clark
3) Joe Medwick (in
   spring training)

4) Bud Metheny
5) Cliff Mapes

133. Post-Playing-Day Pursuits

1) e		11) c	
2) l		12) r	
3) k		13) t	
4) m		14) h	
5) j		15) s	
6) d		16) b	
7) o		17) g	
8) i		18) n	
9) p		19) a	
10) q		20) f	

134. The National Pastime

1) e		11) f	
2) g		12) o	
3) n		13) q	
4) m		14) h	
5) l		15) i	
6) j		16) c	
7) e		17) k	
8) s		18) t	
9) p		19) a	
10) d		20) b	

135. Yankee Killers

1) Walter Johnson	6) Red Faber
2) Lefty Grove	7) Stan Coveleski
3) Ed Cicotte	8) Bob Feller
4) Early Wynn	9) Chief Bender
5) Hal Newhouser	10) Hooks Dauss

136. Yankees at the Met

1) Yogi Berra
2) Duke Carmel
3) Bob Friend
4) Phil Linz
5) Hal Reniff
6) Jesse Gonder
7) Tom Sturdivant
8) Marv Throneberry
9) Charlie Smith
10) Elliott Maddox
11) Jack Aker
12) Ron Swoboda
13) Ralph Terry
14) Gene Woodling
15) Doc Medich
16) Billy Cowan
17) Dave Kingman
18) Billy Gardner
19) Bill Sudakis
20) Sandy Alomar

137. Where Did They Play?

1) Catcher
2) Outfield
3) Catcher
4) Infield
5) Catcher
6) Infield
7) Infield
8) Infield
9) Catcher
10) Infield
11) Infield
12) Outfield
13) Infield
14) Infield
15) Outfield
16) Outfield
17) Infield
18) Outfield
19) Infield
20) Outfield
21) Outfield
22) Catcher
23) Outfield
24) Outfield
25) Pitcher

138. High Average

1) g (1979 Red Sox)
2) j (1987)
3) e (1974 White Sox)
4) a (1978)
5) i (1980)
6) b (1978–79 Padres)
7) c (1977)
8) f (1980 Rangers)
9) d (1979)
10) h (1975)

139. Home Run High

1) g (1977)
2) d (1980)
3) b (1979)
4) j (1980)
5) a (1977 & 1987)
6) h (1977)
7) e (1980)
8) c (1982)
9) f (1980)
10) i (1980)

140. Yanks with 100 Ribbies

1) Bob Meusel
2) Wally Pipp
3) Tony Lazzeri
4) Ben Chapman
5) Lyn Lary
6) Bill Dickey
7) George Selkirk
8) Joe Gordon
9) Charlie Keller
10) Nick Etten
11) Johnny Lindell
12) Tommy Henrich
13) Joe Pepitone
14) Thurman Munson
15) Graig Nettles
16) Dave Winfield
17) Don Mattingly

141. 100 Run Men

1) Wally Pipp
2) Roger Peckinpaugh
3) Bob Meusel
4) Whitey Witt
5) Joe Dugan
6) Earle Combs
7) Tony Lazzeri
8) Ben Chapman
9) Joe Sewell
10) Lyn Lary
11) Red Rolfe
12) Frankie Crosetti
13) Tommy Henrich
14) George Selkirk
15) Joe Gordon
16) George Stirnweiss
17) Phil Rizzuto
18) Tony Kubek
19) Roy White
20) Bobby Murcer
21) Dave Winfield
22) Rickey Henderson
23) Don Mattingly

142. .300 Hitters

1) Phil Rizzuto
2) Joe Gordon
3) George Stirnweiss
4) Johnny Lindell
5) George McQuinn
6) Tommy Henrich
7) Bobby Brown
8) Hank Bauer
9) Gil McDougald
10) Gene Woodling
11) Irv Noren
12) Andy Carey
13) Norm Siebern
14) Bobby Richardson
15) Johnny Blanchard
16) Danny Cater
17) Elliott Maddox
18) Chris Chambliss
19) Jerry Mumphrey
20) Lou Piniella
21) Ken Griffey
22) Don Baylor
23) Don Mattingly
24) Dave Winfield
25) Rickey Henderson
26) Willie Randolph
27) Claudell Washington

143. Players in the Big Apple

1) Y–G–D
2) Y–G–D
3) Y–G
4) Y–D
5) Y–G
6) Y–G–D
7) Y–G–D
8) Y–G–D
9) Y–D
10) Y–D
11) Y–G
12) Y–G–D
13) Y–G
14) Y–G
15) Y–G–D
16) Y–D
17) Y–D
18) Y–G
19) Y–G–D
20) Y–G–D
21) Y–D
22) Y–D
23) Y–G–D
24) Y–D
25) Y–D

Historical Interlude
Number Twenty

Game Six of the 1947 World Series was a nightmare for Yankee fans.

Al Gionfriddo, who had scored the tying run of Game Four, prevented the tying run from scoring in Game Six with one of the most sensational defensive plays in World Series history.

Game Five had been decided by Joe DiMaggio's solo shot against Rex Barney. The Yankees, who had had hopes of wrapping up the Series in Game Six, ran afoul of Gionfriddo once more. With the Dodgers leading 8–5 in the bottom of the sixth, Brooklyn manager Burt Shotton went to his bench again and inserted Gionfriddo in left field as a defensive replacement. (DiMaggio years later said that the thing about the upcoming play that incensed him at the time was that Gionfriddo was playing him much too shallow. It should have been a routine play instead of a sensational catch, DiMaggio said.)

Nevertheless, Gionfriddo justified the move. DiMaggio hit a towering blast to the 415-foot sign in deep left center. But Gionfriddo, who got a good jump on the ball, made an unbelievable catch at the bullpen fence. If he had not gotten to the ball, the game would have been tied. The Dodgers turned out to win the game, 8–6. So the catch, at the time, turned out to be a game-saving catch and a Series-saving grab. The Yankees won the seventh and decisive game, 5–2. (By the way, Gionfriddo never played another game in the major leagues.)

Whom, by the way, did Gionfriddo replace in left field on that October afternoon?

Answer: Eddie Miksis

CHAPTER TWENTY-ONE

Today's Yankees

144. THEY'RE STILL PLAYING

See how many players you can identify from the information and clues that follow. Many of the players are now or were with different teams. You can use the same player more than once.

1) _____ Who was the only pitcher to be banned from post-season play for using a foreign substance in his glove?

2) _____ Who is the pitcher who has defeated every existing major league club?

3) _____ A 21–8 pitcher with the 1984–85 Yankees, he hurled a no-hitter against the 1986 Angels.

4) _____ MVP of the 1983 World Series, this veteran of 20 major league seasons, who played with the Yankees from 1973–76, has performed in the Fall Classic with both the Orioles and the Dodgers.

5) _____ Who is the former Yankee relief pitcher who has more than 300 career saves?

6) _____ Who was the 1988 Yankee pitcher who three years in his career won more than 20 games in the American League?

7) _____ Who is the former Yankee catcher—he played in the 1988 World Series—who batted .296 with 13 homers for the 1985 Bombers?

8) _____ Name the son of a veteran World Series performer (1964, 1967–68 Cardinals, and 1972 Reds) who played in seven games for the 1984 Yankees.

9) _____ Name the 1987 Yankee who won the Rookie-of-the-Year Award in 1983.

10) _____ Who is the former Yankee who, while a member of the 1974 Bombers, hit a record-tying 11 home runs in April?

11) _____ Who is the one-time Yankee (1982) who as a member of the 1979 Mets hit a pinch-hit home run in the All-Star Game?

12) _____ Name the Yankee whose brother Terry played defensive back for the 1977 Packers.

13) _____ Name the former Yankee infielder who is a nephew of Gene Mauch.

14) _____ Who is the Yankee player who in 1973 was selected in the draft by the Atlanta Hawks, the Utah Suns, and the Minnesota Vikings?

15) _____ Who was the 1988 Yankee who batted .571 in the 1974 World Series?

16) _____ Who is the present-day Yankee pitcher who as a rookie won both of his decisions in the 1981 Division Series?

17) _____ Whose son Agee is a basketball forward at Fullerton State?

18) _____ Who is the former Yankee (1983–85) who set a record when he was thrown out twice (1974 Orioles) attempting to steal in one inning?

19) _____ Three times he led his minor league in home runs, he has hit 147 major league four-base blows, but only seven of them were hit with the 1981–83 Yankees.

20) _____ Who was the Yankee catcher who pitched two games in 1987?

21) _____ This present-day Yankee pitcher became the youngest White Sox hurler to post 20 wins in a season when he picked up 22 decisions in 1983.

22) _____ An 11–4 pitcher with a Western Division club in 1987, the Yankees sent him to the minors at the start of the 1988 season.

23) _____ Who is the Yankee pitcher who tied a major league record when he struck out the side on nine pitches in 1984?

24) _____ Name the 1988 Yankee who was the Comeback Player of the Year thirteen years ago.

25) _____ Who is the Yankee who established an American League record for most at bats (677) by a left-handed batter in one season?

26) _____ Who is the Yankee who in 1985–87 averaged 26 home runs per season in his first three full seasons in the majors?

27) _____ Who is the Yankee player who didn't hit a grand slam home run in his first four full seasons in the majors, but then hit a record six in his fifth year?

28) _____ Name the 1988 Yankee pitcher who twice has won 20 games with the Yankees and once won 20 with a National League team.

29) _____ Who was the 1982–84 Yankee relief pitcher who was the losing pitcher in the 1987 All-Star Game?

30) _____ Who is the catcher who was shuttled from the White Sox to the Yankees and back to the White Sox during the 1984–86 seasons?

31) _____ Who was the 1978–83 Yankee pitcher who saved 20 games during the strike-abbreviated 1981 season?

32) _____ In 1979 this 1978–81 Yankee established an American League record for the most wins (14) by a rookie relief pitcher in one season.

33) _____ Who was the 1988 Yankee who established a National League record when he received at least one walk in 16 consecutive games?

34) _____ Who was the 13-game winner with the 1988 Yankees who once pitched a no-hitter against the Dodgers?

35) _____ Seventy-one of his 338 career homers were hit with the 1983–85 Yankees.

36) _____ Who was the player, released by the 1988 Yankees early in the season, who ended up catching for the Red Sox, the winners of the Eastern Division?

37) _____ Who is the Yankee who hit a major league record-tying and an American League record-breaking 35 home runs as the lead-off batter in a game?

38) _____ Name the 1988 Yankee pitcher who is 6–2 in post-season play.

39) _____ Name the player, acquired midway through

the 1988 season, who has averaged 25 home runs a year from 1986–88.

40) _____ Who was the 1988 Yankee who hit .300 for the first time in his twelfth major league season?

41) _____ He and his father hit 407 career homers.

42) _____ Who was the 1988 Yankee who in 1987 made a record-tying three errors in one inning at first base?

43) _____ In 1981 he established a major league record for the most consecutive strikeouts (8) by a relief pitcher in one game.

44) _____ In 1982–84 this former Yankee infielder (1978–79) averaged 44 stolen bases a year; in 1986 he tied a major league record for the most doubles (4) in a game.

45) _____ Eleven years before he stole 14 bases with the 1986 Yankees, he swiped a record-tying three bags in a championship game.

46) _____ Name the Yankee who in 1986 established an American League record with nine lead-off homers in a game.

47) _____ Name the 1980 Yankee—he batted .223 with nine homers—who two years later tied the major league record of eight strikeouts in two consecutive games.

48) _____ Who is the Yankee with more than 200 hits in three consecutive seasons?

49) _____ Name the 1985–87 Yankee who hit a total of 42 home runs while alternating between Columbus and New York.

50) _____ Who is the Yankee who from 1984–87 had no more than a five-point spread in his batting average?

51) _____ Who is the Yankee who won 14 games as a starter in 1983 and 12 games as a reliever in 1985? (He had less than half the innings in relief that he had as a starter.)

52) _____ Who was the 4–2 winner for the 1987 Yankees who opted to play in Japan in 1988?

53) _____ Who is the Yankee who hit 28 home runs with the 1982 Twins?

54) _____ Whose father pinch-hit safely twice against the Yankees in the 1964 World Series?

55) _____ Who was the 1985–87 Yankee pitcher who

in 1981 hurled eight scoreless innings in the Division Series and 10 scoreless frames in the Championship Series without registering a victory?

56) _____ Who was the Yankee starter in the 1976 World Series who is winless in five decisions in post-season play?

57) _____ Who is the 1985–86 Yankee who with the 1983 Pirates set a record when he reached base seven times on catcher's interference?

58) _____ In 1977 this former Yankee (1973–76) tied a major-league record for the most double plays (3) by a catcher in one game, and in 1983 he established a World Series record for the most long hits (5) in a five-game Series.

59) _____ Who is the player who has eight times led the American League in stolen bases?

60) _____ Name the 1988 Yankee pitcher who one year tied for the American League lead in wild pitches (17) and intentional bases (17) on balls.

61) _____ Name the 1987 Yankee who while a member of another team averaged 31 homers a year in his first three (1983–85) major-league seasons.

62) _____ In 1984 he led the International League with a .335 batting average, but he couldn't make it with the Yankees; instead he moved on to the 1986 White Sox-Mariners with whom he hit .300.

63) _____ Name the player who after he left the Yankees tied a National League record for the most home runs (7) in six consecutive games.

64) _____ A winner of a total of 25 games with the 1982–83 Yankees, he was a Cy-Young-Award candidate with the 1987 Phillies.

65) _____ Whose 16 wins in 1987 tied a fifteen-year-career season best?

66) _____ Name the 18–6 Yankee pitcher in 1986 who is now in the National League.

67) _____ Who is the Yankee infielder who has hit .308 in four All-Star games?

68) _____ Forty-six saves is whose major league record?

69) _____ Winner of 190 major league games, the best he could do with the 1981–83 Yankees was a combined 4–4.

70) _____ A Yankee infielder from 1982–84, he is the son of a former major league infielder with the same first name.

71) _____ Signed as a free agent in 1984, he was a combined 15–10 in 1985–86 with disappointing ERAs of 4.88 and 7.54.

72) _____ Who is the Yankee who once hit 34 home runs in one season for a National League team?

73) _____ Rickey Henderson and what other 1988 Yankee have stolen 30-plus bases in a season at least four times?

74) _____ Who is the relief pitcher who tied the record for the most saves in a six-game World Series?

75) _____ Who was the 1981 Yankee who established a Championship Series record by getting two hits in one inning?

76) _____ Who was the .303 batter with the 1983 Yankees who once hit a record four consecutive home runs for the 1975 Orioles in two consecutive games?

77) _____ In 1986 this 1984–85 Yankee pitcher set an American League record when he struck out the first seven batters of a game.

78) _____ Unable to break into the lineup behind Willie Randolph at second base, he moved on to another American League team where he batted .310 and .307 in back-to-back years.

79) _____ Who was the 1982–86 Yankee who played on world championship teams, one of which beat the Yankees, in back-to-back (1975–76) years, and later hit better than .300 twice in five years in the Bronx?

80) _____ Who is the catcher who played one game for the Yankees in the 1978 World Series and three games each for the A's and Tigers, respectively, in the 1981 and 1987 ALCS?

81) _____ A son of a 27-game winner in 1944, this 84-game career winner fell flat with the 1987 Yankees, losing all four of his decisions and posting a 6.60 ERA.

82) _____ Though he has never hit more than 17 home runs in a season, he has twice (for other teams) hit three home runs in a game.

83) _____ Who lost his only World Series decision twelve years ago?

84) _____ Who was the 1985–87 Yankee pitcher who had to wait the longest time (twenty-one years) of any World Series performer before he made his appearance?

85) _____ Who is the Yankee pitcher who in 1975 set a Championship Series record by striking out 14 batters in a nine-inning game?

86) _____ Who was the 1988 Yankee who as a non-Yankee played in two Championship Series in the American League and one in the National League?

87) _____ Who is the present-day Red Sox player who was the only Yankee to homer in his first Championship Series at bat?

88) _____ Who is the present-day Yankee pitcher who is 5–2 in post-season play?

89) _____ Name the player who has driven home more than 100 runs in six of the last seven years.

90) _____ Who is the Yankee pitcher who in 1983 with another team lost the most games (2) and allowed the most home runs (4) in a five-game World Series?

91) _____ Who is the present-day National League pitcher who got the decision in a fight with Billy Martin when they were both with the 1986 Yankees?

92) _____ He played with the 1985–87 Yankees and then moved to the Mariners with Steve Trout.

93) _____ Who is the former Yankee (1973–76) who later tied the record for most doubles (4) in a five-game World Series?

94) _____ Who has hit safely in a record-tying seven consecutive All-Star games?

95) _____ Who was the 1983–85 Yankee who appeared in three consecutive World Series with three different teams?

96) _____ Who got a Yankee record 238 hits in one season?

97) _____ Who hit .322 with 25 homers and 107 RBI in 1988?

98) _____ Who is the part-time outfielder who hit .308 with 11 homers and 64 RBI in 1988?

99) _____ Who was the Yankees' best-winning pitcher in 1988?

100) _____ Who was the 1988 Yankee pitcher tied with Robin Roberts for career (286) wins?

Answers

144: Today's Yankees

1) Jay Howell (1988 Dodgers)
2) Doyle Alexander
3) Joe Cowley
4) Rick Dempsey
5) Goose Gossage
6) Ron Guidry (1978, 1983, 1985)
7) Ron Hassey
8) Stan Javier (Julian)
9) Ron Kittle (White Sox)
10) Graig Nettles
11) Lee Mazzilli
12) Willie Randolph
13) Roy Smalley
14) Dave Winfield
15) Claudell Washington (A's)
16) Dave Righetti
17) Gary Ward
18) Don Baylor
19) Steve Balboni
20) Rick Cerone
21) Richard Dotson (24)
22) Lee Guetterman
23) Ron Guidry
24) Tommy John (Dodgers)
25) Don Mattingly (1986)
26) Mike Pagliarulo
27) Don Mattingly (1987)
28) Tommy John
29) Jay Howell (A's)
30) Ron Hassey
31) Goose Gossage

32) Ron Davis
33) Jack Clark (1987 Cardinals)
34) John Candelaria (1976 Pirates)
35) Don Baylor
36) Rick Cerone
37) Rickey Henderson
38) Tommy John (4–1 in playoffs and 2–1 in World Series)
39) Ken Phelps
40) Willie Randolph (.305 in 1987)
41) Dale Berra (Yogi, 358; Dale, 49)
42) Jack Clark (1987 Cardinals)
43) Ron Davis
44) Damaso Garcia
45) Ken Griffey (1975 Reds)
46) Rickey Henderson
47) Ruppert Jones
48) Don Mattingly (1984–86)
49) Dan Pasqua
50) Mike Pagliarulo (.239, .239, .238, and .234)
51) Dave Righetti
52) Bill Gullickson
53) Gary Ward
54) Joel Skinner (Bob with the Cardinals)
55) Joe Niekro
56) Doyle Alexander (0–4 in ALCS and 0–1 in World Series action)
57) Dale Berra
58) Rick Dempsey

59) Rickey Henderson (1980–86 and 1988)
60) Tommy John (1970 White Sox)
61) Ron Kittle (White Sox)
62) Scott Bradley
63) Graig Nettles (1984 Padres)
64) Shane Rawley
65) Rick Rhoden (1977 Dodgers)
66) Dennis Rasmussen (Reds)
67) Willie Randolph
68) Dave Righetti (1986)
69) Rick Reuschel
70) Roy Smalley
71) Ed Whitson
72) Dave Winfield (1979 Padres)
73) Claudell Washington
74) Goose Gossage
75) Graig Nettles
76) Don Baylor
77) Joe Cowley (White Sox)
78) Damaso Garcia (Blue Jays)
79) Ken Griffey
80) Mike Heath
81) Steve Trout
82) Claudell Washington (1979 White Sox and 1980 Mets)
83) Rick Rhoden (1977 Dodgers)
84) Joe Niekro (Twins)
85) John Candelaria (Pirates)

86) Claudell Washington (1974–75 A's and 1982 Braves)
87) Rick Cerone (1980)
88) Ron Guidry (3–1 in World Series and 2–1 in ALCS)
89) Dave Winfield
90) Charles Hudson (Phillies)
91) Ed Whitson
92) Henry Cotto
93) Rick Dempsey (1983 Orioles)
94) Dave Winfield (1982–87)
95) Don Baylor (1986 Red Sox, 1987 Twins, and 1988 A's)
96) Don Mattingly (1986)
97) Dave Winfield
98) Claudell Washington
99) John Candelaria (13)
100) Tommy John

CHAPTER TWENTY-TWO

Super Seasons

145. THE REGULARS

Fill in the blanks with the Yankee players who match up with their respective categories: year, position, batting average, home runs, and runs batted in, for regular players; and year, position, wins, losses, and earned run average for pitchers. One hint is given for each player identification. (*Italics* denote league leader.)

	Year	Pos.	BA	HR	RBI
1) _____	1904	RF	.343	2	40

Joe DiMaggio broke his unofficial record 44-game consecutive hitting streak.

2) _____	1904	LF	.283	6	22

With the Red Sox in 1903, he became the first player to hit two home runs in one World Series game.

3) _____	1911	1B	.315	3	62

Five years later he won a batting title in the National League.

4) _____	1919	3B	.293	10	83

He won four home-run titles with another team.

5) _____	1920	2B	.314	4	97

At the end of the season, he was traded to the Red Sox in a deal that brought Waite Hoyt and Wally Schang to the Yankees.

6) _____	1921	RF	.378	*59*	*171*

He totaled a record 457 bases that year.

7) _____	1922	1B	.329	9	90

He won two home-run titles with the Yankees.

	Year	Pos.	BA	HR	RBI
8) _____	1923	2B	.284	10	82

In the 1922–23 World Series he hit three home runs.

	Year	Pos.	BA	HR	RBI
9) _____	1925	LF	.290	*33*	138

He and his brother Emil played left field for opposing teams in the 1921–23 World Series.

	Year	Pos.	BA	HR	RBI
10) _____	1927	CF	.356	6	64

He was the lead-off batter for "Murderers' Row."

	Year	Pos.	BA	HR	RBI
11) _____	1928	SS	.319	4	63

He played against the Yankees in two World Series.

	Year	Pos.	BA	HR	RBI
12) _____	1929	2B	.354	18	106

He later played with two National League teams in New York in the same season.

	Year	Pos.	BA	HR	RBI
13) _____	1931	3B	.302	6	64

In 1932–33, his last years in the majors, he struck out three and four times, respectively.

	Year	Pos.	BA	HR	RBI
14) _____	1931	SS	.280	10	107

After batting .309, .289, and .280 in his first three seasons with the Yankees, he slumped to .232 and .220 in 1932–33 and was dealt to the Red Sox in 1934.

	Year	Pos.	BA	HR	RBI
15) _____	1931	LF	.315	17	122

He batted .300 for five major league teams.

	Year	Pos.	BA	HR	RBI
16) _____	1934	1B	*.363*	*49*	*165*

He led the American League in home runs three times.

	Year	Pos.	BA	HR	RBI
17) _____	1936	SS	.288	15	78

He twice led the league in strikeouts and once in stolen bases.

	Year	Pos.	BA	HR	RBI
18) _____	1936	RF	.308	18	107

In 1935 he took Babe Ruth's place as the Yankees' regular right fielder.

	Year	Pos.	BA	HR	RBI
19) _____	1936	C	.362	22	107

In 1937 he drove home 133 runs.

	Year	Pos.	BA	HR	RBI
20) _____	1937	CF	.346	46	167

He owns the sixth all-time-high (.579) slugging percentage.

	Year	Pos.	BA	HR	RBI
21) _____	1939	3B	.329	14	80

He later managed the Tigers.

	Year	Pos.	BA	HR	RBI
22) _____	1940	2B	.281	30	103

He had his highest home run season production (32) with another American League team.

	Year	Pos.	BA	HR	RBI

23) _____ 1941 LF .298 33 122

He batted .438 in his rookie (1939) World Series.

24) _____ 1944 CF .300 18 103

He hit an impact home run on the next-to-last day of the 1949 season.

25) _____ 1944 1B .293 22 91

He won the home-run title that year.

26) _____ 1945 2B *.309* 10 64

He led the American League in stolen bases in 1944 and 1945.

27) _____ 1947 1B .304 13 80

In 1944 he gave the Browns one of their two all-time World Series victories with a two-run home run off Mort Cooper of the Cardinals.

28) _____ 1948 RF .308 25 100

He led the American League in triples in both 1947 and 1948.

29) _____ 1950 2B .287 6 69

He spent the better part of 1952 and 1953 in Korea.

30) _____ 1950 SS .324 7 66

He won the MVP Award that year.

31) _____ 1950 C .322 28 124

He drove home more than 100 runs in each season from 1953–56.

32) _____ 1952 1B .280 18 59

His four home runs in World Series play were key hits in three Yankee victories.

33) _____ 1952 LF .309 12 63

He hit better than .300 for four American League teams.

34) _____ 1954 LF .319 12 66

He batted better than .300 for the 1957 Cards and the 1959 Cubs.

35) _____ 1956 SS .311 13 56

He played in the World Series in eight of his ten major league seasons.

36) _____ 1956 CF *.353* *52* *130*

He became the second Yankee to win the Triple Crown.

	Year	Pos.	BA	HR	RBI

37) _____ 1950 RF .320 13 70

In the 1956–58 World Series he hit a total of seven home runs.

38) _____ 1957 SS .297 3 39

He won the Rookie-of-the-Year Award that season.

39) _____ 1960 1B .309 26 91

In the three seasons before the Yankees traded him to a team in the National League, he hit 26, 28, and 23 home runs, respectively.

40) _____ 1961 RF .269 *61* *142*

He led the American League in RBI in both 1960 and 1961.

41) _____ 1961 C .305 21 54

He had only 243 at-bats that year.

42) _____ 1961 C .348 21 77

He won the MVP Award in 1963.

43) _____ 1962 2B .302 8 59

He was the only member of a losing team to win the World Series MVP Award.

44) _____ 1962 SS .286 20 93

His father caught in the major leagues.

45) _____ 1962 3B .272 18 68

He and his brother Ken played third base for opposing teams in the 1964 World Series.

46) _____ 1964 1B .251 28 100

He hit 27 home runs in 1963 and 31 in 1966.

47) _____ 1971 CF .331 25 94

He finished second in the batting race to Tony Oliva.

48) _____ 1976 1B .293 17 96

He won the Rookie-of-the-Year Award with another team.

49) _____ 1977 CF .326 12 69

In 1975 he stole more bases in one season than any other Angel.

50) _____ 1977 3B .255 37 107

He won a home-run title.

51) _____ 1977 C .308 18 100

He won the Rookie-of-the-Year Award in 1970.

	Year	Pos.	BA	HR	RBI
52) _____	1977	DH	.330	12	45

He won the Rookie-of-the-Year Award with another team.

	Year	Pos.	BA	HR	RBI
53) _____	1978	SS	.243	5	40

Red Sox fans will never forget him.

	Year	Pos.	BA	HR	RBI
54) _____	1980	RF	.300	*41*	111

He never hit .300 before or after that season.

	Year	Pos.	BA	HR	RBI
55) _____	1983	DH	.303	21	85

He has hit 25 or more home runs for four American League teams.

	Year	Pos.	BA	HR	RBI
56) _____	1985	CF	.314	24	72

He has hit .300 four times, twice with the Yankees and twice with a West Coast team.

	Year	Pos.	BA	HR	RBI
57) _____	1985	1B	.324	35	*145*

He led the American League in doubles in each of the 1984–86 seasons.

	Year	Pos.	BA	HR	RBI
58) _____	1987	2B	.305	7	67

Seven times in his Yankee career he stole more than 20 bases in a season.

	Year	Pos.	BA	HR	RBI
59) _____	1988	RF	.322	25	107

In 1979 he hit 34 home runs and drove home 118 runs with a National League club.

	Year	Pos.	BA	HR	RBI
60) _____	1988	CF	.308	11	64

He hit .308 with the 1975 Oakland A's.

146. THE PITCHERS

	Year	Pos.	Wins	Losses	ERA
1) _____	1904	P	*41*	12	1.82

In 1901 he led the Pirates in winning (.677) percentage.

	Year	Pos.	Wins	Losses	ERA
2) _____	1906	P	*27*	17	2.34

The following year he led the league with 21 losses.

	Year	Pos.	Wins	Losses	ERA
3) _____	1910	P	26	5	1.65

In 1914 he won 20 games with Buffalo in the Federal League.

	Year	Pos.	Wins	Losses	ERA

4) _____ 1914 P 17 9 1.94
With the Indians in 1920, he won 20 games during the regular season.

5) _____ 1915 P 18 11 2.11
In 1919 he was 14–5 with the Reds and 0–1 against the Black Sox in the World Series.

6) _____ 1920 P 20 13 *2.45*
He lost a game for the Athletics in the "Miracle Braves'" 1914 World Series sweep.

7) _____ 1921 P *27* 9 3.05
He was 20–9 with the 1924 Reds.

8) _____ 1923 P 21 8 3.63
He won 23 games in 1921 and lost 20 contests in 1919 when he was with the Red Sox.

9) _____ 1924 P 21 9 2.83
He was with the Red Sox before he peaked with the Yankees, and he ended up with the Red Sox.

10) _____ 1927 P 22 7 *2.63*
He lost a World Series game with the 1931 Athletics.

11) _____ 1928 P *24* 13 3.38
He later became an umpire.

12) _____ 1934 P *26* 5 *2.33*
Three times (1934, 1937, and 1938) he led the league in shutouts.

13) _____ 1936 P 19 7 3.71
He won one game without a loss in each of the World Series from 1936–39.

14) _____ 1937 P 13 4 4.17
Six times he led American League relief pitchers in wins, and four times he led them in saves.

15) _____ 1938 P 21 7 3.31
He began his career in Boston and ended it in Chicago.

16) _____ 1942 P 21 5 2.27
His son Bill won 75 games in the majors.

17) _____ 1943 P 20 4 1.64
He won the MVP Award that year.

18) _____ 1947 P 14 5 3.07
An arm injury prevented him from being a recipient

of the Yankees' record-tying 19-game winning streak that year.

	Year	Pos.	Wins	Losses	ERA
19) _____	1949	P	21	10	3.34

He posted a 2.24 ERA in six World Series.

| 20) _____ | 1949 | P | 13 | 8 | 2.59 |

In 1947 and 1949 he led the league in relief wins, losses, and saves.

| 21) _____ | 1952 | P | 20 | 8 | *2.06* |

In 1953 he was 7–1 with 13 saves out of the bullpen.

| 22) _____ | 1953 | P | 16 | 4 | *2.42* |

In four seasons with the White Sox he won 50 games and lost 49.

| 23) _____ | 1954 | P | 20 | 6 | 3.26 |

He was the last rookie before Tom Browning of the 1985 Reds to win 20 games in a season.

| 24) _____ | 1954 | P | 6 | 6 | 3.16 |

He led the league with 22 saves that year.

| 25) _____ | 1956 | P | 18 | 9 | 3.85 |

He pitched a shutout in his only World Series start.

| 26) _____ | 1957 | P | 11 | 5 | *2.45* |

In 1961 he was 6–3 for the team he pitched against in the final game of the 1960 World Series.

| 27) _____ | 1958 | P | *21* | 7 | 2.97 |

He won the Cy Young Award that year.

| 28) _____ | 1961 | P | 15 | 5 | 2.19 |

He saved a league-leading 29 games that year.

| 29) _____ | 1962 | P | *23* | 12 | 3.19 |

He made the final pitch of two seventh games in the World Series.

| 30) _____ | 1963 | P | *24* | 7 | 2.74 |

He won the Cy Young Award in 1961.

| 31) _____ | 1963 | P | 21 | 7 | 2.53 |

Eight years after he finished his first career (1970), he made a comeback with the Braves.

| 32) _____ | 1968 | P | 21 | 12 | 2.45 |

In 1965 he won 20 games; in 1966 he lost 20 games.

| 33) _____ | 1970 | P | 20 | 11 | 2.91 |

From 1969–72 he averaged 17 wins a year.

	Year	Pos.	Wins	Losses	ERA
34) _____	1972	P	9	5	1.91

He saved 35 games that season.

| 35) _____ | 1975 | P | *23* | 14 | 2.58 |

He won four World Series games for another team.

| 36) _____ | 1978 | P | *25* | 3 | 1.74 |

In a game in 1984 he struck out the side on nine pitches.

| 37) _____ | 1978 | P | 20 | 9 | 2.99 |

The following year he was 4–6.

| 38) _____ | 1979 | P | 21 | 9 | 2.97 |

In World Series play he was 1–1 pitching against the Yankees and 1–0 pitching for them.

| 39) _____ | 1980 | P | 6 | 2 | 2.27 |

He saved a league-high 33 games that year.

| 40) _____ | 1986 | P | 8 | 8 | 2.45 |

Possessor of the Yankees' all-time save mark, he came to the Yankees in a trade for Sparky Lyle.

Answers

145: The Regulars

1) Willie Keeler
2) Patsy Dougherty
3) Hal Chase
4) Frank Baker (1911–14 Athletics)
5) Del Pratt
6) Babe Ruth
7) Wally Pipp (1916–17)
8) Aaron Ward
9) Bob Meusel
10) Earle Combs
11) Mark Koenig (1932 Cubs and 1936 Giants)
12) Tony Lazzeri (1939 Dodgers and Giants)
13) Joe Sewell
14) Lyn Lary
15) Ben Chapman (Yankees, Red Sox, Indians, Senators, and Phillies)
16) Lou Gehrig (1931, 1934, and 1936)
17) Frank Crosetti
18) George Selkirk (1935)
19) Bill Dickey
20) Joe DiMaggio
21) Red Rolfe (1949–52)
22) Joe Gordon (1948 Indians)
23) Charlie Keller
24) Johnny Lindell
25) Nick Etten
26) George Stirnweiss
27) George McQuinn
28) Tommy Henrich

29) Jerry Coleman
30) Phil Rizzuto
31) Yogi Berra
32) Joe Collins
33) Gene Woodling (Yanks, Indians, Orioles, and Senators)
34) Irv Noren
35) Gil McDougald
36) Mickey Mantle
37) Hank Bauer
38) Tony Kubek
39) Bill Skowron
40) Roger Maris
41) Johnny Blanchard
42) Elston Howard
43) Bobby Richardson (1960)
44) Tom Tresh (Mike)
45) Clete Boyer (Yankees and Cardinals)
46) Joe Pepitone
47) Bobby Murcer
48) Chris Chambliss (1971 Indians)
49) Mickey Rivers
50) Graig Nettles (1976)
51) Thurman Munson
52) Lou Piniella (1969 Royals)
53) Bucky Dent
54) Reggie Jackson
55) Don Baylor (Angels, Orioles, Yankees, and Red Sox)
56) Rickey Henderson (A's)
57) Don Mattingly
58) Willie Randolph
59) Dave Winfield (Padres)
60) Claudell Washington

146. The Pitchers

1) Jack Chesbro
2) Al Orth
3) Russ Ford
4) Ray Caldwell
5) Ray Fisher
6) Bob Shawkey
7) Carl Mays
8) Sam Jones
9) Herb Pennock
10) Waite Hoyt
11) George Pipgras
12) Lefty Gomez
13) Monte Pearson
14) Johnny Murphy
15) Red Ruffing
16) Ernie Bonham
17) Spud Chandler
18) Frank Shea
19) Vic Raschi
20) Joe Page
21) Allie Reynolds
22) Eddie Lopat
23) Bob Grim
24) Johnny Sain
25) Johnny Kucks (1956)
26) Bobby Shantz (Pirates)
27) Bob Turley
28) Luis Arroyo
29) Ralph Terry (1960 and 1962)
30) Whitey Ford
31) Jim Bouton
32) Mel Stottlemyre
33) Fritz Peterson
34) Sparky Lyle
35) Catfish Hunter (A's)
36) Ron Guidry
37) Ed Figueroa
38) Tommy John (for and against the Dodgers)
39) Goose Gossage
40) Dave Righetti

CHAPTER TWENTY-THREE

Championship Series

147. AMERICAN LEAGUE EASTERN DIVISION PLAYOFF AND CHAMPIONSHIP SERIES

1976 ALCS
Game One

1) _____ Who was the third baseman whose throwing error gave the Yankees all the runs (2) they needed to win their first playoff game, 2–1?

2) _____ Who was the four-game World Series winner with another team who won his first Championship Series start with the Yankees?

Game Two

3) _____ Can you recall whose double put the Royals ahead to stay in their 7–3 victory? (He hit .268 lifetime and got a total of four hits in three Championship Series.)

4) _____ Who was the Yankee nemesis who pitched five and two-thirds innings of almost perfect relief to pick up the win?

Game Three

5) _____ Who was the former Pirate mound star who with relief help from Sparky Lyle chalked up a 5–3 win for the Yankees?

6) _____ Who was the .524 Championship Series hitter that year who hit a two-run homer for the Yankees?

Game Four

7) _____ Who was the diminutive Royal shortstop who got three hits en route to Kansas City's 7–4 victory?

8) _____ Who was the Yankee—he hit a club-high five home runs in ALCS play—who connected for two circuit clouts in the loss?

Game Five

9) _____ Whose three-run home run in the top of the eighth inning tied the score at 6–6?

10) _____ Whose sudden-death home run in the bottom of the ninth inning gave the Yankees their first ALCS victory?

1977 ALCS
Game One

11) _____ Who was the former member of the Reds' 1975–76 world championship teams who lost the first game for the Yankees, 7–2?

12) _____ Who was the .300-hitting 100-RBI man whose homer provided the Yankees with their two runs?

Game Two

13) _____ Who was the 16-game Yankee winner who evened the Series with a three-hitter, 6–2?

14) _____ Who was the designated-hitter—he hit more pinch-hit home runs than any other player—who provided the Yankee offense with a solo home run and a run-producing double?

Game Three

15) _____ Who was the Brooklyn-born 20-game winner who four-hit the Yankees to give the Royals a two game-to-one lead? The score was 6–2.

16) _____ Whose pinch-hit double in the sixth inning—he hit three home runs in the 1980 World Series—scored two runs and broke the game open?

Game Four

17) _____ Who was the Yankee outfielder whose four hits keyed the 6–4 Yankee victory?

18) _____ Who was the relief pitcher, ineffective the day before, whose five and one-third innings of scoreless relief helped the Yankees even the Series?

Game Five

19) _____ Who was the Yankee star who was benched—he drove home a key run with a pinch-hit single—against left-hander Paul Splittorff?

20) _____ Whose sacrifice fly gave the Yankees the go-ahead run in the 5–3 ALCS clincher? Mickey Rivers' single had tied the score in the ninth inning.

21) _____ Who was the 47–75 lifetime pitcher who won the first game of the playoffs, 7–1? Then a Yankee, he won a game in the World Series, too.

22) _____ Who was the .227 hitter in Championship Series action—he hit .357 in World Series play—who accounted for five runs, scoring two and driving home three with three hits, including a double and a home run?

Game Two

23) _____ Who was the Yankee 20-game winner who lost his second game without a win in Championship Series play?

24) _____ Who was the Royal lefty, a former Yankee, who picked up the 10–4 win?

Game Three

25) _____ Who was the Royal standout who hit three home runs in the 6–5 loss?

26) _____ Whose two-run home run into the monument section decided the game in the Yankees' favor?

Game Four

27) _____ Who was the 25-game winner who picked up the win, with ninth-inning help from Goose Gossage, to give the Yankees the Championship clincher, 2–1?

28) _____ Whose sixth-inning home run made the difference?

1980 ALCS
Game One

29) _____ Who was the former Yankee starter who outdueled Ron Guidry in the opener, 7-2?

30) _____ Who was the Royal who hit his fifth home run in Championship Series play?

Game Two

31) _____ Who was the Royal pitcher who evened his record at 2-2 against the Yankees in post-season play?

32) _____ Who was the Royal bullpen ace who picked up a save in the 3-2 Kansas City win?

Game Three

33) _____ Whose three-run homer in the seventh inning gave Kansas City its first American League pennant?

34) _____ Who was the relief pitcher for the Yankees who surrendered the game-winner?

1981 EDP
Game One

35) _____ A .238 hitter with 10 home runs in 1981, this outfielder's two-run homer in the four-run fifth inning highlighted a 5-3 Yankee win.

36) _____ An effective middle-inning reliever for the Yankees, he picked up the win coming to the rescue of Ron Guidry.

Game Two

37) _____ Who, in addition to Ron Davis and Goose Gossage, combined to strike out 14 batters en route to a 3-0 win? (He is a present-day reliever.)

38) _____ Reggie Jackson and what future Yankee manager accounted for all of the Yankee runs with homers?

Game Three

39) _____ Whose eighth-inning homer—he once got five hits in a World Series game—broke a 3-3 tie en route to a 5-3 Brewer win?

40) _____ Who was the all-time save specialist who protected the Brewer win?

Game Four

41) _____ Who was the future Cy-Young-Award-winner who registered the victory?

42) _____ Whose two-out double in the fourth inning proved to be the game-winning hit in the Brewers' 2-1 victory? (He tied for the home run championship the year before.)

Game Five

43) _____ Who was the Yankee "starter" who picked up the win in relief of Ron Guidry? (He was the Rookie of the Year in 1981.)

44) _____ Who picked up his third save of the Series while locking up the Yankee pennant?

45) _____ Whose three-run double in the first inning scored all of the Yankees' runs in their 3–1 victory over the A's?
46) _____ Who was the losing manager in the Series?

Game Two

47) _____ In a 13–3 romp Graig Nettles and what .291 lifetime hitter slammed three-run homers for the Yankees?
48) _____ Who pitched five and two-thirds innings of shutout relief to gain the victory? (He lost three games in that year's World Series.)

Game Three

49) _____ Who won his third game without a loss in post-season play that year?
50) _____ Whose home run in the sixth inning broke a scoreless tie en route to a 4–0 Yankee win and another Pinstripe pennant? (He hit .333 in the Series. The preceding year he hit .385.)

148. AMERICAN LEAGUE CHAMPIONSHIP SERIES

Match the following players with their records in American League Championship Series play: Reggie Jackson, Graig Nettles, Mickey Rivers, Cliff Johnson, Chris Chambliss, Lou Piniella, Rick Cerone, Don Baylor, Roy White, Willie Randolph, Jim Hunter, Sparky Lyle, Ken Holtzman, Tommy John, and George Frazier. Some of them were with the Yankees when they set their marks; some were not. Names may be used more than once.

1) _____ He had an American League record-tying two pinch-hit singles in 1981.

2) _____ He set a record with a .386 career average.

3) _____ In 1981 he drove home a record nine runs in a three-game Series.

4) _____ He played in a record 10 Championship Series.

5) _____ In 1980 he tied a record when he hit a home run in his first Championship Series game at bat.

6) _____ He grounded into an American League record-tying four double plays.

7) _____ He was the only player in the history of the Championship Series to steal home.

8) _____ He drove home a record 10 runs in a five-game Series.

9) _____ He won a record-tying four consecutive games.

10) _____ He struck out an American League record-tying five batters as a relief pitcher in one game.

11) _____ He started a record 10 games.

12) _____ He pinch-hit officially a record-tying five times.

13) _____ He pitched a record nineteen and one-third consecutive scoreless innings.

14) _____ He drew an American League record-tying five walks in a five-game Series.

15) _____ He and his teammate Chris Chambliss got an American League record-tying five consecutive hits in the 1976 ALCS.

16) _____ He played a record fifteen years between his first and last Championship Series.

17) _____ In 1973 he pitched an American League record-tying 11 innings in one game.

18) _____ He pitched in an American League record-tying four games in a five-game Series.

19) _____ In 1980 he hit a record-tying inside-the-park homer, and in 1981 he got a record-tying two hits in one inning.

20) _____ He got a record-tying 11 hits in a five-game Series.

149. .400 HITTERS

Eight Yankees have hit .400 or better in Championship Series play. One of them has done it twice. How many of them can you recall? Respective averages provide an added incentive. See if you can match up the players. Also, can you remember the manager who led the Yankees in the most Championship Series as a Pinstripe pilot?

1) _____ .524 (1976) [twice]
2) _____ .500 (1980)
3) _____ .500 (1981)
4) _____ .500 (1981)
5) _____ .462 (1978)
6) _____ .458 (1978)
7) _____ .435 (1976)
8) _____ .400 (1977)
9) _____ .400 (1978) [twice]
10) _____ (1978 and 1981)

Answers

147: American League Eastern Division Playoff and Championship Series

1) George Brett
2) Catfish Hunter
3) Tom Poquette
4) Paul Splittorff
5) Doc Ellis
6) Chris Chambliss
7) Fred Patek
8) Graig Nettles
9) George Brett
10) Chris Chambliss
11) Don Gullett
12) Thurman Munson
13) Ron Guidry
14) Cliff Johnson
15) Dennis Leonard
16) Amos Otis
17) Mickey Rivers
18) Sparky Lyle
19) Reggie Jackson
20) Willie Randolph
21) Jim Beattie
22) Reggie Jackson
23) Ed Figueroa
24) Larry Gura
25) George Brett
26) Thurman Munson
27) Ron Guidry
28) Roy White
29) Larry Gura
30) George Brett
31) Dennis Leonard
32) Dan Quisenberry
33) George Brett

34) Goose Gossage
35) Oscar Gamble
36) Ron Davis
37) Dave Righetti
38) Lou Piniella
39) Paul Molitor
40) Rollie Fingers
41) Pete Vuckovich
42) Ben Oglivie
43) Dave Righetti
44) Goose Gossage
45) Graig Nettles
46) Billy Martin
47) Lou Piniella
48) George Frazier
49) Dave Righetti
50) Willie Randolph

148: American League Championship Series

1) Lou Piniella
2) Mickey Rivers
3) Graig Nettles
4) Reggie Jackson
5) Rick Cerone
6) Willie Randolph
7) Reggie Jackson (1972)
8) Don Baylor (1982
   Angels)
9) Tommy John
10) George Frazier
11) Catfish Hunter
12) Cliff Johnson
13) Ken Holtzman
    (1973–75 A's)
14) Roy White (1976)
15) Mickey Rivers
16) Graig Nettles (1969
    Twins—1984 Padres)

17) Ken Holtzman
18) Sparky Lyle
19) Graig Nettles
20) Chris Chambliss (1976)

149: .400 Hitters

1) Chris Chambliss
2) Bob Watson
3) Graig Nettles or
   Jerry Mumphrey
4) Graig Nettles or
   Jerry Mumphrey
5) Reggie Jackson
6) Mickey Rivers
7) Thurman Munson
8) Cliff Johnson
9) Chris Chambliss
10) Bob Lenon

The Scorebook

YOUR WINNING PERCENTAGE

Give yourself one point for each correct answer, and total your correct answers chapter by chapter. Then compare your winning percentage with the Yankee winning percentages listed.

Chapter 1. _____   Chapter 13. _____
Chapter 2. _____   Chapter 14. _____
Chapter 3. _____   Chapter 15. _____
Chapter 4. _____   Chapter 16. _____
Chapter 5. _____   Chapter 17. _____
Chapter 6. _____   Chapter 18. _____
Chapter 7. _____   Chapter 19. _____
Chapter 8. _____   Chapter 20. _____
Chapter 9. _____   Chapter 21. _____
Chapter 10. _____   Chapter 22. _____
Chapter 11. _____   Chapter 23. _____
Chapter 12. _____

TOTAL: _____

Use this formula to obtain your winning percentage:

Total correct answers _____

divided by 2,900

= _____ YOUR WINNING PERCENTAGE

YANKEE WINNING PERCENTAGES

An * denotes a championship and a dot, a pennant winner.

.714 (1927)*	.613 (1978)*	.537 (1984)
.702 (1939)*	.611 (1964)•	.533 (1945)
.695 (1932)*	.610 (1922)•	.528 (1988)
.673 (1961)*	.610 (1934)	.519 (1916)
.669 (1942)•	.610 (1948)	.519 (1975)
.669 (1954)	.610 (1976)•	.513 (1959)
.667 (1936)*	.609 (1904)	.512 (1968)
.662 (1937)*	.607 (1933)	.510 (1972)
.656 (1928)*	.602 (1985)	.506 (1971)
.656 (1941)*	.597 (1935)	.500 (1911)
.656 (1953)*	.597 (1958)*	.497 (1969)
.651 (1938)*	.596 (1906)	.494 (1973)
.646 (1963)•	.593 (1962)*	.490 (1909)
.645 (1923)*	.591 (1926)•	.481 (1982)
.641 (1921)•	.586 (1924)	.488 (1918)
.636 (1943)*	.576 (1919)	.477 (1905)
.636 (1949)*	.574 (1970)	.475 (1965)
.636 (1950)*	.571 (1929)	.473 (1907)
.636 (1951)*	.571 (1940)	.464 (1917)
.636 (1957)•	.568 (1910)	.455 (1914)
.636 (1980)	.565 (1946)	.454 (1915)
.630 (1947)*	.562 (1983)	.448 (1925)
.630 (1949)*	.558 (1930)	.444 (1967)
.630 (1956)*	.556 (1979)	.440 (1966)
.630 (1960)•	.556 (1986)	.429 (1908)
.623 (1955)•	.551 (1981)•	.377 (1913)
.617 (1920)	.549 (1974)	.331 (1908)
.617 (1952)*	.549 (1987)	.329 (1912)
.617 (1977)*	.539 (1944)*	
.614 (1931)	.537 (1903)